# Praise for Harold Schechter's True-Crime Masterpieces

### THE A TO Z ENCYCLOPEDIA OF SERIAL KILLERS
by Harold Schechter and David Everitt

"The scholarship is both genuine and fascinating."
—*The Boston Book Review*

"This grisly tome will tell you all you ever wanted to know (and more) about everything from 'Axe Murderers' to 'Zombies.' . . . Schechter knows his subject matter. . . ."
—*Rocky Mountain News* (Denver)

"The ultimate reference on this fascinating phenomenon."
—*PI Magazine*

### DEVIANT
The Shocking True Story of Ed Gein, the Original "Psycho"

"A solidly researched, well-written account of the Gein story."
—*Milwaukee Journal*

"[A] grisly, wonderful book . . . a scrupulously researched and complexly sympathetic biography of the craziest killer in American history."
—*Film Quarterly*

## DERANGED
### The Shocking True Story of America's Most Fiendish Killer!

"This biography of the ultimate dirty old man, Albert Fish . . . pedophile, sadist, coprophiliac, murderer, cannibal, and self-torturer . . . [is] as horrifying as any novel could be."

—*American Libraries*

"Compelling . . . grippingly fascinating-repulsive."

—*Booklist*

"Reads like fiction but it's chillingly real. . . . What Albert Fish did . . . would chill the bones of Edgar Allan Poe."

—*Philadelphia Inquirer*

## DEPRAVED
### The Shocking True Story of America's First Serial Killer

"A meticulously researched, brilliantly detailed and above all riveting account of Dr. H. H. Holmes, a nineteenth-century serial killer who embodied the ferociously dark side of America's seemingly timeless preoccupations with ambition, money, and power. Schechter has done his usual sterling job in resurrecting this amazing tale."

—Caleb Carr, bestselling author of *The Alienist*

"This is *must* reading for crime buffs. *Depraved* demonstrates that sadistic psychopaths are not a modern-day phenomenon. . . . Gruesome, awesome, compelling reporting."

—Ann Rule

"An astonishing piece of popular history. I unhesitatingly recommend [it] . . . to round out your understanding of the true depth, meaning, and perversity on [this] uniquely American brand of mayhem."

—*The Boston Book Review*

"Destined to be a true-crime classic. . . . As chilling as *The Silence of the Lambs* and as bloodcurdling as the best Stephen King novel. . . . It will deprive you of sleep, and take your attention away from everything else on your schedule until you finish it."

—*Flint* (MI) *Journal*

"[Schechter's] writing keeps you turning the pages. . . ."

—*Syracuse Herald-American*

## Critical Acclaim for Harold Schechter's
## Novel Based on the Legend of Ed Gein . . .

### *OUTCRY*
**Voted Best Paperback Original of 1997 by *Rocky Mountain News***

"This is a scary book. . . ."

—*Rocky Mountain News* (Denver)

"FOUR STARS. Harold Schechter, an internationally acclaimed expert on true-crime murders by psychopathic serial killers, changes his medium by scribing a brilliant fictional account of these monsters. . . . All the characters are terrifyingly real. . . . Serial-killer aficionados need to read this thrilling tale that makes most of the subgenre seem cartoonish in comparison."

—Paintedrock.com

"Schechter is unsurpassed. . . . Terrifying. . . . You will feel compelled to grip this novel in your hand until you finish."

—*Clues* magazine

**Pocket Books by Harold Schechter**

The A–Z Encyclopedia of Serial Killers
  *(with David Everitt)*
Bestial
Depraved
Deranged
Deviant
Outcry
Nevermore

# DEVIANT

## The Shocking
## True Story of the Original
## "Psycho"

# Harold Schechter

POCKET BOOKS
New York   London   Toronto   Sydney

POCKET BOOKS, a division of Simon & Schuster Inc.
1230 Avenue of the Americas, New York, NY 10020

ISBN-13: 978-0-671-02546-5
ISBN-10:   0-671-02546-5

First Pocket Books trade paperback printing October 1998

30  29  28  27  26  25  24  23  22  21

Cover design by Brigid Pearson
Cover photo courtesy of AP/Wide World Photos

Printed in the U.S.A.

The man that wandereth out of the
   way of understanding
Shall remain in the congregation of
   the dead.

Proverbs 21:16

# A NOTE ON PRONUNCIATION

ALTHOUGH THE SPELLING OF *Gein* would lead one to believe that the name rhymes with *fine*, it is actually pronounced with a long *e*, as in *fiend*.

# PROLOGUE

In 1960, a maniac dressed in the clothes of his long-dead mother took a kitchen knife to a beauty in a bathtub and permanently altered the face of American horror. The murder occurred, of course, in Alfred Hitchcock's *Psycho*, a movie that not only changed the way an entire generation of filmgoers felt about being alone in the shower but also gave birth to a new kind of cinematic bogeyman. *Psycho*'s monster was not a Transylvanian vampire or a slithery, tentacled creature from outer space but a shy, stammering bachelor with a boyish grin, a bland personality, and the utterly colorless name of Norman Bates.

Although Norman never married, he has, during the past two decades, produced a multitude of offspring—an entire race of cinematic psychos who, following in his footsteps, have stalked and slaughtered countless young victims in movies with titles like *Bloodthirsty Butchers*, *Meatcleaver Massacre*, and *Driller Killer*. For all their extravagant goriness, however, few, if any, of these films can begin to match the supremely nightmarish power of *Psycho*.

To a great extent, that power derives from Hitchcock's diabolical ability to undermine our faith in the essential stability of our world. Like Norman's first victim, Marion Crane, we are propelled on a trip down a very slippery road, one that carries us inexorably away from the familiar sights and signposts of the everyday world into a terrifying irrational night realm. Before we know it, we have come upon a place where the most ordinary situations and settings are suddenly transformed into the stuff of our deepest fears—where, in a single awful instant, a motel bathroom becomes a chamber of horrors; where an affable, perfectly harmless-looking fellow metamorphoses into a crazed, knife-wielding transvestite; and where a helpless old lady turns out to be a leering corpse, decked out in a knitted shawl and grizzled wig. By the time the trip is over, we step away from the screen with the gratitude of a dreamer just awakened from a particularly harrowing nightmare, thankful that the ordeal we have just lived through was only a fiction and persuaded that nothing in the real world could ever be as horrific as such a fantasy.

Of all the shocks associated with *Psycho*, than, perhaps the greatest shock is this:

It is based on the truth. There really was a Norman Bates.

His name wasn't Norman, and he didn't run a motel. But on an isolated farmstead in the heartland of America, during the bland, balmy days of the Eisenhower era, there lived a quiet and reclusive bachelor with a lopsided grin and a diffident manner. During the day, his neighbors knew him as a slightly strange but accommodating man, the kind who could always be counted on to help with the threshing or lend a hand with a chore. It never occurred to any of them that his life was dominated by the overpowering presence of his dead mother or that his nights were spent performing the darkest and most appalling rituals. A robber of graves, a butcher of women's bodies, a transvestite who dressed himself not in the clothes but in the very skin of his victims, he pursued his unspeakable deeds for years without detection. And when his atrocities were finally brought to light, they set off a spasm of national revulsion whose aftereffects are still felt today. They also inspired a writer named Robert Bloch to use them as the basis of a novel called *Psycho*, which, one year later, Alfred Hitchcock turned into the most frightening movie ever made. But compared to what really happened in Wisconsin thirty-odd years ago, *Psycho* is as reassuring as a fairy tale.

# PART 1

# Bloodlines

# 1

*"By the end of the nineteenth century, country towns had become charnel houses and the counties that surrounded them had become places of dry bones."*

MICHAEL LESY, *Wisconsin Death Trip*

Wisconsin, the natives will boast, is a garden state, and as you head north on the highway from Madison on a limpid spring day, you see at once that the claim is simple truth. On either side, the road is lined with postcard-pretty vistas—massive red barns, silos like silver bullets, tranquil white farmhouses nestled in thick groves of trees. The rich, rolling pastures are dotted with ponds, cattle graze lazily on the slopes, and the soil is dark and loamy. An air of prosperity pervades the landscape, as palpable as the aroma of freshly mown hay. One hundred years ago, the writer Hamlin Garland described this part of the state as a "panorama of delight," and the region remains as picturesque as ever. This is Kodak country. Brightly painted billboards invite travelers to family restaurants, farmers' markets, and campgrounds. A roadside advertisement for the American Breeder's Service promotes business with the kind of gently self-mocking good humor characteristic of America's heartland: "I Heard It through the Bovine."

Thirty miles farther north, the landscape changes. The farms thin out; the countryside seems devoid of inhabitants. Occasionally, the highway passes through an improbably small town, a one-street village lined with a general store, a gas station, a tavern, a church, and a handful of white clapboard houses. Even with your speed cut down to thirty, you make it through the entire length of the village within a few seconds. Then you are out in the country again, traveling for miles without passing another vehicle or spotting a

3

single creature, except, perhaps, for a solitary red-winged blackbird settling on a fencepost or the rigid corpse of a run-over deer sprawled stiff-legged by the roadside. Still, the landscape is intensely pretty here, perhaps even more seductively peaceful than the farmland to the south. Here, Wisconsin seems less like a garden state or a vast, thriving dairyland than a lush, sprawling park, an endless expanse of bright green meadows and thickly wooded hills.

It is not until you cross over into the south-central plain area, sixty or so miles north of the capital, that you feel you have suddenly entered a different—and far less hospitable—world. Though the signs along the shoulder offer a variety of neighborly greetings—"Marquette County 4-H Club Welcomes You," "Welcome to Waushara, Christmas Tree Capital of the World"—the area has a lonely and distinctly desolate air. The few ramshackle farms you pass look as though they haven't been worked in years. Across a yard littered with the rusting scraps of farm machinery, a wasted old man, dressed in ragged bib overalls and supported by a pair of wooden canes, makes his way painfully toward a tumbledown barn. The sense of hardship and privation here is as tangible as the smug prosperity of the south. Every part of the landscape seems bleak and ungiving. The grass looks parched; the sky, even on a perfect spring day, presses down on you; and the soil is a faded pink, the same sickly color that the makers of children's crayons (in the days before anyone recognized the inherent racism of the label) used to call "flesh."

To some Wisconsinites, this flat and infertile section of the state is known as "sand country."

Others have called it Wisconsin's "great dead heart."

Within the past twenty years, parts of this region have been resuscitated by advances in agricultural technology. Sophisticated irrigation equipment in particular has given the dead heart some life and kept it beating. Hundreds of failed, ramshackle farms have been razed, replaced by high-yield potato fields. Scattered throughout the countryside are modest ranch houses, some with satellite-dish antennas and backyard pools. Still, this has always been a poor and underpopulated land, oppressive in its emptiness, where most of the inhabitants have struggled to eke out a living in remote and isolated farm communities—places with humble, quintessentially American names: Friendship. Wild Rose. Plainfield.

Plainfield—the name seems particularly well suited for a place so flat and featureless that even an official state guidebook characterizes it as completely "nondescript." It's surprising to discover, then, that the name doesn't refer to the region at all. It was bestowed on the town by one of its founding fathers, a transplanted New Englander named Elijah Waterman, who settled there in 1849, put up a twelve-by-six shanty which served as both his home and the area's only hotel, and christened the town in honor of his birthplace in Plainfield, Vermont. Within thirty years, the little village boasted several churches, a bank, a weekly newspaper, and a variety of businesses: three general stores, two blacksmiths, a drugstore, a tailor shop, a farm-implement warehouse, a gristmill.

The population remained small, however, never rising much above eight hundred inhabitants, most of them poor, struggling farmers, toiling to wrest even a marginal living out of the dry, stony soil—growing some rye, raising a little livestock, cultivating potatoes that often turned out to be too inferior to sell as food and had to be hauled by the wagonload to the local starch factory. The land mocked their efforts. Everything about it seemed to speak of barrenness and futility, even the big lake set in the southeast corner of the township, whose name reflected the sterility of the surrounding countryside: Sand Lake, the settlers called it.

In spite of all they had to contend with—the poverty, the crushing isolation, the unremitting struggle with the hard, unyielding land—the people of Plainfield took pride in their community. It was a solid, decent, neighborly place where old-fashioned values prevailed—where the whole town would turn out for the grade-schoolers' annual Christmas operetta, where Mrs. Duane Wilson's potluck dinner for the Plainfield Homemakers was a special event, and where Merle Beckley's trip to the National 4-H Congress would make front-page news in the local paper. Even the minuscule size of their village—a small strip of houses and stores with a single paved road running through it—was a source of affectionate good humor. One thing about Plainfield, the townsfolk would josh, you never have to worry about kids hanging around the street corners. There aren't any street corners.

Plainfield, they would tell you, was a nice place to live.

Of course, they had their full share of tragedy and disaster, too. Fires raged through the town on several occasions, consuming most of the buildings on Main Street. Cyclones, blizzards, and savage Midwestern thunderstorms took lives, killed cattle, and occasionally destroyed entire farms. Men were shot in hunting accidents, maimed by farm machinery, or left paralyzed when their pickups went skidding off icy roads or collided with trains. And suicide and murder took their toll. Indeed, for many years, the nice little community of Plainfield was identified in local history books as the site of a particularly vicious killing that occurred at the very beginning of the town's existence.

It happened in 1853, just five years after the first settler to the Plainfield area established the town by marking off a tract of land and setting up a simple log dwelling. A local squatter known as Firman was on a trip to Milwaukee, where he met a New Yorker named Cartwright, who was looking to migrate with his family to the Midwest. The territory around Plainfield—Waushara County—desperately needed more settlers, and Firman was willing to give Cartwright forty acres of his own property to entice the Easterner to the area. Cartwright accepted the offer.

For a short while, things went smoothly between the two men. But Firman was of a volatile and, according to contemporary accounts, lawless character. It wasn't long before he picked a quarrel with Cartwright over some trifling matter. The bad feelings between the two men intensified. Finally, Firman tried to oust Cartwright and his family from the land, claiming it as his own and accusing them of trespassing. The matter ended up in litigation. On the day the issue was to be decided, Firman failed to make it to court. The case was decided in favor of Cartwright, who decided to celebrate by stopping off in the barroom of the Boyington Hotel at Wautoma, the county seat. There he ran into Firman.

The men exchanged angry words, until, stung by a particularly bitter insult, Firman sprang upon Cartwright and knocked him out of his chair. Cartwright fell backward, hitting a potbellied stove, which tumbled over, scattering live coals across the floor. Cartwright jumped to his feet and fled the building, pursued by Firman, who caught him by the collar, wrestled him to the ground, and dug his thumbs into Cartwright's eyes. Unable to break Firman's hold, Cartwright groped for his back pocket, pulled out a pistol, and fired into his enemy's body. At the third discharge, Firman emitted a deep moan and slumped to the ground. He died within the hour, and Cartwright was immediately arrested.

Cartwright was held in jail at Oshkosh until he was released on bail. In the meantime, the friends of Firman—a bunch as wild and disreputable as the deceased—had promised to lynch the killer if he ever came back to Waushara County. Ignoring the threat, Cartwright returned to his home. On the second night following his arrival, Firman's cronies attempted to make good on their word and broke into Cartwright's house. Cartwright, armed with a rifle, stationed himself in the attic, his weapon leveled at the ladder. The first of the mob to show his head above the floor was shot and killed instantly. The crowd hurriedly withdrew from the house and held a parley. Deciding to burn Cartwright out, they began to kindle a fire at one corner of his house. Cartwright immediately poked his rifle through a chink in the logs and felled another of the party.

Again, the lynch mob pulled back, held a hurried conference, and this time concocted a devious plan. One of their members, a constable, was dispatched to the home of a judge named Walker, who resided in Plainfield. Walker was roused from his bed and apprised of the situation. The treacherous constable then presented Walker with a seemingly reasonable offer. If the judge would persuade Cartwright to turn himself over to the constable, the lynch mob would disperse. Cartwright would be escorted, under the constable's protection, to the Oshkosh jail, where he would remain until he could be tried for Firman's murder. The unsuspecting Walker agreed to do what he could and proceeded to Cartwright's home. The beleaguered man listened to the judge, agreed to the terms, bid farewell to his wife and children, and started from his home.

A nineteenth-century history book describes the "dread culmination of the tragedy." Cartwright, Walker, and the constable "had not proceeded twenty yards from the house when they were surrounded by the mob. Cartwright was taken from the constable, who made no resistance, put into a sleigh by the crowd, and driven rapidly to Plainfield, where a pole was run out of the upper story of the hay barn belonging to the tavern. A rope was attached thereto and several bunches of shingles were piled up for Cartwright to stand on. Walker, who had followed and was appealing to the mob to desist, was told that if he did not leave he would be hanged with Cartwright.

"The rope was noosed about Cartwright's neck, the shingles were pushed from under him, and he was left hanging until he was dead. Then the rope was untied from the pole and attached to the rear of the sleigh, and Cartwright's body was dragged behind the sleigh to his home and thrown into his house, where his horror-stricken wife and children had been wondering at his fate.

"To the shame of the good name of Waushara County, the human fiends who participated in this murderous outrage against law and right were never punished nor even prosecuted, though many if not all of them were known."

\* \* \*

The story of Firman and Cartwright and the "dread culmination" of their feud remained, for many years, the most sensational episode in the history of Plainfield. To many of the townspeople, it seemed woefully unfair that their honest little village should be associated with such an infamous event.

How could they have known that living in their midst was a "human fiend" immeasurably more depraved than any nineteenth-century lynch mob, a man who would (to the enduring dismay of its inhabitants) make the name of Plainfield, Wisconsin, forever synonymous with darkness, insanity, and unimaginable horror?

# 2

*"Although it is the mother who contributes mostly in producing the conditions which we are going to describe, we usually find in the history of schizophrenics that both parents have failed the child, often for different reasons. Frequently the combination is as follows: A domineering, nagging, and hostile mother, who gives the child no chance to assert himself, is married to a dependent, weak man, too weak to help the child. A father who dares not protect the child . . . because he is not able to oppose her strong personality is just as crippling to the child as the mother is."*

SILVANO ARIETI, *Interpretation of Schizophrenia*

From the very beginning, it was a family that fate seemed to have singled out for tragedy.

The first struck in 1879, the kind of calamity that can blight a man's life, poison his future, and, indeed, leave its ruinous mark on the destiny of his children.

At the time, George Gein's family was living on a farm in Coon Valley, Wisconsin, about fifteen miles outside of La Crosse. One overcast morning, George's mother, father, and older sister climbed into the buckboard and set off for town on an errand.

They never returned.

The Mississippi River was at high water, and the wagon was caught in a flash flood. The elder Gein, his wife, and his firstborn child drowned in the dark, bitter torrent, and George was left orphaned and alone. He was three years old.

His maternal grandparents, stern, Scottish immigrants who lived on a nearby farm, took him into their home. There are few available details about this or any other stage of George Gein's life. He was, after all, just an obscure Midwestern provincial, unluckier than most, whom history has no reason at all to remember, except as the father of an authentic American monster. Indeed, the most notable fact about George Gein's life is how utterly insignificant, how much of a nonentity, he appeared to be, even (perhaps especially) in the eyes of the family he later established.

Following his elementary-school education, George Gein apprenticed himself to a local blacksmith. He spent several years laboring over the anvil and forge. And then one day during his early twenties, he left his grandparents' farm for good and, like so many country people before and after him, headed off for the nearest city.

Within a short time of his arrival in La Crosse, he seems to have established a pattern of drifting from one occupation to another. He sold insurance for a while, tried his hand at carpentry, and worked in a tannery, at the city power plant, and on the Chicago, Milwaukee & St. Paul Railway. Perhaps his difficulty in holding down a job had something to do with his growing attachment to the bottle. Increasingly, George would repair to a saloon after work and drink up much of his pay. Red-eyed and befuddled, he would sink into black moods of anger and self-pity, brooding on the rotten hand life had dealt him. The world was against him. He'd been made into an orphan when he was just a baby and brought up in a grim and loveless home. It was enough to make a man lose faith in the goodness of God. At other times, he would lapse into bitter self-recrimination. His misfortunes were his own fault. He would never amount to anything. He was worthless, incompetent, a complete and hopeless failure—as a worker, a provider, and a man.

Given the genuine hardships he'd had to deal with from the time he was a toddler, most people would have regarded George Gein's low opinion of himself as far too harsh a judgment. But in this respect—as in so many others—George Gein's wife was not like most people.

Her name was Augusta, and she came from a large and industrious family whose dour, demanding patriarch had emigrated from Germany in 1870 and settled in La Crosse. George Gein was twenty-four when he met her; Augusta was nineteen. Even then, she was a person to be reckoned with—a thickset, buxom woman with a broad, coarse-featured face permanently fixed in a look of fierce determination and complete self-assurance. Devoutly—even fanatically—religious, she had been brought up to obey a rigid code of conduct, which her father had not hesitated to reinforce with regular beatings. Augusta was continuously outraged by the flagrant immorality of the modern world. Wherever she looked, she saw a looseness of behavior that seemed shockingly, sinfully at variance with the strict Old World values of her household. Life, she knew, was serious business—a matter of endless hard work, unwavering thrift, and extreme self-denial.

She was, in the end, her father's daughter—a stern disciplinarian, self-righteous, domineering, and inflexible, who never doubted for a moment the absolute correctness of her beliefs or her right to impose them, by whatever means possible, on the people around her.

What she and George saw in each other is mostly a matter of conjecture. George would have been marrying into a large and, in many ways, close-knit family. Augusta had half a dozen siblings at home, with other relatives living nearby, including a cousin named Fred who was a coworker of George's at the David, Medary & Platz Tannery. To a man who had been bereft of his own family at such an early age, there must have been something powerfully appealing about becoming a member of so sizable a clan. And George could hardly have helped being impressed by Augusta's imposing personality, her formidable energies, and her evident capabilities in practical affairs.

For her part, Augusta, who had never been besieged by suitors, may well have been taken by George's prepossessing appearance. He was a strong, straight man with a reserved, even dignified, manner. Indeed, later in life, his neighbors would take him for a retired minister. And, like Augusta, he was a practicing Lutheran (though of a decidedly less fervid stripe). From his rather formal bearing and quiet behavior, she would have had no way of knowing about his growing alcoholism or about those deeper, unhealed wounds that would increasingly incapacitate him. Or perhaps his fundamental weaknesses were, in fact, evident to her and only served to make him more attractive. From all accounts, she was a woman who may well have preferred the kind of husband she could bend easily to her own will.

They were wed on December 4, 1899. Like almost everything else in the lives of these ill-fated people, their marriage, from all available evidence, had the quality of a particularly lacerating nightmare.

In charge of her own household and joined to a man of feckless and increasingly unreliable character, Augusta quickly assumed the role of domestic tyrant. Her own deformities of character—her harshness, rigidity, and fierce intolerance—became ever more pronounced. Her husband was worthless, good for nothing. She sneered at him openly, called him a lazy dog and worse. In spite of his broad back and blacksmith's muscles, he was a weakling, afraid of hard work. It was she who possessed all the strength. He had no spirit, no ambition. Worst of all, he could not seem to hold on to a job. And when she discovered, as she quickly did, how much of his meager earnings disappeared inside the local taverns, her fury— inflamed even more by her religious beliefs—was immeasurable. Her husband became an object unworthy of even her contempt.

George responded to his wife's undisguised hatred by withdraw- ing more deeply into himself. He refused to speak. When Augusta was not ordering him about or deriding his inadequacies, a poison- ous silence prevailed in their house. Occasionally, however, after returning from the tavern and being greeted with an especially vicious tongue-lashing, he would lose control and flail out at Augusta's face, hitting her open-handed again and again. Augusta would sink to the floor, wailing and shouting insults. Afterward, she would draw herself to her knees and pray fervently for her hus- band's death.

Perhaps, she thought, a child would comfort her in her trials, even serve as an ally in her struggles with George. About sexual matters, Augusta's views were characteristically extreme. Sex unsanctified by marriage was an unpardonable sin, an abomination. Between husband and wife, carnal relations were a loathsome duty to be tolerated for the sake of procreation. She was revolted by the very thought of the act. Increasingly, Augusta's perceptions were becom- ing warped into something very much like madness. The world was a sink of corruption, La Crosse a city of Babylonian excess. The women she saw on the streets, with their brazen airs and shameless smiles, were no better than harlots. Still, she craved the solace of a child. And so she allowed her despised husband to come to her bed.

The fruit of that loveless union was a robust boy, Henry, born on January 17, 1902. His life would be hard and isolated, and his death, forty years later, in the prime of his manhood, would be only one of the many dark mysteries that would come to surround the offspring of George and Augusta Gein.

Once again, George found himself out of a job. Augusta decided that there was only one possible solution, one chance for the family to avert economic disaster—George must work for himself. Two of her brothers were successful merchants in La Crosse, purveyors of "staple and fancy groceries." Business increased every year, and the city could easily accommodate another such store. In 1909, George Gein became proprietor of a small meat and grocery shop at 914 Caledonia Street.

It didn't take long, however, for problems to manifest themselves. George clearly could not make it on his own. Augusta knew what had to be done. She already had complete charge of their domestic life. Now she must take total control of their business affairs as well. The entries in the 1909 and 1911 La Crosse City Directories speak volumes, not only about George's increasingly pitiable position in the world but also about the nature of his and Augusta's relationship. In the earlier volume, George Gein is listed as the owner of the store. Two years later, Augusta is named as the proprietor. The entry for George Gein reads "clerk."

In the meantime, they had had another child. Though Augusta did not feel especially close to her firstborn, she attributed her detachment to the child's gender. It was, after all, a boy. Things would be different with a daughter. And so she clenched her teeth and allowed her husband to commit the foul deed upon her again. During the weeks that followed, she prayed every night for the Lord to bless her with a baby girl.

On August 27, 1906, Augusta gave birth to her second child. He was a boy, and they named him Edward Theodore. When Augusta first heard she had delivered a second male child, she felt bitter, betrayed. But Augusta was not the kind to give in to despair. She was made of stronger stuff. And so she took the swaddled newborn in her arms and made a sacred vow.

This one would not grow up to be like all the rest of them. Men. Those lustful, sweating, foul-mouthed creatures who made use of women's bodies in such filthy ways. This one, she promised, would be different.

Augusta would see to that.

# 3

*"A boy's best friend is his mother."*
NORMAN BATES,
in Alfred Hitchcock's *Psycho*

**Y**ears later, he would be asked the same question, time and again: "Tell us something about her, Eddie. What was your mother like?"

As soon as he started to think about her, his eyes would fill with tears and his throat grow so swollen that he'd have trouble swallowing. She was pure goodness, he'd finally say. Not like the others. They got what was coming to them. But she didn't deserve so much suffering.

All her life, she had slaved and prayed and struggled to save him from the evils of the world. And he had tried to be as good as possible. But somehow, he always seemed to fail her.

He remembered the time she had put a few coins in his hand and instructed him to go to the German bakery a block from their home to buy a loaf of bread. They were still living in La Crosse, so he couldn't have been more than seven. Somehow, by the time he reached the shop, the coins were gone. For a long time, he stood on the street corner, fighting back tears, terrified to go home. When he finally did find the courage to return and confess, his voice convulsed by sobs, she looked down at him with that mixture of bitterness and sorrow that never failed to fill him with the deepest self-hatred. "You dreadful child," she had said in a quiet, heartbroken voice more awful than any scream. "Only a mother could love you."

*She* would never have made such a stupid, unforgivable mistake. Whatever needed to be done, Augusta Gein could always be

14

counted on to do it right, without foul-ups or complaints. She was, by far, the ablest one in the family. And the strongest.

When he thought back to his childhood, he usually pictured her standing in their old grocery shop, an immense, looming presence who did nearly all the work—waited on the customers, handled the cash register, kept the books. Meanwhile, her poor excuse of a husband—his father—shuffled about the store in that shrunken, defeated way of his, rearranging the goods on the shelves according to her directions and occasionally delivering groceries.

If Augusta had any flaws, her younger son wasn't aware of them. He knew that it might be a sacrilege even to think it, but in his eyes she was no less infallible than God. He recalled a time (it was, in fact, his earliest memory of her) when he was just a toddler. He was standing at the top of the staircase in their old house on Gould Street. Somehow, he lost his balance and felt himself being pulled—or pushed?—down the steep flight of wooden steps by a powerful force. Panic turned his insides to ice. Suddenly, he felt a crushing grip close around his right arm. His mother was behind him, a wild look on her face, shaking him, shouting at him. He burst into clamorous tears, overcome by a rush of violently conflicting emotions—fright, relief, guilt. Why was she so angry with him? He had no idea, but he knew he must have done something terrible to make her so furious. Misery washed over him. It was all his fault.

From that point on—even into his middle age—he placed all his reliance on her. She alone could be counted on to rescue him from life's dangers.

There was one other memory he had of his childhood in La Crosse.

Behind the meat and grocery store was a windowless, wooden outbuilding which he was forbidden to enter. As a result, it exerted a tremendous fascination. He had seen animals being led into the rear of the shack—big-eyed heifers and grunting pigs—and on several occasions had heard a fearful bellowing coming from behind its sagging boards. Curiosity blazed in him.

One day, when his parents weren't around, he went out through the back door of the grocery and stepped quickly to the prohibited place. The door was opened a crack, enough for him to peer inside.

There, hanging upside down from a chain in the ceiling, was a slaughtered hog. His father stood to one side of the animal, holding it steady, while his mother slipped a long-bladed knife down the length of its belly, pulled open the flaps, reached inside, and began to work at the glistening ropes of its bowels, which slid out of the carcass and into a large metal tub at her feet. Both his parents had on long leather aprons spattered with blood.

He must have made some sort of noise, because his mother turned completely around to look at him.

For the rest of his life, he remembered the moment with an uncanny clarity: the dangling beast, its carcass split open, its guts slopping onto the ground; his mother standing beside it, blood and slime smeared down the length of her body.

Years later, when they asked him about Augusta, he would say, "She was like nobody else in the world."

Then, like the rotting, reawakened corpses in those horror magazines he enjoyed reading so much, the wretchedness would rise up in him from some buried place deep inside, and, though he was by then a man in his early fifties, he would begin to cry as noisily and helplessly as a baby.

# 4

*"City people, attracted by the cheap price of land, came out seeking new opportunity. . . . When they arrived, they found, instead of the pastoral life they had envisioned, merely interminable, unclocked labor, logging, stumping, stoning, draining, fencing, and breaking ground. The region demands a toll of at least one failure for each piece of land successfully brought to cultivation; of the relatively poor land left, much could be sold and resold, and ruin settler after settler, without ever becoming more productive than a sand dune."*

*Wisconsin: A Guide to the Badger State*

By the time Eddie was seven, Augusta had become the uncontested head of the family—its driving force and decision maker—and in 1913, she decided that the Geins would become farmers. Her hard years of labor in the store, toiling day and night and keeping a close eye on every penny, had paid off. She had managed to accumulate enough money for a modest farm. The Geins would become landowners, people of means. There was a good living to be made from dairy cows and rye. And she had another motive, too: she would be getting herself and her family, particularly little Eddie, far away from the evil influences of the city.

Late that year, the Geins moved to a small dairy farm in the lowlands near Camp Douglas, forty miles east of La Crosse. For unknown reasons, they remained there for less than a year. Perhaps Augusta, always on the lookout for a way to improve the family's fortunes, saw an opportunity to purchase an even larger piece of land. Or perhaps she felt that even at that distance, they were still living too close to La Crosse, which, in her burgeoning religious mania, she had come to regard as a latter-day Sodom.

Whatever the case, in 1914, the Gein family made the second—

and final—move, to a one-hundred-ninety-five-acre farm in Plainfield known to the locals as the old John Greenfield place. At a time
when property ownership was almost entirely in the hands of men,
land records show that the Plainfield farm was purchased by and
deeded to, not George, but Augusta Gein.

Augusta was happy with the new homestead, and, in truth, it was
a substantial place, particularly by the standards of that underprivi-
leged area. The house itself was a trim two-story affair, an L-shaped
white frame building with a parlor, a kitchen, and a pair of
bedrooms on the first floor and five more rooms upstairs. The
outbuildings included a fair-sized barn, a chicken coop, and an
equipment shack. There was also a shedlike summer kitchen that
had been built onto one end of the house, with a connecting door
opening into the regular kitchen.

Augusta promptly set about arranging the rooms with the sparse
but solid furnishings she had gradually acquired during the years of
her marriage. The best pieces were reserved for the parlor, which
contained a handsome cherry bureau, its breakfront decorated with
a simple leaf design; a stout wooden rocker with elaborately carved
arm supports; a small pine bookcase, its five narrow shelves neatly
stacked with leather-bound volumes; a large Oriental carpet,
slightly threadbare but with a rich geometric pattern; and a number
of pictures on the walls, including family portraits in heavy gilded
frames and (Augusta's favorite) a reproduction painting of Christ
gazing skyward at an angel.

Augusta was, of course, a fastidious homemaker who insisted that
her house be kept, as she put it, "as neat as a pin." She was fiercely
proud of her perfectionism. There might be richer people in the
world but none who maintained a tidier place. The Gein home
wasn't a mansion, but it would never look anything less than
absolutely clean and orderly—not, at any rate, as long as Augusta
was alive.

There was another feature of their new homestead that Augusta
grew to appreciate as the Geins settled into their new lives: its
extreme isolation. The farm was situated six miles west of Plainfield
village, a significant distance in the days of dirt roads and wagon
travel, when farmers rarely ventured from home and the monthly
trip to the general store in town was a major event. Their nearest
neighbors were the Johnson family, whose farmhouse was located a
little less than a quarter-mile down the road. Otherwise, the Geins

were surrounded by nothing but meadows, marshland, scattered clumps of trees, and acre upon acre of pale, sandy soil.

The remoteness of her farm suited Augusta just fine. It hadn't taken her long to conclude that the religious and moral standards of Plainfield were scandalously low. In her increasingly warped vision, the decent, hard-working, God-fearing townsfolk were a disreputable and untrustworthy lot. Augusta felt herself far too good for them. The less she had to do with them, the better. Since Plainfield boasted a Catholic, a Methodist, and a Baptist—but no Lutheran—church, there was even less reason to mingle with her neighbors. She herself would handle her sons' moral and religious training. On those rare occasions when she was compelled to travel to town, she could feel the resentment emanating from the merchants she had to deal with and the people she passed on the street. Perhaps they could sense her superiority simply from the way she bore herself. Or perhaps, having ridden by her farm, they were envious of how well-cared-for it was.

Augusta didn't mind being shunned by the people of Plainfield. Indeed, she wanted no part of such a backslidden, vice-prone community. Her boys provided all the companionship she needed. The farm would be her own self-contained little world.

Much as she might have liked to, Augusta couldn't keep her sons entirely cut off from the world. When Eddie was eight, he began attending the Roche-a-Cri grade school, a tiny one-room building with a dozen students altogether. Later, Roche-a-Cri merged with another country school, the White School, and it was there that Eddie Gein completed his formal education at age sixteen after graduating from the eighth grade. Eddie was a capable if unexceptional student, who managed well enough in all his subjects. (Years later, in the early days of his notoriety, when he was placed under intense psychiatric scrutiny and subjected to a battery of tests, his I.Q. would be recorded as average.) He was a particularly good reader. Indeed, throughout his life, he busied himself with books and magazines on varied and, at times, quite unusual subjects.

Books were a good way to relax, he believed. And you could learn lots of things from them, too.

But although Eddie did passably well in his studies, his school years were not a particularly happy time. He felt overwhelmingly alone, hopelessly cut off from his classmates. They related to each other so easily—griping about their chores, exchanging scraps of local gossip they had picked up at the dinner table, talking excitedly about the big fire down at Conover's Warehouse or the upcoming Donkey Derby at Plainfield Auditorium. Eager to be accepted, he watched how they acted and tried to imitate their behavior. But somehow he could never fit in.

On a few occasions during his childhood and adolescence, he seemed to be coming close to making a real connection. But as soon as he would return home and tell his mother about his newfound friend, she would immediately begin raising objections. The boy's family had a bad reputation. There were dark rumors about the father's past, and the mother was known to be a woman of questionable virtue. Augusta wouldn't have a son of hers associating with people like that. How could Eddie behave in such a way? By now, her voice would have risen to a scream. Was she raising a fool?

Eddie would begin to blubber and retreat to his room. The next day, he would go to school and avoid even looking at the other boy.

From the point of view of his peers, there was definitely something a little different about Eddie Gein. At no point in his life—not, at any rate, until his simmering psychosis erupted into full-blown dementia—did anyone perceive that he might be a dangerously disturbed individual. And, in fact, it would have taken a fairly sophisticated eye to see in young Eddie's behavior—his social incompetence, for example, and increasing isolation—the signs of incipient madness. But there were things about Eddie that certainly struck his schoolmates as peculiar—the way his eyes kept shifting around whenever he tried to talk to you; the odd, lopsided grin he always wore, even when the conversation had to do with the deer-hunting accident that killed Eugene Johnson or old man Beckley's heart attack; his habit of laughing at weirdly inappropriate times, as though he were listening to some strange, private joke that no one else could hear.

Sometimes, one of the girls would turn around in her seat and catch him staring at her with a look of such peculiar intensity that, even at that early age, she would feel vaguely unclean—violated. And there were times when a few of the boys would be huddled together, whispering about sex. Eddie, approaching the group and overhearing the talk, would blush furiously and back away as fast as he could.

That was another thing about Eddie that his schoolmates of both sexes recognized from an early age. He didn't seem to be like other boys. There was something about his mannerisms—the softness of his voice, the meekness of his posture, the nervous fluttering motions his hands made when he talked—that struck them as distinctly girlish. He had another effeminate trait, too. He cried very easily. He certainly couldn't take a joke. They remembered the time Eddie got teased about his eye. He had a fat, fleshy growth on the corner of his left eyelid. It wasn't really disfiguring, but it made his eyelid droop. Once, one of the boys made a comment about it—not anything mean, really, just a joke about Eddie's "saggy-baggy eye." Eddie's shit-eating grin had instantly dissolved, and, in front of all of them, he began to sob like a little girl.

As far as Eddie was concerned, all these things about his schoolmates—their teasing, their insensitivity, and especially their dirty talk—only confirmed his mother's omniscience. She was right about everything. Outside the close confines of the family, the world was a hard and wicked place.

Not that conditions within the Gein family were any less difficult. No matter how doggedly they worked it, their hardscrabble farm yielded barely enough food to provide for the family's subsistence. The fruitless struggle with the soil was a backbreaking job, particularly since George could no longer be counted on to do his share of work. By the time Eddie was a teenager, his father's main occupations seemed to be loafing, liquor consumption, and abusing his wife and children. He had often whipped the boys when he got drunk. By now—though both Eddie and Henry were small, slightly built young men—they were too big to be beaten. But George could still rant and rave. During one of his alcoholic rampages, he had even accused his wife of adultery. Considering the pathological prudishness of Augusta's sexual attitudes—not to mention her refusal to associate with any of her neighbors—it seems clear that George's mental condition was, by this point, no more stable than his wife's.

Even had she been so inclined, Augusta would scarcely have had the time to indulge in infidelity, since, besides her housework, she now had to take on some of the chores that her husband would no longer deign to do. Indeed, now that the boys were grown up enough to travel into town and buy the monthly provisions, she never left the farm at all. Life in Plainfield had turned out to be a brutal business, but Augusta refused to abandon it. Divorce was unthinkable, a fundamental violation of her religious beliefs. If the Lord had meant to burden her with a bestial husband and a life of unrelenting labor, then she would not set herself against His will.

Cut off from all social contacts, completely separated from the life of the community, condemned to an existence of crushing poverty in a remote and desolate region with two tormented and inimical parents, Eddie—never emotionally strong to begin with—was retreating farther and farther into a private world of fantasy. The Gein farm may not have been productive, but it was proving to be a fertile breeding ground for madness.

As Eddie and Henry grew to manhood and George sank ever deeper into the black pit of his melancholia, Augusta took to harping, with increasing and obsessive frequency, on a single, strident theme: the wickedness of modern women. From newspaper photos and magazine illustrations, she knew the way they dressed, with their short skirts, powders, and lipstick. They were tainted, fallen creatures, and the women of Plainfield, she would admonish her sons, were the worst.

When heavy rains fell and outdoor work was impossible, she would settle into her rocker in the damp, dimly lit parlor and, with the boys at her feet, tell them the story of Noah, prophesying the coming of another flood to wash away women's sins. Or, reaching for the heavy family Bible, she would rest it on her lap, open it to the *Book of Revelations*, and read:

> So he carried me away in the spirit into the wilderness: and I saw a woman sit upon a scarlet coloured beast, full of names of blasphemy, having seven heads and ten horns. And the woman was arrayed in purple and scarlet colour, and decked with gold and precious stones and pearls, having a golden cup in her hand, full of abominations and filthiness of her fornication: and upon her forehead was a name written, "MYSTERY, BABYLON THE GREAT, THE MOTHER OF HARLOTS AND ABOMINATIONS OF THE EARTH."

At other times, her eyes squeezed tight and her voice quavering, she would begin to rock back and forth in her chair and recite passages from *Proverbs*, which she had committed to memory:

> The lips of a strange woman drop honey,
> And her mouth is smoother than oil:
> But her latter end is bitter as wormwood,
> Sharp as a two-edged sword.

Now therefore, my sons, hearken unto me,
And depart not from the words of my mouth.
Remove thy way far from her,
And come not nigh the door of her house.

For why shouldest thou, my son, be ravished
with a strange woman,
And embrace the bosom of a stranger?

What, my son? and what, O son of my womb?
And what, O son of my vows?
Give not thy strength unto women,
Nor thy ways to that which destroyeth kings.

Then, reaching down and taking each of her boys by the hand, she would make them swear to her that they would keep themselves uncontaminated by women. If their lusts became too pressing to resist, she would say, even the sin of Onan was preferable to the vileness of fornication.

It would be hard for any child to withstand such a constant assault, though Henry apparently struggled a bit against Augusta's teachings. On a few occasions during his late adolescence, he made several doomed attempts to socialize with local girls. But his will was no match for his mother's. Finally, he resigned himself to bachelorhood, a condition that seemed characteristic of Augusta's male relations. Like several of her brothers, who never took wives, Augusta's two sons would remain unattached—bound to no other woman but their mother—for as long as they lived.

In Henry's case, that wouldn't be very long.

*"You can do nothing to bring the dead to life, but you can do much to save the living from death."*

From a family medical guide, found
among Edward Gein's possessions

They went in shockingly rapid succession.

By the time George reached his early sixties, the hurts he had borne for a lifetime—some of them self-inflicted, others the result of his wretched luck and catastrophic marriage—had taken a devastating toll on his health. All the years of heavy drinking, hard times, and domestic misery had left him broken in body and soul. By 1937, he was a wasted man, a helpless invalid, completely dependent on the family that detested and feared him.

Three years later, when George was sixty-six, his hard and cheerless life came to an end. His funeral was held on April 4, 1940, at R. A. Goult's combination furniture store and funeral home, with the Reverend Wendell Bennetts of the Plainfield Methodist Church officiating.

The obituary that appeared in the local papers was a model of postmortem sentimentality, focusing on the poignant facts of George's orphanhood and concluding with a tearful tribute to the dear departed that, given the realities of George Gein's family life, seems like a particularly cruel joke:

### GEORGE GEIN DIES

George Gein, 66, was born August 4, 1873, and passed away April 1, 1940.

His mother and father and little sister preceded him in death. They were gone to town and he was staying at home because of the high water, as it was raising in the Mississippi river. The father, mother, and sister never returned, leaving him an orphan boy. This flood occurred in Vernon county a good many years ago.

He lived in La Crosse until 1914, then going to Plainfield, where he since resided.

He is survived by his wife and two sons, Henry and Edward.

He had suffered considerably for the past three years, but his sufferings were eased by his faith in God.

He was a good husband and father and will be missed by all who knew him.

George Gein's death did not represent a serious loss to his family. Quite the contrary. As far as his sons were concerned, it relieved them of a particularly galling task. For as long as they could remember, the old man hadn't been good for much of anything (except boozing and meanness), and in the last few years of his life, he had added to their troubles by requiring continual care.

But even without the burden of a sick and unloved parent to take care of, life remained grueling for the Geins. Their efforts to eke out a living from the farm were both unending and almost entirely futile. In all the years they had lived there, the family hadn't been able to scrape together enough money to afford a single improvement. In every essential respect, their house remained the same as it had been in 1914, unequipped with either electricity or indoor plumbing. The only major change was in the deterioration of its once trim exterior. With its flaking gray paint, splintered front steps, poorly patched roof, and sagging porch, the house Augusta had once been so proud of looked weatherworn and increasingly dilapidated.

By this time, the most devastating war in the history of humankind was well under way, but neither of the brothers would be involved. Henry was too old for military service. Eddie was still eligible for the draft, but when he traveled to Milwaukee in 1942 for his physical exam, the army rejected him because of the growth on his left eyelid, which slightly impaired his vision.

He was thirty-six years old at the time, and the one-hundred-thirty-mile journey he made to Milwaukee was the farthest from home he had ever been. Or would ever be in his life.

Following the death of their father, the brothers undertook a variety of odd jobs away from the farm to bring in a bit of extra money. Eddie found occasional work in the Plainfield vicinity as a handyman—hanging windows, patching roofs, painting houses, repairing fences. He also did some babysitting. The kids were always glad to see Eddie. He would roughhouse with the boys and do silly magic tricks for the girls or tell them creepy stories about headhunters and cannibals from the adventure magazines he read all the time. In the winter he would join in their snowball fights and in summer treat them to ice cream.

As a youngster, he had never felt at ease with his peers. But now that he was grown up, he related more comfortably to children than to other adults. Around people his own age, he felt self-conscious and insecure. He wasn't sure how to act or what to say to them, particularly the women.

As far as the people who hired him were concerned, Eddie Gein, unlike his stuck-up, holier-than-thou mother, was a good neighbor. True, he had his peculiarities. He didn't say much, and it was always hard to tell what he might be thinking, since his lips were constantly forming into that sly, unsettling grin. But given his family background, a few eccentricities were only to be expected. For the most part, they regarded the soft-spoken little bachelor as a decent sort— a mite foolish, maybe, but a polite and dependable fellow.

Of the two brothers, Henry was considered the harder worker. He had always been more independent than Eddie, and, during the early 1940s, he found more and more employment away from the family farm. He worked for a road-building contractor, set poles and strung wires for a power and utility company, and, at one point, was hired by a neighbor to act as a foreman, overseeing a crew of Jamaican farm laborers.

Eddie had a deep admiration for his older brother. "He's the only man in the area who can handle those guys," he'd tell his neighbors when they asked if Henry was having any trouble managing the Jamaicans. Henry and Eddie had always had a good relationship, sharing chores, going fishing together, hunting their property for rabbits and squirrels. Sure, they had their share of arguments— what brothers didn't? One particular sore point had to do with their mother. On more than one occasion, Henry suggested that Eddie's attachment to Augusta was overly close. He never actually spoke disrespectfully of their mother. But Eddie could sense that Henry had some serious questions about her hold over her younger son.

Eddie was astonished. He had always believed that Henry shared his own view of Augusta, regarding her as infallible, faultless, a saint on earth. Henry's implied criticism of Augusta came as a real shock to Eddie. It was something he just couldn't understand.

And it was something he would never forget.

The single indisputable fact about Henry Gein's sudden death at age forty-three is that it occurred on Tuesday, May 16, 1944, while he and Eddie were fighting a runaway fire on some marshland near their home. According to some accounts, the blaze began accidentally. According to others, it was started deliberately to burn off the dry grass. Eddie would later claim that setting the fire was Henry's idea. "I coaxed him and tried to keep him home," Eddie would tell his interrogators, years after the tragedy. "But he just kept at me 'til I took him there." At the time it happened, though, newspapers reported that it was Eddie who insisted on burning the marsh that day, and that Henry had come along to help.

But the biggest question surrounding the tragedy is, of course, the precise manner of Henry's death.

As Eddie later told it, when a strong wind suddenly blew up and the fire got out of control, he quickly moved to one end of the marsh and struggled to extinguish the blaze before it reached a stand of pines on the perimeter of the field. After managing to put out the fire, he returned to look for his brother, but darkness had fallen and he couldn't locate Henry. Eddie then rounded up a search party that included Deputy Sheriff Frank Engle and took them back to the marsh.

As soon as they arrived, Eddie led them straight to the place where his older brother was lying facedown and very obviously dead. Several odd things immediately struck the searchers. First, though the corpse was stretched out on a scorched piece of ground, there were no signs that Henry had been injured by the flames. His clothes were soot-covered but otherwise undamaged, and the exposed parts of his body were similarly free of burns. Moreover, when the men bent to look more carefully at Henry, they noticed what seemed to be some funny bruises on his head.

The strangest thing of all was the way Eddie had guided them directly to the death site, though he apparently hadn't been able to locate his brother earlier. When they mentioned that to Eddie, he only shrugged and agreed with them. "Funny how that works," he observed.

District Attorney Earl Kileen, County Coroner George Blader, and Dr. Ingersoll of Plainfield were immediately called to the scene. As the weekly newspaper the *Waushara Argus* reported in its issue of Thursday, May 18: "It was determined by the medical authority present that death was due to asphyxiation. After an investigation by the coroner it was decided that an inquest was not necessary, as foul play did not enter into the death of Mr. Gein."

Clearly, no one could seriously imagine that Henry was the victim of murder—at least, no one could imagine it then. Years later, of course, when his brother's true nature stood revealed to a horror-stricken world, the very peculiar circumstances surrounding Henry's abrupt demise would be instantly called to mind, and the phrase "Cain and Abel" would be bandied about by lots of people around Plainfield.

But for now, the matter was considered closed. Henry, some said, had simply been overcome by the smoke and the heat and had hit his head on a rock when he collapsed. Certainly, he wouldn't be the first middle-aged farmer from those parts to succumb while doing battle with a raging marsh fire. Others maintained that Henry had had a bad heart, and the struggle with the flames had brought on a coronary. But, though some of them criticized Eddie for his strangely unfeeling response, no one believed for a moment that he was in any way to blame. He might be a bit of an oddball, but the notion that the meek little man was capable of hurting, let alone killing, anyone was too silly to entertain.

And so, in the third week of May 1944, Goult's funeral parlor had itself another customer, and Eddie Gein had his mother all to himself.

But not for very long.

For all her adult life, Augusta had been not just the head of her family but its backbone, too. Single-handedly, she had kept the house in perfect order, educated her two sons in the tenets of her faith, and managed the family business. She even did a man's share of the chores around the farm. To Eddie, she was a miracle of physical and spiritual fortitude. Even now, in his late thirties, whenever he thought or dreamed about her, she appeared in his mind as a towering being, impossibly large, a figure of immeasurable strength and willpower.

And so it came as an enormous shock to him when, shortly after Henry's death, Augusta suddenly complained of feeling terribly faint and sickly. She needed a doctor. By the time Eddie's pickup pulled up at the Wild Rose hospital, she was so weak that she had to be transported to the examination room in a wheelchair. Eddie sat on a bench in the corridor, twisting his plaid deerhunter's cap in his hands and blinking nervously. After an agonizing wait, a doctor appeared and solemnly informed him that his mother had suffered a stroke.

During her hospitalization, Eddie stayed at her bedside every day, for as many hours as he was allowed. Finally, she was discharged. Eddie—whose slight, wiry frame gave no real indication of his considerable strength—took her home, carried her inside the house, and laid her in her bed. When he looked down at her drawn, twisted face, a wave of pity and horror washed over him. He had never seen her look so frail and ravaged. But at the same time, he felt strangely exhilarated by her helplessness. She was entirely in his care. After all these years, he had a chance to prove his worth to her. Perhaps she would even acknowledge his efforts. He imagined her reaching out to embrace him, to grasp him to her bosom in gratitude and love. He could not remember a time when she had ever held him closely.

He waited on her every need. She never complained, simply lay there in bed and told him, as best she could manage, what work needed to be done. In the evenings, he would sit by her side and read to her by lamplight. Often, she would tell him to recite from Psalm 6:

> O Lord, rebuke me not in thine anger,
> Neither chasten me in thy hot displeasure.
> Have mercy upon me, O Lord; for I am weak;
> O Lord, heal me; for my bones are vexed.
> My soul is also sore vexed:
> But thou, O Lord, how long?
> Return, O Lord, deliver my soul:
> O save me for thy mercies' sake.
> For in death there is no remembrance of thee:
> In the grave who shall give thee thanks?
> I am weary with my groaning;
> All the night make I my bed to swim;
> I water my couch with my tears.
> Mine eye is consumed because of grief;
> It waxeth old because of all mine enemies.
> Depart from me, all ye workers of iniquity;
> For the Lord hath heard the voice of my weeping.
> The Lord hath heard my supplication.
> The Lord will receive my prayer.

Slowly, she began to recover her strength. By mid-1945, she was ready to try walking. Eddie stood near her bed and offered a hand, but she shoved him off—"Move away, boy, I can manage myself"—and struggled to her feet.

Eddie felt elated to see her on her feet again, though her failure to acknowledge the care he had provided during her long recuperation left him slightly crestfallen. But the important thing was to see her healthy, to have his mother back again.

Then something horrible happened.

It was the winter of 1945. The Gein farm still had some livestock, and Augusta announced that they must have straw for fodder. Eddie would go to a neighbor named Smith to arrange for a purchase, and she would accompany him to oversee the transaction.

Whenever Eddie told the story afterward, his voice would tremble with fury and grief.

As Eddie and Augusta drove into the yard, Smith—a sullen, quarrelsome fellow with a notoriously short temper—was laying into a mongrel puppy with a heavy stick. As the dog yowled in pain, the woman Smith lived with—out of wedlock, according to Augusta—appeared on the porch and began screeching at Smith, gesticulating wildly and begging him to stop. Smith continued beating the pup until it lay dead at his feet, while the woman wept and shrieked curses at him.

Augusta was shaken by the scene. Strangely, it was the sight of the woman—"Smith's harlot," Augusta called her—that seemed to upset her most.

Less than a week after the incident at Smith's farm, Augusta suffered a second stroke. Eddie rushed her back to the hospital, but on December 29, 1945, at the age of sixty-seven, she died.

The curtness of her obituary in the *Plainfield Sun* suggests something about the community's feelings toward Augusta. Henry's death had been front-page news, and even George had received a respectful farewell. By contrast, the entire obituary for Augusta reads as follows: "Mrs. Augusta Gein died at the Wild Rose hospital on December 29th of cerebral brain hemorrhage. The body was brought to the Goult funeral home where services were held Dec. 31, Rev. C. H. Wiese officiating. She is survived by one son, Edward, who lives on the home farm southwest of here."

Several of Augusta's siblings attended the funeral, but otherwise no one besides Eddie showed up. Eddie was beyond caring. If anything, he was glad that so few people were present. He wept like a child—his face was smeared with tears and snot—and he would have been embarrassed to have his neighbors see him in such a miserable state. But he simply couldn't control his grief. He had lost his only friend and one true love.

And he was absolutely alone in the world.

For millions of Eddie's countrymen, it was a time of thanksgiving and celebration. Just a few months earlier, the long, terrible war had finally come to an end. Looking into the future, America saw nothing but bright days ahead, and, in fact, the coming years would be an especially sunny time in the life of the nation.

But for Eddie Gein—and for the little Wisconsin town that harbored him—darkness had just begun to descend.

# PART 2

# The
# Deadhouse

# PART 2

## The Deadhouse

# 6

*"It is perhaps worthwhile to add here that not all those suffering from a typical psychosis, even when the disorder is serious in degree, give an obvious impression of derangement."*

HERVEY CLECKLEY, *The Mask of Sanity*

Small-town life is notorious for its lack of privacy. When you reside in a community whose entire population could easily be housed in a single New York City apartment building, you are likely to feel that every one of your neighbors is privy to the most intimate facts of your personal life and that you are on equally familiar terms with the details of theirs. Living in Plainfield, some folks would tell you, was like sharing a bed with every man, woman, and child in town. There aren't many secrets that stay hidden for long.

This image of the intense, often oppressive intimacy of small-town living has a great deal of truth to it, of course. But it is also true that many people who really do share the same bed—men and women who have been married so long that even their faces have begun to look alike—manage to conceal major secrets from each other, often for the better part of a lifetime. It is also the case that, precisely because they live in such tight proximity, small-town dwellers retain a necessary measure of privacy by tacitly agreeing to avoid knowing certain things about each other. Denial, after all, is a basic psychological mechanism which operates even in the minds of the most dedicated busybodies and gossips. Like the parent who refuses to face the most disturbing signs of maladjustment in a favorite child, small-town dwellers will often manage to dismiss, explain away, or turn a blind eye to the extreme peculiarities of their neighbors.

Moreover, for all their very real friendliness and hospitality,

Midwesterners tend to be a reticent bunch, regarding certain personal matters as inappropriate subjects for conversation or examination. They also have a pronounced—and very American— tendency to take people at face value and to pay as little attention as possible to the darker side of human nature.

All of this perhaps helps to explain how a middle-aged bachelor could live in a tightly knit community of just over six hundred people, all of whom knew him by name, and, for more than a decade, get away with murder—and worse.

There is another factor, too. Beginning in 1945, and for the dozen years that followed, Plainfield was only one of the places Eddie Gein inhabited. For much of that time, he dwelled in a world so utterly remote and nightmarish that no normal person could possibly have known of its existence or guessed at its terrible secrets.

As far as the citizens of Plainfield could see, Augusta Gein's death hadn't changed Eddie much. He was the same soft-spoken, mild-mannered individual he had always been—a little awkward around people but a polite and accommodating fellow, who would never say no to a neighbor who needed help sawing firewood, hauling grain, or repairing a barn. When Bob Hill's car broke down or Georgia Foster had to go off on an errand and needed someone to sit with her children, Eddie could always be counted on to lend a hand. He'd go out of his way to do his fellow townsfolk a favor.

True, there were a few detectable differences in Eddie. His appearance, never exactly well groomed to begin with, had become noticeably more unkempt. His jaw was often covered with a full week's growth of stubble, and it was clear to anyone who stood within an arm's length of him that he could stand to bathe a good deal more often than he did. Indeed, some of the shopkeepers in town—who generally looked down their noses a bit at the "hay-seeds" from the surrounding countryside—had very little use for Eddie Gein. James Severns, for one—the proprietor of the Plainfield barbershop—regarded Eddie with undisguised disdain. In the barber's eyes, the little man with his salt-and-pepper stubble and ragged homemade haircut was a sorry sight, a "filthy thing."

To anyone who had occasion to pass by Eddie's property, it was evident that the Gein farmstead had also undergone a marked decline in appearance since Augusta's death. Now that he was all alone, Eddie had simply stopped working the place. The front yard was overgrown with weeds, and the pastures were receding to woodland. The last few head of livestock were gone, sold off by Eddie to pay for his mother's funeral. Unused pieces of farming equipment—cultivator, fanning mill, manure spreader—sat rusting in the barnyard.

Because Eddie had such minimal needs, he managed to support himself by leasing a few acres of land to neighboring farmers and hiring himself out as a handyman. For a while, he did work for the township, clearing brush from the roadsides in summer and plowing snow in winter. Since his land was lying fallow, he was also entitled to a small government subsidy through a state soil-conservation program.

Though a few of the townsfolk took his neglect of the farm as a sign of shiftlessness in Eddie, most of his neighbors considered him an able and hard-working hand. When threshing time came, Eddie was often hired on as one of the crew. Slight as he looked, he had the strength and endurance that come from a lifetime of manual labor. Floyd Reid—who worked alongside Eddie many a time, on threshing crews and at the local lumber mill—was one of those who regarded Gein as "the most dependable person in the county." And unlike some of the other men, Eddie never used cuss words or spoke out of turn. He was always quiet and well mannered.

Take the way he behaved during dinnertime. When a farmer got together a threshing crew to help harvest his crops, it was his wife's responsibility to provide the workers with a solid midday meal— roast beef, baked beans, mashed potatoes, pickles, relishes, hot bread and rolls, freshly churned butter, homemade cottage cheese, jellies, preserves, and assorted fruit pies and cakes, all washed down with fresh milk or iced tea or strong, steaming coffee. As the men filed into the house through the kitchen door, brushing the dust off their heavy bib overalls or mopping their faces with the faded red kerchiefs they kept knotted around their necks, Eddie would hang back, waiting until the last of the crew was seated before finding himself a place.

Often, when the meal was finished and the other men had all stepped back outside to stretch out in the grass for a while, relax, and have a smoke, Eddie would linger at the table, gazing fixedly at the farmer's wife and daughters as they bustled about the kitchen. Many of the females—even the very young ones—felt a little disconcerted by the way Eddie sat there inspecting them, his lips twisted into that strange little leering half-smile of his. But they also couldn't help feeling a bit sorry for him. His life was so terribly lonely. And he never seemed to mean any harm or disrespect by the looks he gave them. In fact, if one of the girls were to stare back at him, he would immediately jump up from his chair and carry his plate, utensils, and drinking glass over to the sink—a courtesy that none of the other men ever saw fit to perform. More than one farmer's wife, touched by Eddie's politeness and by the awful solitariness of his existence, resolved to bake an extra batch of holiday cookies for the forlorn little bachelor come Christmastime and deliver it herself to his home.

Not many of the farmers, though, shared their wives' sentimental view of Eddie. Indeed, though they considered him a capable enough worker, some of the men treated Eddie as an outright chucklehead, the perfect patsy for a good practical joke. Generally, after the day's harvesting was done, the crew would unwind with a tub of iced beer. On a few occasions, one of the fellows would hand Eddie a bottle that had been half filled with brandy. Eddie would guzzle it down without noticing the difference, and, before you knew it, his droopy eyelid would begin to sag even more.

Then there was the time someone planted a smoke bomb under the hood of Eddie's pickup. Even those men who didn't approve of such childish doings—men like Floyd Reid, who felt sorry for Gein and regarded his oddness as the inevitable consequence of his sadly disadvantaged upbringing—couldn't help but smile at the look on Eddie's face as he came tumbling out of his truck when the smoke bomb went off.

For all the stamina he displayed on the job, there was something distinctly, even gratingly, womanish about the shy little bachelor—"weak-acting," Gyle Ellis called it, whereas Otto Frank tended to think of Eddie as "another Casper Milquetoast." Eddie claimed, for instance, to be squeamish about blood, and—though he commonly hunted rabbit and squirrel, often in the company of Bob Hill and other local boys he had befriended—he would never kill a deer, he said, because he couldn't stand to see it dressed out.

Eddie's professed aversion to bloodshed was peculiar not only because he'd spent most of his life on a farm, where butchering animals was a standard part of his existence, but also because he seemed so preoccupied with violence. Eddie was a great one for reading and had a particular affection for true crime magazines, the kind with lurid covers of half-naked girls being assaulted by beefy men in trench coats and black leather masks. Eddie couldn't get enough of these publications and was constantly recounting, for the benefit of anyone who would listen, some especially juicy lust

killing he had just read about in the latest issue of *Inside Crime* or
*Startling Detective.* Murder was one of his favorite topics of conversation. In the company of men, he also tended to talk about women,
though his comments—how cute Irene Hill looked or how "nice
and plump" Bernice Worden had become—sounded more like the
utterances of a schoolboy than the responses of a forty-year-old
man.

Of course, Eddie wasn't found in the company of men very often.
Though the people he came in contact with—the farmers, house-
wives, and merchants of Plainfield—couldn't see it, Eddie was, by
the early 1950s, in full retreat—from society, from reality, from
sanity itself. More and more of his time was spent in the darkness of
his decaying farmhouse. In the past, he would kill some time
occasionally at the Plainfield ice cream parlor or at the big indoor
roller-skating rink in the neighboring village of Hancock. Now,
except to do an odd job or run an errand, he rarely went anywhere.
In fact, there seemed to be only one place in the area he continued
to visit with any regularity: Mary Hogan's tavern.

Situated in the tiny town of Pine Grove, about seven miles from
the village of Plainfield, Hogan's establishment was an odd-looking
place. Built of concrete blocks with a semicylindrical roof of cor-
rugated metal, it looked less like a roadside tavern than a warehouse topped with a Blatz Beer sign.

Having been raised by an abusive, alcoholic father and a fanatically moralistic mother who viewed liquor as only slightly less vile
than sex, Eddie wasn't much of a drinker. But he did indulge in a
beer now and then. His real reason for visiting Mary Hogan's place,
though, was not to drink or socialize—he could have accomplished
those goals in a number of taverns closer to home—but to observe
the proprietress. Eddie was transfixed by her.

A formidable middle-aged woman who weighted nearly two
hundred pounds and spoke with a heavy German accent, Mary
Hogan bore—at least in Eddie's eyes—an unmistakable resemblance to his own mother. What made her so fascinating to him,
however, were not just the similarities but, even more, the glaring
differences between the two. Augusta had been a saint on earth, the
purest, most pious woman in the world. Hogan, by contrast, was a
foul-mouthed tavern keeper with a shady, even sinister past. Few
hard facts would ever be known about her, but according to rumor,
she was twice divorced, had connections to the mob (she had moved
to rural Wisconsin from Chicago some years before), and was even

reputed to have been a big-city madam. To Eddie, she was like some kind of perverse mirror image of Augusta, as evil as his mother had been good.

Thinking about the two of them together that way made Eddie feel dizzy. How could God have allowed his mother to waste away and die, while suffering this Hogan creature to live? He couldn't figure it out.

One thing was for sure, though. God couldn't possibly permit such a flagrant injustice to go on for very long. Deep in his bones, Eddie just knew that was true.

7

*"The bond between a mother and her child is often beyond comprehension—a slight, unexpected stirring from the baby's nursery can awaken her from deepest slumber, an almost sixth sense warns of imminent danger to her little one. But does the sense of peril end at what is taken by most to be death? Or can a mother commune with her child even as she lies in the grave?"*

BETH SCOTT and MICHAEL NORMAN, *Haunted Heartland*

It is early evening on a drizzly fall day, several years after the death of Augusta Gein. Her bachelor son, now in his mid-forties, has just returned home, having spent the afternoon performing an errand for his neighbors, Lester and Irene Hill, proprietors of a tiny country store in West Plainfield. The Hills purchase their provisions from a warehouse in Wisconsin Rapids, twenty-some miles from Plainfield, and Eddie, having very little else to do with his time, often volunteers to make the trip into the city when the Hills are too busy to pick up their supplies.

A cold gust of wind blows the rain across Eddie's stubbled face as he moves across the sagging rear porch of his house, the warped, weatherworn boards creaking under his feet. He pushes open the door into the dank and lightless summer kitchen, letting his watery blue eyes grow accustomed to the dark. He listens for a moment to the mice as they scurry for the corners. Above his head, cobwebs tremble in the blackness between the ceiling and rafters. Nothing else in this place stirs. Apart from the rodents and spiders, Eddie is alone.

Moving carefully across the trash-littered floor—around decaying cartons of household junk, piles of moldering feed sacks, a couple of rank, mildewed mattresses—he steps to the heavy wooden door on the opposite wall of the shed, enters his kitchen, and puts a match to the oil lamp on the table. The lamp flickers to life beneath the kitchen window, clearly visible behind a curtain so motheaten and tattered that it is nearly transparent. Eddie gazes at the windowpanes, but the glass is coated with such a thick layer of grime that it gives back no reflection.

It is cold in the house, and Eddie keeps on his plaid flannel jacket and deerhunter's cap as he prepares his evening meal. Throwing a few sticks of wood into his ancient cookstove, he gets a small fire going, just big enough to warm up his usual pork-and-beans supper. There's no need for a pot. Eddie just takes an opener to the lid, then set the can right on the stovetop.

Reaching into his mouth, he removes the moist lump of Wrigley's he has been chewing and carefully adds it to his gum collection, which he hoards in a one-pound Maxwell House coffee tin on a shelf, along with his other dustcoated treasures. A gas mask. A bunch of used medicine bottles. Three old radios (still workable, though of limited use in a house with no electricity). A boxful of plastic whistles, toy airplanes, and other breakfast-cereal premiums. A decomposing sponge rubber ball. Two sets of yellowed dentures. A wash basin full of sand. His special handmade bowls.

Eddie sticks a finger into the beans and, satisfied with their temperature, empties them into one of the bowls. He rummages through the jumble of unwashed utensils in his sink and comes up with a spoon. Then, carrying the spoon and bowl in one hand and his oil lamp in the other, he makes his way out of the kitchen.

The floor is so crowded with filth and debris—food scraps, rodent droppings, grimy rags, empty food cans and oatmeal containers, cardboard boxes overflowing with crime magazines, a half-empty sack of plaster, a stiffened horsehide buggy robe—that, even in the daytime, Eddie cannot negotiate it easily. Now, in the dim circle of light shed by his oil lamp, he cannot avoid stepping into an ash pile or knocking his shins against a rusted metal tub filled with bits of twine, tattered children's clothes, and shards of broken china.

As he traverses the kitchen, his shadow slides across the items he has tacked onto one of the dingy, flaking walls. A dozen promotional calendars, a few dating back to the 1930s. An automobile reflector disk inscribed "Accidents Spoil Fun." A card from the telephone company reading "In Case of Fire, Call 505." (Eddie does not own a telephone.)

Then, passing beneath a pair of deer antlers, a rusty horseshoe, and a withered Christmas wreath, all mounted over the doorway and dripping with cobwebs, he steps inside his bedroom.

It is the only other room in the house that Eddie ever enters. Beyond it lies the Sacred Place, boarded off by Eddie years before. The second story is visited only by an occasional squirrel scuttling down through the chimney.

Eddie sets his oil lamp and handmade bowl on a wooden crate. Because its underside is so irregular (Eddie has tried to file down some of the bumps, but with limited success), the bowl threatens to tip over, and Eddie takes a moment to balance it on the crate top. Then, picking up a few sticks of kindling from the floor, he starts a fire in the potbellied stove near his bed.

The room is, if possible, even more squalid than the kitchen, a chaos of discarded food tins, empty cartons, crumpled newspapers, corroded hand tools, old musical instruments (including a broken accordion and a violin without strings), and a three-foot stack of tattered coveralls. A clothesline hung with soiled handkerchiefs is strung above Eddie's iron bedstead. Amid the insane clutter and filth, the only objects that seem to have been treated with care are Eddie's firearms: two .22-caliber rifles, a .22 pistol, a 7.65-millimeter Mauser, and a 12-gauge shotgun.

Outside, the rain has stopped falling, but—though a full moon has emerged from behind the clouds—no light enters the room. Its two windows have been tar-papered shut.

Seating himself on his sagging, grease-stained mattress, Eddie sifts through the pile of books and periodicals at his feet and selects his reading matter for the evening: a pulp magazine called *Man's Action*, with a lurid cover painting of an impossibly big-breasted blonde, outfitted in a Gestapo uniform and applying a riding crop to the naked back of a writhing concentration-camp prisoner. Then, picking up his food, he takes a mouthful of the viscous mixture, opens the magazine on his lap, and begins to read.

Lately, he has been studying accounts of Nazi barbarities, and tonight, as he spoons down his supper, he pores over a story that relates, in loving detail, the atrocities committed by Ilse Koch, the infamous "Bitch of Buchenwald," accused of collecting human heads and using the tattooed skin of her victims for lampshades and book bindings. He also likes reading about the deeds of Irma Grese, the angelic-looking nineteen-year-old SS warder who wore a sky-blue jacket that matched the color of her eyes, kept a horse whip stuck in one of her jackboots, and performed her primary duty—selecting enfeebled women and children for extermination at the Auschwitz and Belsen death camps—with uncommon zeal and enjoyment.

Eddie's tastes, of course, aren't limited to Nazi horror stories. He has a special fondness for South Seas adventure yarns, particularly ones concerning cannibals and headhunters. Only recently, he came across a supposedly true-life narrative that he can't seem to get out of his mind. It concerned a man who murdered a wealthy acquaintance and escaped on his yacht, only to be shipwrecked on a Polynesian isle, where he was captured, tortured, and flayed by the natives. Of particular interest to Eddie was the graphic description of the process used to shrink and preserve the victim's head, though he also enjoyed the part about the drum that had been fashioned by stretching the skin of the dead man's abdomen across a hollow gourd.

Stories about exhumations are also among Eddie's favorites. He has read everything he can get his hands on about the English "resurrection men," or "body snatchers," who peddled corpses to nineteenth-century anatomy schools. Another story set in nineteenth-century Britain, about a club of depraved young aristocrats who dug up corpses of beautiful young women and put them to unspeakable uses, has left an equally lasting mark on Eddie's fantasy life.

Lately, Eddie's imagination has been fired by an astounding tale unfolding in papers and newsweeklies across the nation. And ex-GI—a good-looking young man from New York City—has traveled to Denmark and undergone an operation that has transformed him into a woman. Eddie is fascinated by this story. Since childhood, he has often daydreamed about becoming a girl and imagined what it would feel like to have female sex parts instead of a penis. For a very long time, of course, his concept of female sex parts was exceptionally imprecise, based entirely on a crude illustration of human reproductive organs in a medical textbook he bought in Wisconsin Rapids. Recently, however, he has been able to study the private parts of several women firsthand. The expression on his face is a perfect mixture of lewdness and contentment as he thinks of these wonderfully intimate and exciting experiences.

When Eddie can't find an interesting magazine article about cannibalism, grave robbing, Nazi war crimes, or sexual mutilation, he relies for entertainment on the local newspapers—particularly the *Wisconsin Rapids Daily Tribune* and the *Plainfield Sun*—searching their pages for stories about killings, car accidents, suicides, or unexplained disappearances.

And there is one other kind of news item he examines with great care and gratification.

He always makes sure to read—and, in certain cases, to tear out and save—the obituaries.

Having scraped the last of the pork and beans from the inside of his bowl, Eddie drops his magazine onto the floor and gazes up at his Trophies dangling from the opposite wall. Their presence comforts him a bit. Still, he feels very lonely tonight. He misses his mother.

He closes his eyes and listens for her. On several occasions since her death, he has heard her voice, quite clearly, telling him to be good. But tonight, he hears only the rattle of the branches in the wind and the mice scuttling across his kitchen floor.

Life in Plainfield has been painfully empty for Eddie since his mother was taken from him. He feels angry and resentful toward his neighbors, who repay his kindness with cruelty and deceit—teasing him, cheating him of his wages, borrowing equipment from him and never giving it back. True, there are exceptions. Some of the womenfolk in particular—like Irene Hill—treat him nicely from time to time, offering him a meal, letting him sit for a while in the living room with the family and watch Red Skelton on TV. But for the most part, Eddie feels friendless and bitterly alone.

Indeed, for a while after his mother's death, he gave serious thought to selling the farmstead and getting as far away as possible. He no longer had any desire to work the place. He thought he would let it reforest itself, get whatever money he could for it, and move to a different part of the country, maybe even a different part of the world. But, in the end, he did not have the energy or the will to do anything.

Nothing has seemed real to him since she went away. He often feels as if he is living in a dream.

He has, in fact, had a number of strange experiences over the past few years—seen, heard, and even smelled such peculiar things that he sometimes thinks he is imagining them. Like the time last spring when he was squirrel hunting on his property. He suddenly had the strongest sensation that someone—or something—was watching him, and when he looked up at the trees, all the leaves were gone, and hunched on every branch was a black, slack-necked buzzard that glared at him with blood-red eyes.

Another time, as he was walking through a field, he glanced down at a pile of yellow leaves and saw a bunch of human faces peeking through it. They grinned at him evilly, and as he turned and ran away, he could hear their mocking laughter.

And then there is the miasma that rises from the ground and fills Eddie's nostrils with a dizzying stench.

Eddie lies absolutely still and tries to visualize his mother's face. For some reason, he can't remember how she looked when she was younger. Whenever he thinks of her now, he pictures her as he saw her last, in her coffin.

For a long time, he was convinced that he could get her back, that his willpower was strong enough to raise her from the grave. On several nights, when the rest of the world was sleeping, he even drove out to the Plainfield cemetery and attempted it. But his efforts were not successful.

There are the others, of course—the women who have become such an important part of his life. But they are a poor substitute for his mother.

Stretched out on his shabby, unmade mattress, he knows what is coming. When it hits him, his whole body begins to tremble, and he has trouble catching his breath.

He bolts from his bed and hurries from the farmhouse.

Outside, the rain has left a clean, almost springlike aroma in the air. But that is not what Eddie smells.

By now, he can barely control himself, so powerful is his craving. Clearly, it has been too long since he last made a visit.

Small Midwestern towns are not renowned for their night life, but Eddie knows at least three places nearby where the women are always waiting and available.

He climbs into his pickup and heads off into the night.

# 8

During a ten-year period, beginning in the late 1940s, Wisconsin law-enforcement officials were baffled by a handful of mysterious disappearances.

An eight-year-old girl named Georgia Weckler was the first. On a sunny Thursday afternoon, May 1, 1947, little Georgia was given a lift home from her grade school in Jefferson, Wisconsin, by a neighbor, Mrs. Carl Floerke, who dropped the girl off by the half-mile lane that led from Highway 12 to the Weckler farmhouse. Mrs. Floerke watched as the girl paused to open her family's roadside letterbox and remove a stack of mail. Then Georgia gave Mrs. Floerke a final wave goodbye and turned up the lane toward home.

She was never seen again.

When the girl failed to show up at home by evening, local lawmen were called in and immediately launched an all-night search, which proved fruitless. By Friday, hundreds of area residents had joined in the hunt, scouring ten square miles of countryside without finding a trace of the missing girl. Farmers and businessmen from around the county also contributed more than eight thousand dollars as a reward for information leading to the Weckler girl's recovery.

The only clue to her disappearance was a black Ford sedan which had been seen backing out of the Wecklers' lane shortly after Mrs. Floerke let Georgia off by the mailbox. Sheriff George Perry of Jefferson discovered deep ruts in the gravel—clearly caused by the rapid spinning of automobile tires—which suggested that the Ford had taken off in a hurry.

On Monday night, Georgia's father—a respected member of the

community who served as town treasurer—went on the radio to appeal for his daughter's release. But when a week had passed without a word from the abductors, Georgia's parents and neighbors could only assume the worst. As the headline article in the May 8, 1947, issue of the *Jefferson Banner* put it, "Lack of any effort on the part of the kidnappers to contact the parents gave rise to fears that her disappearance may have been the work of a perverted mind."

The same sort of mind was at work once again in the case of a pretty teenaged girl named Evelyn Hartley, the daughter of a biology professor at Wisconsin State College in La Crosse. A fifteen-year-old honor student at Central High School, Evelyn occasionally babysat for family friends, and at six-thirty P.M. on Saturday, October 24, 1953, she arrived at the home of her father's colleague, Professor Viggo Rasmussen, to take care of the Rasmussens' twenty-month-old daughter, Janis, while the parents attended Wisconsin State's homecoming game.

Evelyn had only been babysitting for a year, and it was her practice to check in with her parents by phone at some point in the evening. But on this night, there was no word from her. Shortly before nine, Richard Hartley picked up the phone and tried reaching his daughter. She didn't answer. Worried, Hartley quickly drove the mile and a half to the Rasmussen home and knocked on the door. Again, no answer. Peering through a picture window, he caught sight of his daughter's eyeglasses and one of her canvas loafers lying in the middle of the living-room floor.

By now his concern had flared into alarm. He searched for a way in, but the doors and first-floor windows were all locked. Then he spotted an open basement window. He also spotted something else: footprints underneath the window. And bloodstains leading away from the house.

Hartley crawled through the window and discovered his daughter's other shoe lying on the basement floor. Upstairs in the living room, the rugs were disarranged, as though they had been disturbed during a scuffle. Hartley quickly notified the police.

During the search that followed, police and sheriff's officers discovered more blood on the lawn, as well as several bloody patches, including a palm print, on the house of a neighbor. Bloodhounds were brought in to follow the trail that led away from the basement window, but the dogs were stopped cold at a spot about two blocks away. Apparently, the girl had been forced into a car at that point.

From the slim evidence they could gather, the police theorized that Evelyn had heard a noise in the basement and went to the top of the stairs to investigate. When she saw the intruder coming up the stairs, she turned and tried to flee. There were indications that she had even managed to reach the front door when she was overtaken. Neighbors reported hearing a single scream at around seven-fifteen, but at the time they had thought nothing of it, assuming it was the sound of children playing.

As in the Weckler case, no word was heard from the abductor. Police Chief George Long told reporters that night that he assumed the girl had been kidnapped. "But not," he added ominously, "for ransom."

Over the next few days, a massive search was conducted—"the most intensive combing" of the region that had ever taken place, according to Chief Long. At least a thousand volunteers—farmers, members of veterans' organizations, Boy Scouts, church groups, students and faculty from Wisconsin State College—joined law-enforcement officers in a fifty-mile hunt that extended into Minnesota. River patrols dredged the waterways, an Air Force helicopter searched the bluffs and woodlands, and every swamp, ravine, culvert, and cave was explored.

By Tuesday, Evelyn's whereabouts remained a mystery, though the searchers had located several pieces of evidence that seemed to confirm the police chief's suspicions. Two blood-smeared items of girls' underclothing—a white pair of panties and a brassiere, identical to the kind worn by the victim—were discovered just off Highway 14, about two miles southeast of La Crosse. And about four miles farther south, near a place called the Sportsview Inn, police found a bloodstained pair of men's trousers.

On Tuesday night, Mr. Hartley issued an emotional appeal for the return of his daughter. His wife, tight-lipped and tearful, refused to speak to any more reporters. "I've answered all the questions I can," she told them. "I don't want to think about it anymore. It's terrible. It's almost beyond bearing." Meanwhile, searchers began using long poles to explore the mounds of soft earth in the fields around the Rasmussen home. By that time, as the *Milwaukee Journal* reported, "every indication was that the search was directed toward finding a corpse."

But the body was never found.

Three more people vanished during this period. And whereas the Weckler and Hartley abductions were committed more than a hundred miles apart from each other, these other disappearances occurred in the same vicinity.

All of them happened around Plainfield.

On November 1, 1952, a forty-three-year-old farmer named Victor "Bunk" Travis—a resident of Adams County, just west of Plainfield—said goodbye to his wife and went off to hunt deer in the company of a Milwaukee acquaintance named Ray Burgess. At some point in the late afternoon, the two stopped for beers at Mac's Bar in Plainfield, where they remained, drinking and chatting, for several hours. At around seven P.M., they left the bar, got into Burgess's car, and drove away.

That was the last that was ever seen of them. The two hunters, along with the car Burgess was driving, simply disappeared. A month later, local lawmen were still searching for the missing men but without much hope of ever finding them.

"What has happened to Travis?" asked the editor of the county newspaper, the *Waushara Argus*. "Why would he leave his pretty young bride of two months, or his mother, without telling her that he didn't expect to be back within a few hours? These questions are stirring the imaginations of the natives of Adams County, a county that has thousands of acres of wilderness. A wilderness that is seldom traversed except in limited fashion during deer hunting season.

"It is wild country," the article concluded. "Country that could hide violence for years and perhaps never give up its secret."

In a sense, the final disappearance was also the least explicable. After all, the abduction of children by psychopathic strangers is every parent's worst nightmare and a common enough occurrence to be a legitimate fear. And heavily armed hunters who spend a chunk of the afternoon drinking beer in a country tavern before venturing back into the woods have been known to come to unhappy ends.

But to the people of Plainfield, the disappearance of Mary Hogan—the two-hundred-pound tavern keeper with the profane tongue and mysterious past—seemed especially baffling. And sinister.

When a Portage County farmer named Seymour Lester walked into Mary Hogan's tavern on the afternoon of Wednesday, December 8, 1954, he was immediately struck by how silent and empty the place seemed. Then he noticed the pool of blood on the floor. Hurrying down the road to the nearest farmhouse, he first telephoned Villas Waterman, town chairman of Pine Grove, then notified the sheriff's office in the city of Stevens Point.

Within a short while, Waterman and Sheriff Harold S. Thompson, along with a number of deputies, arrived on the scene and saw at a glance that Hogan had fallen victim to foul play. A spent .32-caliber cartridge lay on the floor next to a large patch of dried blood. The patch was streaked, as though a body had been dragged through it. A bloody trail led outside the door to a spot in the parking area where the body had apparently been loaded into a pickup truck.

Realizing that he needed additional help, Thompson contacted the state crime lab at Madison, whose investigators carefully searched the tavern for fingerprints and other clues. A farm-to-farm check was made in Portage and surrounding counties, and an alert was transmitted to the police in Chicago, Hogan's previous home. But the authorities were unable to turn up a single lead.

On December 8, 1955, the anniversary of Hogan's disappearance, Ed Marolla, editor of Plainfield's weekly newspaper, the *Sun*, ran a front-page column headlined "What Happened to Mary Hogan?" A year later, in the issue of December 15, 1956, he was still asking the same question:

> After two full years, complete mystery surrounds the disappearance of Mary Hogan who apparently was shot and dragged from her Town of Pine Grove tavern on December 8, 1954.
>
> Nothing, absolutely nothing, has come to light, and the questions concerning the whereabouts of Mary Hogan's body are as unknown today as they were on that bleak December day when a neighbor stepped into the tavern to find a strangely silent building and blood splotched on the floor. . . .
>
> Following the disappearance of Mary Hogan, a series of crimes took place in the Almond area some miles to the east but along the same highway. Other crimes were committed at Wild Rose and at Plainfield. Some of these crimes were partly solved by the confessions of a town of Almond man.
>
> But in so far as the Mary Hogan case is concerned, it is still a complete and deep, dark mystery. Speculation is still rife about what happened to her, and people still talk about Mary Hogan. Was it something out of her past that caught up with her? Or was it just plain local hoodlums who perpetrated the crime?

Was the body of Mary Hogan taken away and cremated somewhere as some people surmise, or does the body of Mary Hogan lie rotting in some lonely Town of Pine Grove or nearby area grave?

The authorities don't know. No one knows—that is, except the murderers themselves.

# 9

*"Wisconsin contains, if the yarns are an indication, more ghosts per square mile than any state in the nation."*

ROBERT E. GARD and L. G. SORDEN, *Wisconsin Lore*

Among the men who occasionally employed Eddie Gein as a handyman was a local farmer and sawmill owner named Elmo Ueeck. Like many of Eddie's acquaintances, Ueeck sometimes twitted the meek little bachelor about women.

One day, shortly after the disappearance of Mary Hogan, Ueeck and Gein were chatting, when the conversation turned—as it so often did in Plainfield during that time—to the subject of the missing tavern keeper.

"Eddie," said Ueeck. "If you had spent more time courting Mary, she'd be cooking for you instead of being missing."

Ueeck would never forget Eddie's response. As he recalled years later, Eddie "rolled his eyes and wiggled his nose like a dog sniffing a skunk." Then he smiled and said, "She's not missing. She's down at the house now."

Coming from anyone else, such a comment might have seemed questionable, if not downright suspicious. But Eddie was always talking crazy like that, so Ueeck didn't make much of it.

Nor did anyone else who heard Eddie make the same remark. Eddie had become increasingly reclusive, but whenever he happened to find himself in the company of other men and the question of Mary Hogan's whereabouts came up, he would always crack the same strange little joke. "She's at the farm right now," Eddie would say, grinning his idiot's grin. "I went and got her in my pickup truck and took her home."

The men would snicker or shake their heads at Eddie's lame attempt at humor.

No one paid much attention. It was just the sort of damn fool remark you'd expect from an oddball like Eddie Gein.

It was about this time that a strange rumor concerning Eddie began circulating around Plainfield.

According to some local youngsters who claimed to have seen the objects in question with their own eyes, there were shrunken heads in Eddie Gein's house.

Bob Hill was one of the people who swore he'd seen the heads. The teenage son of Irene and Lester Hill, the West Plainfield storekeepers, Bob was the closest thing Eddie had to a friend. He hunted rabbits with the older man, accompanied him to movie shows and an occasional high-school baseball game, and was one of the few individuals who had ever been inside Gein's dark, decrepit house.

It was on one of those visits, the teenager declared, that Eddie had brought out and shown him a pair of preserved human heads—creepy things, with leathery skin, long matted hair, and hollow eye sockets. When Bob asked Eddie where they came from, the little man replied that they were genuine South Seas shrunken heads, sent by a cousin who had fought in the Philippines during the war.

Several other Plainfield youngsters saw the heads, too. Not far from Eddie's farm lived a family with two young sons—a teenager and his eight-year-old brother. Every now and then, the pair would come over for a visit. Eddie and the older boy would play cards in the kitchen, while the eight-year-old amused himself with some of the intriguing objects scattered around Eddie's floor.

Years afterward, as a middle-aged man, the younger of the two brothers would relate a particularly disquieting episode that took place on one of those occasions. "Cards didn't fascinate me at that particular time, but Eddie had other things, like a tool that would punch holes in leather or paper. I'd spend my time doing that while my brother and Eddie played cards.

"One of these times when we were over there, I ran out of paper and asked Eddie where I could get more. He told me to go into his bedroom. When I went around the corner, there were three heads hanging on that door. Just the heads—the faces were dried and they had hair on them. Remember those African movies with the shrunken heads? That's what they looked like. Not really shrunken. I'd have to say they were the actual size of the head. But skin, hair, all that.

"I didn't say nothing. When we walked home, I asked my brother what the heads could be, and he told me they were probably Halloween get-ups. And I was young enough that I believed it.

"I never asked Eddie about it. But from that particular time or shortly thereafter, Eddie no longer let my brother or me into the house."

In a town as small and sealed-off as Plainfield, gossip spreads like the flu, and it wasn't long before the entire community had heard the reports of Eddie Gein's peculiar possessions. Still, no one was especially disturbed or even surprised by the story. A set of souvenir shrunken heads from the South Pacific was exactly the sort of collectible you'd expect someone like Eddie Gein to own.

Indeed, the hearsay about Eddie Gein's heads became a kind of joke around Plainfield. At some point during this period, Eddie had a notion to move away from his old farmstead and approached two of his neighbors, Donald and Georgia Foster of West Plainfield, with a proposition. According to Mrs. Foster, who later described the incident for reporters, "Ed came around and wanted to know if we'd like to trade our house for his farm. We have only an acre or so of land here and we thought the idea was worth considering, so we went out to look his place over.

"We looked into all the rooms except the front bedroom and one room right off what I suppose was originally the dining room but that Ed used for a bedroom and a living room. He had the door closed to that one room. He said it was just an old pantry and was filled with junk.

"We didn't see anything to make us suspicious. The place was awfully dirty and full of stuff piled all over the floor. It was pretty dark, too. He had those dirty old curtains at the windows, so we couldn't see much.

"The kids have always brought back stories about him having shrunken heads there. So when we were upstairs in his house, I kidded Ed about it. I pointed to one of the bedrooms and I said, 'Is that where you keep your shrunken heads?' He gave me a funny look. My husband looked at me, too, and I wished I hadn't said it. But then Ed gave that little grin of his and pointed to another room.

" 'No,' he said, 'they're in this other room over here.'

"People were always kidding Ed about things like that."

For various reasons—Eddie's increasing weirdness, the story of his shrunken heads, the progressively rundown appearance of his property—the old Gein farmhouse gradually developed a reputation among the children of Plainfield as a haunted house.

Especially toward evening, when the darkness started to gather around the dismal, lonely place and the only light to be seen from Eddie's house was the somber glow of an oil lamp behind his moldering kitchen curtains, it was easy to believe that evil really did live within those walls. Roger Johnson, son of Eddie's nearest neighbor, remembers vividly how, when walking home from a friend's house at dusk along the road that led past the Gein farm, he would "save all his energy up for that last hundred yards" and then "run like hell" until he was well clear of Eddie's place.

"It wasn't that I feared Eddie," Roger would later explain. "I feared the house."

The grownups, of course, would listen to these fears and smile. After all, every small town in America has its own haunted house, some tumbledown place inhabited by a harmless old eccentric who has been transformed by the colorful imaginations of the neighborhood children into a monster, a ghoul, a fairy-tale ogre—the kind of fiend who lurks in the gloom of his parlor, carving knife in hand, just waiting for an unwary child to knock on the door.

But every parent knows that this is just one of the many wild fantasies young children are prone to. In real life, such creatures simply do not exist.

One thing is certain: if Eddie's young neighbors were spooked by the mere look of his gloomy old farmhouse, it's fortunate for them that they weren't around on those nights when a far more ghastly sight could be seen in his front yard—the figure of what seemed to be a naked elderly female with wiry gray hair, mottled flesh, withered dugs, and the face of a corpse.

Indeed, to see this grotesque apparition, you might well have imagined (had you known of Eddie's belief in the power of his will) that his efforts to raise his mother had succeeded after all and that the creature cavorting obscenely in the moonlight was the resurrected person of Augusta Gein herself.

It was a sight that would have supplied any of Eddie's impressionable young neighbors with a lifetime's worth of nightmares. It might even have persuaded their parents that the stories about Eddie Gein's house of horrors were more than just childish make-believe.

# 10

*"Death nor the marble prison my love sleeps in*
*Shall keep her body lockt up from mine arms."*

Anonymous, *The Second Maiden's Tragedy*

Her name is Eleanor Adams; her age, fifty-one. Wife of Floyd
Adams of Plainfield and mother of two adult children, George and
Barbara.

Tonight, though her family has no way of knowing, she is alone
with Eddie Gein.

Eddie has known her by sight for many years, though he has
never spoken so much as a word to her. But on this balmy August
night, driven by those desperate urges that seem to come from
someplace outside himself, like the proddings of an evil spirit, he
has gone and fetched her to his remote, decaying farmhouse.

At the moment, she is stretched out on his soiled mattress, her
features illuminated by the dingy glow of his oil lamp. Though she
is surrounded by the souvenirs of Eddie's other conquests, she has
no way of knowing what is about to happen to her.

Eddie hovers over the bed, ogling his prize. There is something
about Mrs. Adams that has always reminded him of Augusta. But
the excitement welling up in him as he stares down at the woman is
like nothing he ever felt for his mother.

A shiver of pleasure snakes through him as he begins to disrobe
her. Mrs. Adams offers no resistance. When her waxy flesh is
exposed to his view, he raises his lamp and moves it slowly down
the length of her body.

He has heard other men refer to women as "dolls," and that is
precisely how he perceives Mrs. Adams—as a doll. But only little
girls play with dolls, he reflects. The thought makes him smile.

Standing by the foot of the bed, he moves her legs apart and, with the lamp in one hand, bends nearer for a better look. Abruptly, he jerks back, repulsed by her smell. Mrs. Adams lies absolutely still.

On a table nearby lie all of Eddie's instruments. He sets the oil lamp down, picks up one of the tools, and then, turning back to his guest, applies himself to his work.

Though his excitement is so intense that it causes his hands to tremble, he proceeds at a leisurely pace. There is no need to hurry. The night has just begun.

And Mrs. Adams, as Eddie knows from experience, will never be missed.

# PART 3

# The Butcher of Plainfield

# 11

*"There once was a man named Ed*
*Who wouldn't take a woman to bed.*
*When he wanted to diddle,*
*He cut out the middle,*
*And hung the rest in the shed."*

Popular limerick, Wisconsin, ca. 1958

The fall of 1957 was a trying time for America, a season of crisis. In late September, the nation was shaken by racial turmoil in Little Rock, Arkansas, where federal paratroopers, ordered in by the President, clashed with redneck mobs bent on blocking the integration of the city's public schools. Less than two weeks later, America's postwar pride in its military and scientific supremacy was rocked by the successful launch of *Sputnik I*, the first man-made satellite to orbit the earth. Later that autumn, the country received still another shock when the White House announced that during the welcoming ceremonies for a visiting dignitary, President Eisenhower had suffered a stroke.

It was a year when sugary singles such as Debbie Reynolds's "Tammy," Tab Hunter's "Young Love," and Pat Boone's "Don't Forbid Me" shot to number one on the record charts. But in the fall of 1957, a stranger kind of music was being heard, too. In its October 28 issue, *Time* magazine reported the release of a sick-humor album containing lyrics such as these:

I love your streak of cruelty, your psychopathic lies,
The homicidal tendencies shining in your eyes.
Don't change your psychic structure,
Weird as it may be . . .

Stay, darling, stay way under par . . .
Stay as sick as you are.

Only a week earlier, *Time* had run a column on the countrywide craze for an even blacker kind of comedy, ghoulish jokes known as "Bloody Marys":

—Mrs. Jones, can Johnny come out to play baseball?
—You know he doesn't have any arms or legs.
—That's okay. We want to use him for second base.

—Mommy, why do I keep walking around in circles?
—Shut up, or I'll nail your other foot to the floor.

We tend to mythicize the fifties, to remember them as a golden age of simplicity and innocence—the era of sock hops, after-school milkshakes at Pop's Sweet Shoppe, and Davy Crockett coonskin caps. Happy Days. But in many ways, the Eisenhower era was an anxious time, fraught with A-bomb fears and haunted by the still recent nightmare of the death-camp horrors. At newsstands and in corner candy stores, clean-cut comic books like *Archie* and *Little Lulu* competed for rack space with publications like *The Vault of Horror* and *Tales from the Crypt*, gore-drenched fantasies in which putrefying corpses return from the grave to take revenge on their murderers and butcher shops proffer prime cuts of human flesh to their unsuspecting customers.

The crises that occurred in the fall of 1957—the ugliness in Little Rock, Russia's sudden leap into space—gave the national sense of confidence and self-esteem a serious battering. And in mid-November of that year, the country would be jolted again, this time by a crime so appalling that, in a very real sense, American culture still hasn't recovered from the shock.

The Wisconsin woods are a hazardous place to be during the state's nine-day hunting season—and not just for deer. By Sunday, November 24, the final day of the 1957 season, the death toll stood at forty thousand bucks and does and thirteen hunters. Two of the men suffered fatal heart attacks while traipsing through the frozen woods. The remaining eleven were killed by stray bullets, generally fired by overeager strangers, though both Eskie Burgess, 44, of Chicago and George Schreiber, 64, of Stratford died at the hands of their own sons. Other hunters got off more easily, suffering serious but nonlethal gunshot wounds (some of them self-inflicted) to various parts of their bodies—legs, shoulders, neck, groin.

Opening weekend is a particularly busy—and deadly—time. During the first three days alone, the kill figure for the 1957 season reached 28,675 deer. Many of the sportsmen who stalk the central Wisconsin wilderness come from Milwaukee and Chicago. The rest are local hunters, who pour into the woods in such profusion that their little rural towns are left all but depopulated of every male capable of managing a rifle.

Of course, trying to bag a spiked-horn buck in freezing Midwestern weather is a rigorous, often frustrating business, and many a hunter will take temporary refuge from the cold in the handiest tavern, fortifying himself with a few stiff drinks before returning to the woods and venting his exasperation on virtually anything that moves. "Better lock up the livestock," the local farmers joke when hunting season commences, and in Marquette County, they like to tell the story of the game warden who stopped a party of inebriated hunters with a milk cow strapped to their car.

When a legal kill is made, the deer is field-dressed—slit open and gutted—tagged, and brought to the nearest inspection spot, which might be a government office or, in smaller communities, a tavern or gas station, designated as an official checkpoint by the state. In the middle of November, a traveler through rural Wisconsin will see the evidence of the hunt all around him—fenders and car roofs draped with the day's kill and filling stations festooned with gaping carcasses.

An icy drizzle was falling on Saturday, November 16, and the land lay buried under three inches of snow. But a bit of inclement weather wouldn't interfere with the hunt—a fact that must certainly have been in Eddie Gein's mind as he sat in the squalor of his kitchen that morning, planning his day's activities. Eddie was one of the few adult males who wouldn't be venturing into the forest. He wasn't a killer of deer, and the prey he was after wouldn't be found in the woods.

It would be found right in Plainfield. And on that day—the start of the 1957 deer-hunting season—Plainfield, Eddie figured, would be nearly deserted.

By the time he finished breakfast, the rain had stopped falling. He put on his jacket and plaid deer hunter's cap, loaded a fuel can and a large glass jug into his maroon '49 Ford sedan, and headed for town. The time was just after eight A.M.

Eddie's first stop was the local Standard station, where he filled the can with kerosene. Then he got back into his Ford and, moments later, pulled up in front of his ultimate destination—Worden's Hardware and Implement Store, situated between a vacant building and an unoccupied house near the east end of Plainfield's business district. He parked his car and, carrying the glass jug, stepped inside the store.

Worden's—which had begun as a harness shop back in the 1890s—was one of Plainfield's oldest commercial establishments. Throughout most of the 1920s, it was co-owned by two men, Leon Worden and Frank Conover, who were also in-laws, Worden having married his business partner's young daughter, Bernice. Worden bought out his partner's interest in 1929, and when he died two years later, his young widow assumed the ownership and operation of the store.

Though a few of her neighbors—perhaps out of envy of her rumored wealth—regarded Bernice Worden as a bit snippy and sharp-tongued, she was held in high regard by most of the community. Indeed, in July 1956, she was the first woman to be honored on the front page of the local newspaper as Plainfield's "Citizen of the Week." A pleasant-featured, solidly built, fifty-eight-year-old widow, Bernice Worden was a devout Methodist, a doting grandmother, and an exceptionally capable business woman, who had purchased the corner building that housed her establishment, expanded her inventory to include modern farm implements and household appliances, and for many years had the distinction of being the only female dealer of International Harvester products in the region. Though most of her time was devoted to business, she occasionally took time off to indulge her passion for fishing.

Even a person as industrious as Bernice Worden, however, couldn't manage all the work by herself (besides being the area's main supplier of hardware, appliances, and farming equipment, Worden's served as the town's freight depot and telegraph office). For that reason, she was assisted on most days by her son, Frank, who had clearly inherited his parents' formidable energies. In addition to his work in the family business, he served for a time as village constable and, later, as both town fire marshal and deputy sheriff.

But on November 16, 1957, Frank was nowhere around. Like much of Plainfield's male population, he was in the woods hunting, just as he had told Eddie Gein he would be when the little man had inquired the day before.

As a result, when Eddie entered Worden's early that Saturday morning, its fifty-year-old proprietress was alone in the store—exactly as Eddie expected.

Mrs. Worden wouldn't have been surprised to see Eddie, since he had stopped by around closing time on Friday to check on the price of antifreeze. But she might not have been entirely pleased. Lately, Eddie had taken to hanging around the store more and more frequently and was beginning to make something of a pest of himself. On one recent occasion, he had actually had the gall to invite her to "try out the floor" at the new roller-skating rink in Hancock. The pale-eyed little man seemed to mean the offer as a joke—he was wearing his silly little smile when he asked—but Mrs. Worden had not been amused. Like most of Plainfield's merchants, she regarded Eddie Gein as little more than the village idiot.

Still, the Geins had been good customers for many years, and Mrs. Worden was not about to treat Eddie with anything less than politeness and cordiality. When he explained that he was there to purchase some antifreeze, she filled up his jug from a steel barrel in her office, took his money, wrote up a sales receipt, and watched as he shambled out the door.

Moments later, Eddie reentered.

He was thinking, he explained, of trading his Marlin rifle—which only fired .22 shorts—for one that could accommodate all three .22 calibers, short, long, and long rifle. He pointed to one of the Marlins lined up in the store's gun rack and asked if he could examine it.

"Sure," Mrs. Worden said. "That's my favorite kind of rifle."

Eddie reached over and slid the weapon out from under the chain that hung across the front of the rack. He began to look the rifle over.

Mrs. Worden moved to the store window and looked outside. Across the street, in front of Gamble's General Store, stood her son-in-law's new red Chevy. "I see Bud has a new car," she said aloud, more to herself than to Eddie. "I do not like Chevrolets."

Standing there with her back to Eddie, she had no way of knowing that at that very moment, he was reaching into his overalls pocket for a .22 shell. Or that in his festering madness, he had begun to perceive the fifty-eight-year-old widow as a wicked creature deserving of divine punishment, the evil antithesis of his own sainted mother—just like Mary Hogan, another middle-aged local businesswoman who had, not very long before, come to a bad end. A very bad end.

That day, Bernard Muschinski, Sr., was manning the gas pumps at his Phillips 66 station directly across the street from Worden's. As he tended to business, he had ample opportunity to notice the early-morning comings and goings at the hardware store—Mrs. Worden returning with her mail at around eight-fifteen, a delivery truck unloading freight just a few minutes later.

Sometime between eight forty-five and nine-thirty, Muschinski saw the Worden's Hardware panel truck pull out of the garage at the rear of the building and head east. Muschinski couldn't tell who was behind the wheel, though he was sure the driver was a man. Still, there was nothing unusual about that. The Wordens often hired local help to haul freight and run deliveries, so Muschinski didn't give the matter a second thought. And he wasn't particularly surprised when, later in the day, he strolled across the street and found the front door locked. Like other people who passed by the store that Saturday and noticed it was empty, he figured that Mrs. Worden had simply decided to close up shop for the opening day of the hunting season, when so many of her customers would be out in the woods.

There *was* one funny thing, though. The lights. It seemed strange to Muschinski that Mrs. Worden would lock up for the weekend and leave them burning.

Elmo Ueeck—the Plainfield farmer who had joked with Eddie Gein about Mary Hogan's disappearance—had gotten lucky that day, bagging a deer within a few hours of the opening of the season. He did feel a twinge of guilt for having nailed the buck in Eddie Gein's woods. Elmo knew that Eddie hated anybody to hunt on his property without permission. But what Eddie didn't know wouldn't hurt him, and there was no particular reason why Eddie had to find out about Elmo's little transgression.

As luck would have it, Elmo was just driving away with his kill tied to his car when he spotted Eddie's maroon Ford barreling down the road in his direction. Ueeck was surprised at how fast Gein's car was traveling. Usually, Eddie drove so slowly you could almost outrun him. Well, there was no way for Ueeck to keep his crime a secret now, not with that fat spiked-horn buck hanging right there across his hood. Elmo figured he had some explaining to do.

Much to his surprise—and relief—Eddie didn't even bother to

slow down. He just stuck his hand out the car window and waved merrily as he sped past. As the day wore on, though, Elmo felt increasingly uneasy about leaving matters where they stood, so in the middle of the afternoon, around three o'clock, he decided to pay a visit to Eddie's place and apologize for shooting the buck on his land. Arriving at the Gein farmstead, he found Eddie on his knees beside his jacked-up Ford, changing tires. There was nothing unusual about that—except that as Elmo moved closer, he discovered that Eddie was replacing his snow treads with regular tires, a very peculiar thing to be doing with three inches of snow on the ground and winter just beginning. Still, Elmo didn't attach too much significance to Eddie's action.

Now, if someone else removed his snow tires at that time of year, thought Elmo, you'd have to say he was crazy or maybe trying to cover up his tracks. But not Eddie Gein. He was always doing odd things like that.

Elmo tried to say he was sorry, but Eddie seemed too preoccupied to care. And so, after hanging around and chewing the fat for a while, Elmo got back into his car and drove home.

A couple of hours later, Eddie had two more visitors to his farm: his teenaged friend Bob Hill and Bob's sister, Darlene. Eddie, who was happily occupied inside his house when the pair arrived, hurried out to meet them in the yard.

The Hills' car wouldn't start, and Bob was wondering if Eddie would mind driving into town for a new battery.

"Sure," Eddie said. "Just let me wash up." His hands were all bloody, he explained, from dressing out a deer.

Eddie's statement didn't set off any alarm bells in young Bob's head. The boy had shot rabbit and red squirrel with the older man many a time and apparently didn't know that Eddie never hunted deer. Or that Gein claimed never to have butchered a large animal, since the sight of blood supposedly made him feel faint.

By the time Eddie returned to the Hills' place with the new battery and helped install it in the car, it was getting pretty late, so Irene invited the little bachelor to stay for supper.

Eddie accepted gladly. Irene set out a hearty meal—pork chops, boiled potatoes, macaroni and cheese, pickles, coffee, and cookies—and the little man dug into it with gusto. He'd had a busy, productive, thoroughly exhilarating day, and he felt hungry as hell.

# 12

*"Edward Gein had two faces. One he showed to the neighbors. The other he showed only to the dead."*

Stevens Points Daily Journal, November 25, 1957

During deer season, Muschinski's filling station served as an official checking facility, where the huntsmen brought their kill to be weighed and tallied. By five in the evening on that gray, bitter Saturday, when Frank Worden returned—empty-handed—from the woods, a string of stiffening carcasses already hung in the gas-station yard. Though Worden hadn't come home with a kill, the season still had eight days to go, and he wasn't discouraged. In fact, he drove directly to Muschinski's to ask a question about the town's yearly big buck contest.

Immediately, Muschinski mentioned that he had seen the Worden truck leave town early that morning and that the store had been closed ever since. Had Frank's mother, Muschinski wondered, decided to go hunting, too?

Worden was puzzled. As far as he knew, his mother had intended to keep the store open all day. Concerned, he went across the street to try the door and discovered that it was, in fact, locked. Since he wasn't carrying a key, he hurried home to fetch one, then quickly returned to the store.

As soon as he stepped inside, he saw that something was terribly wrong.

The cash register was missing from its counter. And the floor was spattered with reddish-brown stains, which led in a trail to the back door and which Worden instantly recognized as blood. A great deal of blood.

Running to the rear, he looked into the driveway. Muschinski was right. The store's panel truck was gone.

Worden was alarmed but didn't panic. He'd been a deputy sheriff for nearly a year and knew how to proceed. He picked up the phone and dialed Sheriff Art Schley at his office in Wautoma, the county seat, about fifteen miles away. Schley could hear the agitation in his deputy's voice as Worden reported what he'd discovered inside the store.

Schley, who had been sheriff for just over a month, immediately phoned the home of his chief deputy, Arnie Fritz, and—in some distress himself—relayed the news. Within minutes, the pair were speeding down to Plainfield.

By the time they arrived, Worden had had a chance to examine the store for clues. "He's done something to her," Worden blurted out as soon as he saw the two officers. When Fritz asked whom he meant, the missing woman's son—by now deeply distraught— answered bitterly and without hesitation.

"Eddie Gein," he said.

Keeping tight control of his emotions, Worden explained why he suspected Gein. "He's been hanging around here a lot lately, bothering my mother to go roller skating and dancing and to movie shows." Just the day before, Worden went on, Gein had come by the store around closing time to check on the price of antifreeze. While there, he had inquired very casually if Frank intended to go hunting on Saturday. Frank—not attaching any particular significance to the question—had confirmed that he meant to be out in the woods first thing in the morning.

Frank then showed Schley and Fritz something he had discovered while awaiting the sheriff's arrival—a slip of paper with his mother's handwriting on it. She had made it out that morning. As far as Frank was concerned, it was a piece of evidence that pointed directly to Gein. It was a sales receipt for antifreeze.

The three men decided that Gein should be located immediately. In the meantime, Fritz had put out a call for help. Before long, lawmen from throughout the region and as far away as Madison— sheriffs, former sheriffs, deputy sheriffs, town marshals, traffic officers, State Crime Lab investigators, and more—were converging on Plainfield. Among the first to arrive on the scene were Marshal Leon "Specks" Murty of the village of Wild Rose; sheriffs Wanerski, Searles, and Artie of Portage, Adams, and Marquette counties; traffic officer Dan Chase; deputies Arden "Poke" Spees and Virgil

"Buck" Batterman; and Captain Lloyd Schoephoerster of the Green Lake County Sheriff's Department.

By seven o'clock, the street in front of the hardware store was filling up with squad cars, their red revolving lights flashing on the gathering crowd of Bernice Worden's neighbors. Uniformed officers and taut-faced farmers huddled in the frigid fall night, their breath rising in puffs as they talked bitterly about the fate of the widow— another woman snatched from their midst, just like Mary Hogan. Only this time, there was a name attached to the mysterious abductor. The name of Eddie Gein.

Over at the Hills', Gein was warming himself with the last few mouthfuls of Irene's coffee. He had, in fact, seemed chilled all evening, and neither the warmth from the kitchen stove nor the Hills' kerosene space heater seemed to make any difference. Irene wondered if the little bachelor was coming down with the flu.

Eddie had moved over to the davenport and was horsing around with one of the Hills' younger children when Jim Vroman, Irene's son-in-law, rushed into the house and began talking excitedly about Bernice Worden's disappearance and the commotion downtown. Eddie sat there listening intently until Vroman was finished, then shook his head and said, "Must have been somebody pretty cold-blooded."

Irene looked at Eddie and suddenly remembered how he had been dining at her house a few years before when the news of Mary Hogan's abduction reached them. "Ed," she said, "how come every time somebody gets banged on the head and hauled away, you're always around?"

Eddie just grinned the way he did and gave a little shrug.

Like any teenager who has just heard the news of some big local trouble, Bob Hill was itching to see the excitement for himself and asked if Eddie would drive him downtown.

Eddie, always obliging, agreed.

The Hills kept their store open late, and it was time for Irene to relieve her husband, who had been taking care of business while the rest of the family ate. As Gein and Bob got ready to leave, Irene bid goodbye to her visitor, then hurried across the snow-encrusted yard to the little grocery. She removed her coat and sent Lester home for his meal.

She hadn't been there more than a few minutes when the front door swung open, letting in a blast of frozen air and two grim-faced men, Officer Dan Chase and Deputy Poke Spees.

Chase had been dispatched to find the suspect and, after making a quick stop at the Gein farmstead and satisfying himself that no one was home, had proceeded to the Hills', where Eddie was known to be a frequent visitor. As soon as the two officers stepped inside the store, they asked Irene if she knew where Eddie was.

"He's sitting in his car right there in my driveway, unless he's taken off," Irene told them. "He's driving my son downtown to see what's going on."

Sure enough, when Chase and Spees went around to the house, they found Gein's car still there, engine idling, tail pipe spewing exhaust vapor into the cold. The Hills' porch light was burning, and in its glow Chase could see Eddie sitting behind the wheel of his Ford with Bob Hill beside him.

Chase tapped on the driver's window, and Gein rolled it down. "Eddie," said Chase, "I'd like to talk to you."

Obediently, Eddie stepped out into the yard and followed the two officers to their squad car, where he got into the back seat with Spees. Positioning himself up front, Chase swiveled to look at the stubble-cheeked little man, who sat there smiling weakly, his watery blue eyes peering out from beneath the peak of the plaid deerhunter's cap planted sideways on his head.

Chase asked Gein exactly how he'd spent the day, from the time he woke up to the present moment, and Eddie proceeded to tell him.

When he finished, Chase asked him to run through the events of the day one more time, beginning with his visit to Worden's. Gein repeated his account.

"Now, Eddie," said Chase after a moment. "You didn't tell the same story come through there that second time."

Eddie blinked once, then said, "Somebody framed me."

"Framed you for what?" asked Chase.

"Well, Mrs. Worden."

Chase leaned closer to his suspect. "What about Mrs. Worden?"

"Well, she's dead, ain't she?"

"Dead!" Chase exclaimed. "How do you know she's dead?"

Eddie's lopsided grin seemed frozen in place. "Well, I heard it."

"Where'd you hear it?"

"I heard them talking about it," Eddie said, straining to sound nonchalant.

By then, whatever doubts Chase had been entertaining about Gein's involvement had completely evaporated. He knew he had his man.

Informing Eddie that he was a suspect in the robbery of Bernice Worden's store, Chase radioed his superior, Sheriff Schley, that the suspect was in custody. Then he started the squad car and pulled out of the yard, leaving the Hills shaking their heads in bewilderment.

They had no way of knowing, of course, that the next time they set eyes on their quiet little neighbor, his name would be known throughout the nation—indeed around the world. Or that they themselves were about to gain widespread and highly unwelcome celebrity as the last people to break bread with America's most notorious maniac.

# 13

*" 'And then—and then I opened the door, and the room was filled with bodies and skeletons of poor dead women, all stained with their blood.'*

*" 'It is not so, nor was it so. And God forbid it should be so,' said Mr. Fox."*

From the English fairy tale "Mr. Fox"

At thirty-two years old, Arthur Schley was a big, imposing man, not overly tall but broad-chested and husky—the kind of small-town sheriff whose very bulk invests him with authority. On the night of November 17, however, Schley was feeling a little unsure of himself. A former employee of the Waushara County Highway Department, he was new on the job and nervous about heading up a murder investigation. Still, things were going well. He was surrounded by a large force of experienced officers, and, though it was not quite eight o'clock, only a couple of hours since he'd received Frank Worden's call, the suspect had already been apprehended. The important thing now was to locate Frank's mother.

Gein's house seemed like the logical place to start looking, and so, accompanied by Captain Schoephoerster, Schley got into his car and headed out of town, arriving a short while later at the lonely, decaying farmstead.

Gein's house looked grim even in broad daylight. On a frozen winter's night, with icicles hanging from the porch roof and dead clumps of weeds poking up through the snow, its desolation was so extreme that even a brave man could be spooked by the sight of it. It was hard to believe that anything human could make its home in such a place.

The two officers moved across the yard, boots crunching in the snow, breaths rising before them like wraiths. They made their way around the house, trying each door in turn, but all of them were tightly locked, except for one—the door leading into the summer kitchen, which was secured with a flimsy latch. Schoephoerster put his boot to the door, and it gave way with a crack. Aiming their flashlights at the junk-littered floor, the men moved carefully around the rotting cartons and rusted farm tools to the opposite side of the shed, where Schoephoerster tried the door that led into the main part of the house. Meanwhile, Schley stepped back and swept his beam around the room. He felt something touch his jacket from behind and turned to see what he had brushed up against.

There, in the beam of his flashlight, dangled a large, dead-white carcass. It was hanging upside down by its feet. Its front had been split completely open, so that its trunk was little more than a dark, gaping hole. The carcass had been decapitated as though someone had sliced the head off for a trophy.

The body had been butchered like a heifer or a dressed-out deer. Only it wasn't an animal. It was the body of a human being, an adult woman. Bernice Worden's body.

The sight was so stupefying that it took a moment for Schley to understand what he was looking at. Then he managed to choke out a few words—"My God, there she is"—before stumbling out of the shed and into the frozen night. He had sunk to his knees in the snow and was vomiting loudly when Schoephoerster came staggering after him.

# 14

*"On horror's head horrors accumulate."*
SHAKESPEARE, *Othello*

Schoephoerster ran to his squad car and radioed the news: Bernice Worden's corpse had been located at Eddie Gein's farm. Then, steeling themselves as best they could, he and Schley reentered the summer kitchen to confront the nightmare that waited inside.

With unsteady hands, they trained their flashlights on the gutted, headless woman suspended by her heels from the ceiling. A crude wooden crossbar—three feet long, bark-covered, and sharpened to a point at both ends—had been shoved through the tendons of one ankle; the other foot had been slit above the heel and secured to the rod with a stout cord. Her arms were held taut at her sides by hemp ropes that ran from her wrists to the crossbar. The bar itself had been hooked to a block-and-tackle and hauled up toward the roof beams. And there—left to keep in the coldness of the shed like a side of beef in a butcher's meat locker—the mutilated remains of the fifty-eight-year-old grandmother hung.

By now, the other officers alerted by Schoephoerster had begun arriving at the farm. These were all individuals—county lawmen, state troopers, crime lab investigators—who were used to seeing harrowing sights, to witnessing the gruesome aftermaths of murders, hunting mishaps, and highway accidents. But, to a man, the sight of Mrs. Worden's decapitated and disemboweled body stunned them into silence. None of them had ever set eyes on anything so appalling.

At that moment, none of them would have believed that the hideously violated corpse of the woman was only the first—and by no means the most unspeakable—of the horrors that Eddie Gein's death farm had in store.

Led by Schoephoerster, the officers moved from the summer kitchen into the main part of the house. It was the first time in years that anyone besides its owner had set foot inside the place. At first, they conducted their investigation by flashlight and kerosene lamp. And in that dim and fitful glow, they discovered that Gein's decaying old farmhouse was the habitation of a creature who could truly be called, without sensationalism or overstatement, a ghoul.

It was clearly a madhouse. The sheer disorder of the place—the sprawling heaps of rubbish, old cartons, tin cans, bottles, tools, newspapers, magazines, food scraps, rags, and much more—was profoundly disconcerting. It was as if Gein had reversed the usual process of garbage disposal and made weekly runs to the town dump to pick up a load of trash for his living quarters. Such chaos was clearly the product of an equally chaotic mind—mental derangement expressed as decor. It quickly became apparent to the explorers that, in the whole rambling house, only a couple of rooms were actually used by its inhabitant. But it was hard to imagine anyone really living—cooking, eating, sleeping—amid such filth and debris.

And then there were the particular items that spoke so plainly of insanity—the coffee can stuffed with lumps of used chewing gum, the cracked and yellowed dentures displayed on a shelf like Fabergé eggs, the wash basin full of sand. But these, of course, were the least disturbing objects in Eddie's crazed collection.

There was, to begin with, the funny-looking soup bowl one of the officers saw sitting on the kitchen table and picked up for closer inspection. The soup bowl turned out to be the sawed-off top of a human skull.

There were other skullcaps scattered around the place. And there were several complete skulls, too, including a pair that had been stuck on Eddie's bedposts as a decoration.

One of the chairs by the kitchen table had a distinctly peculiar look to it. When Captain Schoephoerster bent to examine it, he discovered that the woven cane seat had been replaced by smooth strips of human skin. The underside was lumpy with fat. Four such chairs were eventually found.

These grotesque furnishings were not the only evidence of Gein's insane handiwork. Indeed, as the investigators quickly discovered, Gein's farm functioned not just as a human slaughterhouse but as the workshop of a fiend. His diseased imagination fed by accounts of Ilse Koch and her human-skin artifacts, Gein had busied himself with the production of similarly abhorrent objects.

As the stunned and disbelieving lawmen poked through the wreckage of the house, they uncovered a variety of articles fabricated from human skin—lampshades, bracelets, a wastebasket, a tom-tom, the sheath of a hunting knife.

Later, they found a belt fashioned out of female nipples and a shade-pull decorated with a pair of woman's lips.

A portable generator was secured, flood lamps were brought in, and the deathly gloom that Gein had inhabited for the past dozen years was finally dissolved in the glare of electric light. Meanwhile, in the bitter darkness outside, a huddling crowd of newsmen was being kept at bay by the police, who had blocked off Gein's house and refused to issue any statements, other than to say that Mrs. Worden's body had been found and that Gein was being held as a suspect.

The reporters could tell, of course, that something extraordinary was going on inside the house. But the only comment that Sheriff Schley would make was that the situation was "just too horrible. Horrible beyond belief."

And indeed, even the investigators working their way through the shambles inside and seeing the newly illuminated horrors with their own eyes were having difficulty crediting their senses.

At one point, for example, Allan Wilimovsky, a crime lab specialist, picked up an old shoebox, glanced inside, and realized with a start that—as inconceivable as it seemed—he had just discovered a sizable collection of female genitalia.

There were nine vulvas altogether. Most were dried and shriveled, though one had been daubed with silver paint and trimmed with a red ribbon. Another—the top-most one—seemed quite fresh. It consisted of a portion of mons veneris with the vagina and anus attached. Looking closely at this specimen, Wilimovsky noticed small crystals clinging to its surface. The recently excised vulva, he realized, had been sprinkled with salt.

Another box contained four human noses. And there was a cardboard Quaker Oats container filled with scraps of human head integument.

Insane as it seemed, some of Gein's loathsome creations were obviously meant to be worn. There were, for example, several pairs of skin puttees—leggings made from actual human legs. Even more ghastly was a garment fashioned from the upper torso of a middle-aged woman. Gein had carefully skinned the top part of her body—breasts included—tanned it, and attached a cord to it so that it could be donned as a kind of vest.

Perhaps the most shocking discovery of all, however, was Eddie's mask collection.

The masks were actually human facial skins that had been painstakingly peeled from the skulls of nine women. They had no eyes, of course, just holes where the eyes had been. But the hair was still attached to the scalps. A few of the masks looked dried out, almost mummified. Others seemed more carefully preserved, as though they had been treated with oil to keep the skin smooth. Some of them still had lipstick on their mouths and looked quite lifelike. For those who knew their faces, it would not have been hard to tell the identities of the victims.

Four of these face-skins had been stuffed with paper and hung on a wall of Eddie's bedroom like hunting trophies. These, as it turned out, were the "shrunken heads" that several of Eddie's young neighbors had glimpsed years earlier, before he had permanently shut the doors of his house to visitors.

Other masks were stored inside plastic or paper bags. One of the officers—Deputy Arnie Fritz—discovered a moth-eaten horsehide robe lying in a heap behind the kitchen door. When he picked it up, he found a brown paper bag stuck within its folds. Opening the bag, he aimed his flashlight inside and saw a mass of dry hair attached to a desiccated skin. Much later, looking back on that moment, Fritz would say that he didn't know what possessed him to do what he did next. Perhaps, like most of the men who went through Eddie's house that first terrible night, the horrors of the place had simply put him into a kind of daze. In any event, what he did at that moment was reach into the bag, take hold of the grisly thing it contained, and raise that thing up to the light. And as he did so, Specks Murty, who was standing nearby, looked over and gasped, "By God. It's Mary Hogan."

The three-year-old mystery of the tavern owner's disappearance had finally been solved.

For the dozens of local lawmen involved, the investigation of Bernice Worden's murder had turned into a macabre form of excavation. Sifting through the rubble of Gein's house was like conducting an archeological dig in hell. Throughout the night, so many body parts were uncovered—shin bones, scalps, scraps of skin, withered breasts, vaginas, lips, noses, heads, and more—that it was impossible to tell how many victims had supplied them. And all these human bits and pieces were contained in a very confined area—the kitchen and downstairs bedroom that Eddie inhabited.

Faced with the boarded-off part of the first floor that lay beyond Gein's living space, the searchers couldn't help but feel a twinge of apprehension. After the things they had turned up in his bedroom and kitchen, it was hard to imagine what horrors he had felt compelled to seal away from view.

The nails were removed. The boards were taken down. And the sight that confronted the investigators did indeed provide a shock, though of a very different kind from any they had yet experienced during that long, punishing night.

What the investigators saw when they removed the boards was a bedroom and parlor in a state of absolute tidiness. Everything was in perfect order—the bed, the bureaus, the rugs, the bookcases, the chairs and side tables and curtains. After the unholy squalor of the rest of the house, the very neatness of these rooms was intensely unsettling.

The nature of the furnishings as well as the clothes that the investigators found meticulously folded away in the dresser drawers made it clear that the rooms had been inhabited by a woman. And the thick coating of dust that lay over everything indicated that this part of the house had not been used—or even entered—in years.

In fact, the lovingly preserved rooms had belonged to Eddie's long-dead mother. Though they didn't know it at the time, the searchers had stumbled upon a shrine. Like Egyptologists breaking into the burial chamber of a pharaoh, the men who entered Augusta Gein's living quarters that night were the first humans to set foot inside that sanctum since it had been sealed off many years before by a worshipper who regarded it as the dwelling place of a god.

Out in the summer kitchen, Allan Wilimovsky of the crime lab had set up a camera and photographed Bernice Worden's remains—still hanging upside down from the rafters—from various angles. By this time, early Sunday morning, other parts of her butchered body had been discovered—her heart in a plastic bag in front of Gein's potbellied stove, a pile of entrails (still warm) wrapped in a newspaper and folded inside an old suit of men's clothes.

As yet, however, no one had located the corpse's head.

Wilimovsky and a crime lab colleague named Halligan began

poking through the heaps of trash scattered around the floor of the summer kitchen. In a corner of the shed lay a pair of stained and tattered mattresses. Lifting the top one by a corner, Halligan saw an old burlap feed sack sandwiched between them. Steam rose from the sack.

Wilimovsky picked up the bag, reached inside, and removed Mrs. Worden's head.

It was smeared with dirt, and there was blood in both nostrils, but the expression on the face looked peaceful. But Eddie had done something to the decapitated head that would have defied belief, except that nothing seemed unbelievable to the investigators anymore. Not after the endless succession of horrors they had witnessed that night.

What Eddie had done was take two ten-penny nails, bend them into hooks, connect them with a two-foot length of twine and stick one nail into each of Bernice Worden's ears. In this way, the head could be hung in Eddie's bedroom as a trophy or wall ornament— the latest acquisition in his collection of monstrous *objets d'art*.

Bernice Worden's body was unhooked from the pulley and placed inside a plastic bag. Along with the severed head, which had been photographed by Wilimovsky and then replaced in the burlap sack, the corpse was transported back to Plainfield, where a postmortem examination was to be conducted at Goult's Funeral Home.

It was five in the morning, Sunday, November 17—twelve hours since Frank Worden had returned from the woods to discover that his mother was missing.

# 15

*"I've never worked on a case quite like this one."*

CHARLES WILSON,
director of the Wisconsin Crime Laboratory

Following his arrest on Saturday night, Eddie was transported to
the town of Wautoma and locked in a cell in the rear of the county
jailhouse. The front of the building served as living quarters for
Sheriff Schley, his wife, and their three daughters.

A trio of deputies stood guard outside Gein's cell—Arden Spees,
Specks Murty, and Dan Chase. Suddenly, around two-thirty in the
morning, Sheriff Schley burst into the jail. After having spent six
hours stuck inside the living nightmare of Gein's horror house, he
was visibly agitated.

Schley looked at Chase. "Has he come clean?" he demanded.

"Not too much," said Chase.

The night of nerve-rending discoveries finally got the better of
Schley. He grabbed the fifty-one-year-old bachelor by the shoulders
and started slamming him up against the wall of the jail.

Instantly, the three deputies sprang at the men and separated
Eddie from Schley's powerful grasp.

The little man was shaken up a bit, but Schley's outburst didn't
manage to dislodge a confession from him. In fact, it produced the
opposite effect. Eddie clammed up even tighter than before.

At four-thirty A.M., Joe Wilimovsky—Allan's brother and the
crime lab's polygraph specialist—arrived at the jail to question the
suspect, an interrogation that would continue, on and off, for more
than twelve hours. At no point during this period did Gein have an

attorney present, nor was he ever advised of his right to counsel. But Gein admitted to nothing.

That Sunday morning, the citizens of Plainfield went off to church knowing only that something horrific had happened in their little village. By then, everyone had heard a few basic facts: that Mrs. Worden had been abducted from her store on Saturday morning; that her truck—its floor and front seat spattered with blood—had been discovered just east of the village by Sheriff Frank Searles of Adams County, in a pine grove that served as the local lovers' lane; that Mrs. Worden's corpse had later been found at the old Gein farmstead; and (though some of them refused to believe it) that meek little Eddie Gein stood accused of the murder.

That was all they knew for sure. But as awful as Mrs. Worden's murder was, something even more enormous had clearly taken place. Police from as far away as Chicago were pouring into Plainfield on their way out to the Gein farm. And the town was under virtual siege by a growing army of reporters, who were camped out at the farm and had set up their headquarters in the offices of the local weekly, the *Plainfield Sun.*

Bizarre and unbelievable stories—whispered talk of unspeakable crimes and unthinkable depravities—circulated among the citizens of Plainfield as they milled on the streets after their Sunday services. As one paper reported, the news blackout imposed by Sheriff Schley had turned the town into a "hothouse of rumor."

The first account of the Plainfield horrors to reach the world outside the isolated little farming community appeared in the Sunday edition of the *Milwaukee Journal.* "MISSING FROM STORE, WIDOW FOUND DEAD," read the headline. The story itself contained only a few bare details. It described Frank Worden's discovery of his mother's abduction, the subsequent discovery of the body "on a farm seven miles away," and the arrest of a suspect. The article reported that Sheriff Schley "would not identify the suspect," though it mentioned that the victim's corpse had been found on the farm of one Edward Gein.

As the day progressed, there were increasing indications from the officers that a story of extraordinary magnitude was about to break. And one of the officers who indicated as much was the dead woman's son, Deputy Sheriff Frank Worden. Though Worden refused to divulge any details, he admitted to reporters that something even worse than his mother's murder was involved. "It's a case that will shock the state of Wisconsin," Worden claimed.

As it turned out, his remark would prove to be a significant understatement.

# 16

*"Yes, she has withered; I feel it on her bosom.—*
*So we must meet again and here?*
*Here, where I as doctor cut her flesh apart,*
*the body which was mine? A frenzy of desire runs through my veins,*
  *once more, once more. . . .*
*In horror I draw back: a desecrator of the dead?*
*Wide is her eye with its own staring gaze—*
*They found me raving in the morning on the floor."*

Anonymous, quoted by Wilhelm Stekel in *Sadism and Masochism*

Late that Sabbath morning, just a short time after her neighbors had filed out of Plainfield's various houses of worship, where candles had been lit and prayers offered for Bernice Worden's soul, the butchered remains of her body lay on a table in the embalming room of Ray Goult's funeral home. Gathered around the table were Goult; Allan Wilimovsky and James Halligan of the State Crime Lab; Sheriff Harold Kroll of Sheboygan County and his deputy, Robert Frewert; and Dr. F. Eigenberger, a pathologist from Neenah, Wisconsin, along with his wife, Cordelia.

The postmortem examination of Mrs. Worden's corpse—a procedure that would last into the late afternoon—was about to begin.

Eigenberger conducted the autopsy while dictating his findings to his wife, a secretary and office manager in a large Sheboygan medical clinic, who jotted the notes on small loose-leaf sheets. Later, these notes were assembled into a finished report. Typed on Sheboygan Memorial Hospital letterhead, Bernice Worden's autopsy report is an exceptionally dismaying document, which makes chillingly clear the full extent not only of Gein's butchery but of the madness that could compel him to use a human body in such a way.

The report begins with a section labeled "General Information":

The body of a murdered and mutilated woman, Mrs. Bernice Worden, had been found in the woodshed of the old Gein farmhouse near Plainfield, Wisconsin. Investigation which had led to this discovery had been started in the hardware store owned and operated by Mrs. Worden, where an incompletely wiped pool of blood had been found. Further observation had led to the belief that the body had been dragged through the store, loaded upon a truck, then transferred to a private car in which the body had allegedly been brought to the place where it was discovered. The body had been found hanging by the heels from the roof bars—decapitated and eviscerated. Head and viscera had been found in the same location, the vulva in a box, the heart in a plastic bag. Before performing the autopsy the above mentioned locations were visited.

Next comes the description of the autopsy itself, beginning with a lengthy section headed "Inspection":

The body was that of an over middle aged, allegedly 58 year old woman, well shaped, and in a good state of nutrition. It had been decapitated at shoulder level by a smooth circular cut which severed skin, all the soft structures and the intervertebral cartilage between the 6th and 7th cervical vertebrae had been cut with a sharp instrument. There was no evidence of jagged edges indicating that no axe or similar implement had been used.

The body had been opened by a median incision from the manubrium sterni and extending in the midline to the area just above the mons veneris. Here the cut circled around the external genitalia for the complete removal of the vulva, lower vagina, and the anus with the lowest portion of the rectum. To accomplish this, the symphysis pubis had been split and the pubic bones widely separated. From the appearance of the cut for evisceration it was concluded that the cut was started from the lower end and terminated above the stomach pit. The reason for this was the somewhat jagged appearance of the cut skin near the chest indicating hesitation in terminating the knife cut.

The vulva and adjoining structures that had been removed were presented in a carton box together with preserved and dried other specimens of the same type. The freshly removed vulva fitted well into the tissue defect of the body. Only few pubic hairs had remained on both sides of the removed organs and a portion of this hairy skin was removed for purposes of identification. Examination of the outer genitalia revealed no evidence of trauma and no conclusion could be reached whether or not sexual intercourse had taken place.

The body cavities had been completely eviscerated together with most of the diaphragm. Inspection of the trunk and extremities revealed how the body had been hoisted by the heels.

There was a deep cut above the Achilles tendon of the right leg and a pointed crossbar made of a rough wooden stick covered by bark had been forced underneath the tendon. The other side of the crossbar had been tied to a cord which was tightly fastened to a cut of the leg above the heel. This cut had severed the Achilles tendon and had necessitated the tying with cord to hold the body securely to the crossbar. The length of the crossbar was estimated as about three feet. Both wrists had been tied with longer hemp ropes to the corresponding ends of the crossbar attached to the feet, thus holding the arms firmly when the body had been suspended by the heels.

Inspection of the skin surface of the body revealed dirt covering the shoulders, mostly the upper dorsal area, and the dirt resembled dry mud in thin scaly crusts. The skin of the back, both arms and legs, less of chest and abdomen was somewhat discolored by dust which showed irregular smudgy areas of heavier covering. Rather striking was the amount of black dust covering both plantar surfaces, dust which appeared somewhat "rubbed in," as if from walking barefoot on a dirty, dusty floor.

Both breasts appeared good sized and, for her age, well formed. They felt medium firm, mostly because the adipose tissue had hardened from the exposure to cold. The right nipple appeared normal, the left was somewhat inverted. Both breasts appeared to lean upward, apparently due to the long suspension by the heels. There was no evidence of mutilation of the breasts.

Inspection of the body (trunk and extremities) revealed no evidence of ante mortem trauma. The exsanguination was complete, only fingernails showed moderate cyanosis. On the left ring finger was a cameo ring. The empty body cavities were glistening and free from blood, appeared as if they had been washed. No fractures of the trunk or extremities were found. The seventh vertebra was removed for further examination by the Wisconsin State Crime Laboratory.

The thoracic and abdominal viscera had been separately kept, wrapped in newspaper and hidden in a bundle of old clothing. These viscera consisted of both lungs with the trachea, the aorta from the base to the abdominal bifurcation, the esophagus, stomach, small and large intestines with mesentary and omentum to the lower rectum. En bloc with this were removed: The spleen, pancreas, adrenals, kidneys with the ureters, upper half of the urine bladder, and internal genital organs. Separately removed had been:

1. Heart (without the pericardium) and this had been kept in a plastic bag.

2. Liver.

The report then proceeds to detail the condition of the individual organs (stomach, intestines, pancreas, liver, and so on) before turning to a description of the capitated head—a particularly significant section from a forensic point of view, since it reveals how Mrs. Worden was killed:

The head with the neck was submitted in a separate cardboard. It fitted with the trunk of the body. The hair was medium short cut, somewhat curly, and appeared soiled with dust and smeared with blood. The color of the hair was dark, showing considerable graying. . . . A roundish hole of the scalp which was difficult to find on outer inspection, measured, when moderately stretched, 0.76 cm. in diameter. The edge of the defect revealed a narrow marginal abrasion. There was no tear in the contour of the opening and no evidence of burn, nor could any powder particles be grossly visualized. This skin defect, suggesting the entrance wound of a bullet, was located to the left of the midline and about 6 cm. above the neck hairline, 3.5 cm. laterally and 2 cm. above the outer occipital protuberantia.

The face appeared covered with dust in irregular distribution. There was no evidence of external trauma to the face. Both eyes were closed. . . . The nose appeared intact on palpation, but there was blood in both nostrils. The left ear had a hooked spike inserted, the tip of which was at the time of examination 2 cm. deep in the external ear canal. There were slight, apparently post mortem excoriations, on the outer border of the ear canal. Blood oozed from this ear in larger quantities than the excoriations indicated.

Tied to the head of the hooked spike was a cord to which another hooked spike of the same size had been attached. This right spike was at the time of examination not inserted in the right ear canal.

The neck revealed no evidence of applied force, like from strangling, no finger or nail imprints, nor scratches. The trachea and larynx appeared normal. The portion of the lower medulla oblongata and the upper cervical spine had been ripped out. This portion of the spinal cord was not found. . . .

Dissection of the brain showed hemorrhages in all ventricular spaces. The actual bullet track through the brain was difficult to visualize. It was evident that the bullet had traversed the brain beneath the corpus callosum passing through the ventricles, and struck the sphenoid bone. To facilitate the localization of the bullet, as there was no exit defect, X-ray pictures were taken and the bullet, apparently of .22 caliber, was located and found within the right orbita beneath the median portion of its roof without destruction to the eyeball. (Bullet turned over to the Wisconsin State Crime Laboratory.) The extensive skull fracture had been the cause for the bleedings from the nose and the right ear canal.

After a brief summation of the findings of a microscopic examination of the brain, lungs, liver, heart, spleen, and kidneys, the autopsy report ends with the pathologist's conclusions regarding the manner of Mrs. Worden's death:

Examination of the decapitated and eviscerated body of Mrs. Bernice Worden revealed as the only cause of death a bullet shot wound in the head which had been fired in the back of the head. The bullet had penetrated the brain anteriorly causing destruction of the vital areas and interventricular hemorrhage as well as extensive skull fractures and some subarachnoid hemorrhage. The bullet had lodged in the left orbit. It had apparently not been a contact nor a very close shot. . . . Death had apparently occurred shortly (seconds or minutes) after the shot had been fired. All the other mutilations of the body had been carried out after death.

Interestingly, Mrs. Eigenberger's original handwritten sheets contain a number of parenthetical comments excluded from the final postmortem report. These brief notations, hastily scribbled on the back of the loose-leaf pages, consist of short, provocative phrases that clearly represent her spontaneous reflections on various aspects of the murder—ideas that struck her while the autopsy was in progress.

At one point, for instance, she observes that Gein's removal of the heart and liver conforms to a "deer hunter's pattern." A bit later, she wonders whether the "seed" for the murder had been "planted by crime comics and movies" (a speculation prompted partly, no doubt, by the discovery of Eddie's massive collection of quasiporno-graphic crime publications and partly by contemporary concerns over excessive comic book violence, a controversial issue in 1950s America).

Perhaps the most striking of Mrs. Eigenberger's jottings, however, appears on the back of the very last page of her notes, where she has written the words "Sex Slayer and the Battered Beauty." What makes this phrase so arresting is its utter incongruity in the context of the postmortem report. In contrast to her husband's detached, clinical language, Mrs. Eigenberger's notation has the shameless-ness of a tabloid headline.

Indeed, her attempt to come up with a titillating catch phrase for the crime anticipates the kind of treatment that the Gein horrors were about to receive in the press. Within twenty-four hours of Mrs. Worden's autopsy, newspapers throughout the Midwest would be full of equally sensational headlines, as journalists tried to find language lurid enough to do justice to Eddie Gein's demented handiwork.

# 17

*"Where last week the talk on North Street was about deer hunting or dairying, Monday it was filled with speculations on matters that are ordinarily far outside the interests of respectable residents of communities like this. Who could have imagined a few days ago that topics like cannibalism and human butchery would be discussed in Plainfield on Monday?"*

*Milwaukee Journal*, November 18, 1957

By the time the story broke late on Sunday, there couldn't have been a soul in central Wisconsin who wasn't aware that a crime of particularly monstrous proportions had been uncovered in Plainfield. But no one was prepared for the facts that finally emerged. The shock of that day's disclosures quickly spread from the Midwest across the nation. Like the young bride in "Bluebeard," who unlocks the door to the forbidden chamber and finds herself staring at a roomful of butchered corpses, America was transfixed by the horror.

Throughout the day, rumors abounded in Plainfield that Ed Gein's isolated farmhouse was in fact a "murder factory," filled with the skeletal remains of at least seven victims. Sheriff Schley maintained a stubborn silence, refusing to speak a word to reporters, though he did release a statement confirming that "several skeletons" and anatomical parts of human bodies have been recovered.

Later that afternoon, several officials on the scene—beginning with the district attorney of Waushara County, Earl Kileen—provided the press with the first detailed account of the findings. For the first time, reporters learned about Mrs. Worden's trussed-up and dressed-out body, about the heads preserved in plastic bags, about the skulls scattered around Gein's rooms, about the furniture and implements fashioned from human skin. Deputy Dave Sharkey of Wood County, who had spent the entire night searching through Gein's farmhouse, offered additional facts, describing among other things Gein's grisly collection of death masks. "I'm of the opinion that some of them are young people," he told newsmen. "Some of them have lipstick on and look perfectly natural."

Far from putting an end to the hearsay, Kileen's and Sharkey's disclosures only added fuel to the rumor mills. The very hideousness of their revelations generated even ghastlier stories, including one that would quickly gain the status of fact—that Gein was not only a butcher of human flesh but a consumer of it as well.

Kileen himself added considerable credibility to this tale when, after supplying newsmen with a graphic description of Mrs. Worden's cleaned-out cadaver, he observed, "It appears to be cannibalism."

It wasn't long before the facts surrounding Bernice Worden's murder—horrific enough to begin with—underwent some significant alterations. Mrs. Worden's heart, for example, which had actually been discovered in a plastic bag near Eddie's stove, was suddenly reported to have been found in a frying pan on one of the burners. The old suit of clothes in which her entrails had been hidden became a refrigerator packed with vital organs, all of them neatly wrapped in brown butcher's paper. Stories began to circulate that the widow's body had been dismembered and her legs hung up to cure in Gein's summer kitchen. Eddie's cellar was rumored to be stocked with quart jars full of human blood.

For the next few weeks in Plainfield, whatever horrors could be imagined were instantly reported as fact. William Senay, owner of Bill's Bar on North Street, described the phenomenon to reporters. "Some guy comes in here and tells a story," said Senay. "Then he goes down the street and tells it again. And by that time he believes it himself."

There was, in fact, another highly sensational charge still to come, one so incredible that it would be greeted with skepticism even by those who had no trouble believing that their reclusive neighbor was a cannibal. Still, it would be hard to dismiss the claim out of hand, since the person who would make it was Eddie Gein himself.

# 18

*"Everyone to his own taste. Mine is for corpses."*

From the trial testimony of
the necrophile Henri Blot

By Monday morning, the land lay under a four-inch blanket of snow. But the frigid conditions didn't deter the investigators, who continued to sift through the squalor of Gein's farm buildings. They also launched a search of his one-hundred-ninety-five-acre property, an undertaking that would end up lasting a week.

The chaos of Gein's house was such that new pieces of evidence were constantly turning up in the clutter. The number of body parts buried amid the debris seemed endless. On Sunday, for example, Kileen had told the press that four human heads had been found inside Gein's house. On Monday, he announced the discovery of six more, some wrapped carefully in plastic bags, others tossed casually under furniture.

Kileen's revelations set off a media blitz. By Monday, the influx of newsmen into Plainfield had turned into a full-fledged invasion. Journalists descended on the stunned little town in droves. There were reporters from all the big regional dailies—the *Milwaukee Journal*, the *Milwaukee Sentinel*, the *Madison Capital Times*, the *Chicago Tribune*, the *Chicago Sun-Times*, the *Minneapolis Star*, the *St. Paul Pioneer Press*, and others. Some of these papers assigned as many as five reporters to cover various angles of the rapidly unfolding story. Writers and photographers arrived from *Life*, *Time*, and *Look* magazines. Television and radio stations sent news teams, and the Associated Press set up a portable wire service in the Local Union Telephone Company office to transmit photographs from Plainfield.

Within a day or so, there would even be correspondents from overseas newspapers.

The intense media interest in the horrors coming to light on Gein's farmstead had as much to do with the locale of the case as with its gruesome nature. By early Monday, it was already evident that the village of Plainfield—a quiet little town in the heart of America's dairyland—was the scene of one of the most sensational crimes in Wisconsin, if not American, history. As yet, no one could say how many murders had actually been committed, but investigators were inclined to believe that the number was substantial. "We know we have at least eleven dead," Deputy Sharkey told reporters. "There might be fifty for that matter."

Indeed, among the many rumors circulating through Waushara County that morning were reports connecting Eddie to every unexplained disappearance that had occurred in Wisconsin during the past ten years. And it was true that a virtual army of investigators from throughout the Midwest—more than one hundred fifty officers, according to one estimate—visited Gein's premises during a forty-eight-hour period to check it for clues to various missing-persons cases. Heading the list of crimes they were hoping to solve were those involving Georgia Weckler, the eight-year-old girl who had vanished in 1947; Victor "Bunk" Travis, the local man missing since 1952; the La Crosse teenager Evelyn Hartley, carried off while babysitting in 1953; and Mary Hogan, the Portage County tavern keeper whose mysterious disappearance in 1954 bore a striking similarity, as more than one local newspaper noted, to the details of Bernice Worden's abduction.

Shortly before eleven o'clock that Monday morning, a major development occurred in the case when prosecutor Kileen told a mob of reporters that Gein had finally broken his thirty-hour silence.

In a statement to Kileen, Gein had acknowledged killing Mrs. Worden, though he insisted he couldn't remember any details of the crime because it all happened while he was in a "daze." A stenographic record of Gein's admission was later released to the press. The section relating to Mrs. Worden's murder reads as follows:

> KILEEN: Now you start from the time you went into the Worden implement store. Tell us exactly what happened the best you can recall.

GEIN: When I went into Mrs. Worden's, I took a glass jug for permanent antifreeze. When I entered the hardware store she came toward me and said, "Do you want a gallon of antifreeze?" and I said, "No, a half gallon." She got out the antifreeze and pumped it out, and I held the jug for her to pour it in and then she pumped out another quart, and I was still holding the jar while she pumped that. Then I paid her with a dollar bill. She gave me back one cent because it was 99 cents.

This is what I can't remember from now on because I don't know just what happened from now on, you see.

She glanced out of the window towards the filling station across the street and said, "They are checking deer there." Then she looked towards the west, out of the west and north windows, and said, "There are more people up town than I thought there would be." She might have said something about the opening of the season, she might have said that.

KILEEN: Do you remember striking her or shooting her?

GEIN: No. This is what got me—whether I took my antifreeze out. That is what I can't remember. It is hard for me to say from now on. My memory is a little vague, but I do remember dragging her across the floor. I remember loading her body in the truck. Then I drove the truck out on the east road at the intersection where 51 and 73 separate east of Plainfield. I drove the truck up in the pine trees. Then I walked to town and got in my car and drove it out there and loaded her body in the back of the car, and also the cash register. I loaded the cash register in the truck when I put her body in there.

Then I drove out to my farm and took the body out of the car and hung it up by the heels in my wood shed.

KILEEN: Tell how you took the blood out and buried it. You used the knife you made from the file to cut her up?

GEIN: That is as close as I can remember. I was in a regular daze like, and I can't swear to it.

KILEEN: Then you said that you took the blood from the body and put that out—buried it out by the toilet house where you pointed out.

GEIN: East of the toilet.

KILEEN: Do you remember what you had the blood in? Was it a pail, bucket, or jar?

GEIN: It must have been a pail.

KILEEN: What kind of pail?

GEIN: Probably galvanized. Probably a 10-quart pail.

KILEEN: Then you proceeded to dress out the body? You told me that you thought you were dressing out a deer.

GEIN: That is the only explanation I can think was in my mind.

Kileen had also raised the question of cannibalism, asking Eddie if he had butchered Mrs. Worden with the intention of eating her. But the little man had been evasive. "On that point," Kileen told reporters, "he still has a lapse of memory."

But the confession of Mrs. Worden's killing was not in itself the most sensational part of Gein's statement to Kileen. After all, Eddie's guilt had never been in doubt, not since Friday evening when Frank Worden searched through his mother's store and turned up the receipt for the antifreeze Gein had purchased that morning. The real shocker had to do with Gein's revelation regarding his unholy collection of human scraps and tatters.

Gein denied that his "trophies"—the faces and heads, vulvas and breasts, noses and lips, skin and bones which littered his hell-house—were the remnants of murder victims. He wasn't a crazed killer at all. In fact, Eddie claimed, Mrs. Worden's murder was an aberration, an accident. When Kileen asked if Gein had ever killed anyone else besides the shopkeeper, Eddie shook his head. "Not to my knowledge," he said.

Then where, Kileen wanted to know, did all the body parts come from?

The answer was simple. From graveyards, said Eddie.

As the lawmen listened in astonishment, Gein explained that for a five-year period, beginning in 1947, he had made a large number of nocturnal visits—as many as forty—to area cemeteries. Most of the time, he had returned home without committing any offense. But on at least nine of those occasions, he had dug up and opened caskets, removed what he wanted, then covered over the coffins again, leaving the violated graves, he assured Kileen, "in apple pie order."

The cadavers were all newly dead women, middle-aged or older, whose obituaries Gein had read in local papers. Eddie had known a number of them while they were alive. Beyond these few facts, Eddie had little to say. All of his grave robbing, he insisted—like the murder of Mrs. Worden—had taken place while he was in a "daze."

\* \* \*

Immediately after Kileen's announcement, at eleven A.M., the fifty-one-year-old suspect, looking frail and wearing what was to become his trademark outfit—rubber boots, red cloth gloves, workshirt buttoned to the neck, woolen jacket, plaid deerhunter's cap—was hustled from the jail to a waiting automobile. Accompanying him were Kileen, Sheriff Schley, and County Judge Boyd Clark.

"He has something he wants to show us," said Kileen.

It was the first time Eddie had appeared in public since his arrest, and as he moved through the throng of reporters, flashbulbs popping all around him, he buried his face behind his shackled hands.

Gein was driven out to his farm, where he took a group of officials on a tour of the premises, pointing out various locations around the property, including the spot behind his outhouse where he had emptied the pail full of blood drained from Mrs. Worden. A crowd of journalists followed close behind. Already, Eddie seemed much more at ease with the news photographers, making no efforts to hide his face from their lenses. On the contrary, he gazed directly at the cameras, smiling for them with his shy little grin.

The pictures taken that morning show a slight, perfectly ordinary-looking, middle-aged rustic who seems about as threatening as a Salvation Army Santa Claus. For the newsmen who snapped those pictures, as well as for the millions of people who would see them that evening on the front pages of papers across the Midwest, it was almost impossible to believe that such a meek-looking fellow was—by his own admission and in the strict sense of the term—a ghoul.

Eddie was returned to the jail at around one P.M., but less than two hours later, he was taken from his cell again and brought to the Waushara County Courthouse, an imposing edifice adorned with a row of Ionic columns and fronted by a handsome pair of statues honoring the heroes who died for the Union and on the battlefields of World War I. There he was arraigned before Judge Clark on a charge of armed robbery, stemming from the theft of Bernice Worden's cash register (containing forty-one dollars), which had been found in Gein's home.

Kileen had told reporters earlier that Gein would be charged with first-degree murder "in a day or two." In the meantime, he was filing the larceny charge at the request of Charles Wilson, director of the State Crime Laboratory, who wanted to hold off on the murder charge until his staff had finished going through the gruesome mass of evidence on Gein's farm.

Brought before the bench, Gein told Judge Clark that he wanted a lawyer and could afford to hire one. The arraignment was adjourned for a week to permit the prisoner to obtain counsel. Bail was set at ten thousand dollars, and Eddie was returned to his cell.

# 19

*"Mostly, Gein liked older, more well-developed women—dead that is."*

JUDGE ROBERT H. GOLLMAR

Late Monday, Lieutenant Vern Weber, chief of detectives of the La Crosse Police Department, arrived in Plainfield to check out the purported uncovering of clues linking Gein to the abduction of Evelyn Hartley. Reports issuing from the farm were scattered and often contradictory, but, according to some accounts, one of the vulvas found among Eddie's genitalia collection was that of a young girl. There were also rumors that clippings on the Hartley case had turned up among the mountainous piles of old newspapers inside Gein's home. When reporters asked Weber if a solution to the four-year-old case was finally at hand, the lieutenant was hopeful but noncommittal. "It looks good, and then again it doesn't look good," he replied.

After spending some time examining the evidence inside Gein's home and interviewing Eddie twice at the Waushara County jailhouse, Weber met once again with the press.

Like every other person who had actually been inside the house or talked directly to Gein, Weber was subjected to an interrogation himself, grilled by a news-hungry mob of reporters who were desperate for any eyewitness descriptions of the contents of the "death farm" or of the man they had dubbed "the mad butcher of Plainfield."

Weber told the journalists that much of Eddie's macabre collection had already been transferred to the crime lab's truck. There he had seen "ten women's heads, some with eyes and some without." A few of the heads "were complete with skulls, others were merely skin." The heads—some of which had been found behind chairs and other pieces of furniture—"were in a very good state of preservation." Weber had asked Eddie about that, and Eddie had replied that he had cured the heads in brine.

Weber said that he had beheld with his own eyes "a chair with a seat which appeared to be made of human skin." The chair, he explained, was "a typical kitchen chair which probably once had a rattan seat." He had also seen "a knife with a handle that appeared to have skin covering."

Weber went on to describe his conversations with Gein. The detective said he was "inclined to believe" Gein's story about being in a daze during his body-snatching expeditions. The little man had told Weber that whenever he felt one of his "grave-robbing spells coming on," he "would pray and that sometimes the prayers would snap him out of it." According to Gein, he had "come out of a spell one time while he was digging up a grave and had stopped" and immediately returned home.

At the same time, he suggested to Weber that his interest in the cadavers was purely scientific. All during his youth, Gein told the detective, "he had wanted to be a doctor." The grave robbing, he implied, was motivated by his intellectual curiosity. He wanted bodies to dissect in order to learn about human anatomy firsthand.

In any event, he insisted he hadn't looted a grave since 1954. "He said maybe his prayers had been answered," Weber told the reporters. Weber discounted the stories of cannibalism. "That's out," he told the reporters. He had asked Gein "strong questions" on that subject. Gein had sworn that "he never ate a bit of that stuff and I don't believe that he did," Weber said.

As for the disappearance of Evelyn Hartley, the lieutenant was inclined to believe that Gein was not, after all, involved. Though one of the cellophane-wrapped heads in Eddie's collection seemed to have come from a younger woman, the face "bore no resemblance whatever" to Evelyn Hartley's. Moreover, Weber said, a pair of tennis shoes which had been recovered at the time of the crime and were believed to belong to the kidnapper were much too large for Gein. "The shoes we found are size eleven-and-a-half," the detective explained. "Gein wears about an eight."

There was, Weber stated, another piece of physical evidence that might conceivably be linked to Gein—a denim jacket which had been discovered just off a highway near La Crosse and was presumed to have been worn by the kidnapper. The jacket had a faded stripe running across its back, as though it had been worn under a harness or suspension belt, the kind used by painters and ironworkers. Since Gein had occasionally worked as a logger, he himself might have used a harness while trimming branches from treetops. But "on the whole," Weber conceded, "I'm not too encouraged about developing anything along that line."

Weber also said that, though Gein had been born in La Crosse and lived there until he was seven, "he claims he hasn't been back since." Gein still had relatives who resided in La Crosse, Weber told the reporters, "and we're going to check with them." Gein's alibi—that on the day of the girl's disappearance he had been doing some odd jobs for a neighbor—would also be checked out.

In the meantime, the heads and skulls discovered in Gein's home were being examined against Evelyn Hartley's dental charts, which had been forwarded to District Attorney Kileen by La Crosse County Criminal Investigator A. M. Josephson.

Weber concluded by offering his personal assessment of Gein. "He is a very sincere, very meek fellow. You'd never believe he'd be the kind of guy to do such a thing. You feel like he needs help awful bad."

This level-headed—even sympathetic—description differed markedly from the picture of Gein as a fiendishly depraved sex-butcher that was being promulgated by the popular press. But it was, in fact, consistent with the reactions of many professionals—lawyers, judges, psychiatrists, nurses, and others—who would have contact with Eddie Gein in the years to come.

Although a link between Gein and Evelyn Hartley was coming to seem increasingly unlikely, there were signs that Eddie's farmhouse might, in fact, contain an answer to the three-year-old mystery of Mary Hogan's disappearance. Gein's possible connection to the apparent murder of the middle-aged tavern keeper was a subject of open speculation by the press. Monday's newspapers ran front-page stories suggesting that a major break in the Hogan case was imminent. Though the information filtering out of the farmhouse was spotty, there were reports that investigators had uncovered a large cache of firearms inside Gein's home and that one of the weapons was a .32 automatic pistol. One of the major clues in the Hogan case was a spent .32-caliber cartridge, which had been found next to a dried puddle of blood on the floor of her tavern the day she disappeared.

It was also known that Portage County authorities, including Sheriff Herbert Wanerski, Undersheriff Myron Groshek, and District Attorney John Haka, had spent several hours questioning Gein, who had steadfastly denied knowing Mrs. Hogan, though he did concede that he had been inside her tavern—located just six miles north of his farm—on several occasions.

Wanerski and his colleagues, however, had no intention of letting up on Gein until they had extracted a confession, since, unbeknownst to the press, they already had in their possession a piece of evidence that left no doubt about his guilt.

What they had was the grisly relic discovered in Eddie's charnel house by Deputy Sheriff Arnold Fritz—Mary Hogan's face, skinned from her skull, softened with oil, and stuffed inside a paper sack.

# 20

*"It's the most revolting thing I've ever seen."*
CORONER RUSSELL DARBY,
after viewing Edward Gein's home

A brutal storm, one of the worst November blizzards Wisconsin had suffered in years, dumped more than a foot of snow onto parts of the state before tapering off on Tuesday. Three people died of heart attacks while shoveling their front walks, another was crushed to death when the ice-laden roof of his carport collapsed on him. Several hunters were lost in the woods; others were stranded in snow-bound camps. The hunting itself came to a virtual halt, the three-day kill figure standing at 28,675 deer.

The savage weather, however, did not deter a crowd of newsmen from making their way out to the Gein farm Tuesday morning. The press had finally received permission to enter Eddie's house.

By then, the State Crime Lab had removed the ghastliest of Gein's possessions from the premises. But even so, the house conveyed an intense impression of madness and morbidity, and, as one reporter noted, the newsmen—after days of clamoring for a peek inside the killer's home—did not seem particularly eager to stay once they found themselves there.

They did, however, remain long enough for a tour of the already infamous "death house," conducted by Deputy Dave Sharkey, who pointed out the spot in the summer kitchen where Mrs. Worden's butchered carcass had dangled from the rafters, the pile of old clothes in Eddie's bedroom under which investigators had found a box full of human skulls, and the kitchen table that held one of Eddie's cranial-cap soup bowls.

News photographers were finally allowed to take pictures of

Eddie's living quarters. The grainy black-and-white photos, which caught the heart-sickening gloom of Gein's household, appeared that evening in papers throughout the Midwest. For the first time, the public got a close inside look at Eddie's madhouse. The papers also printed shots of various crime lab investigators sifting through the remaining contents of the rooms. Since nothing of Eddie's graveyard gleanings was left in the house, the caption writers had to rely on lurid speculations to create the necessary titillation. One typical photograph showed a couple of investigators shining a flashlight on a perfectly ordinary-looking woman's handbag, presumably "in an attempt to determine whether it is made of leather or human skin."

The most vivid description of Gein's dwelling, however, was provided by a *Milwaukee Journal* staff writer named Robert W. Wells in a lengthy piece headlined "INCREDIBLY DIRTY HOUSE WAS HOME OF SLAYER." The article captured both the unimaginable filthiness of the house and the crazy incongruity of its contents. Wells evoked a place where a picture of Christ gazing skyward at an angel might hang on one wall and the eyeless face of a female corpse on another. Where a stack of old children's books with titles like *Dorothy Dale, A Girl of Today* might lie on a table alongside a book on embalming. Where a pile of Crackerjack premiums—plastic whistles, toy airplanes—might share shelf space with a section of human skull. Though Wells's piece conjured up the overpowering creepiness of the ghoul's abode, it ended on a distinctly poignant note, one that called attention not to Gein's derangement but to his terrifying isolation:

> The little man who lived here amid his mad collections, in a state of disorder that few of the animals who were his closest neighbors would have tolerated, had most of the doors and windows sealed with heavy tarpaper or thick, dirty draperies.
>
> Inside the decaying house the four rooms which he used were so filled with junk that even so slight a man as Gein must have had difficulty moving about.
>
> There was plenty of space that could have been his for the taking, however—the nearly empty upstairs with its five uncluttered rooms; and the two downstairs rooms which he had sealed up securely and dedicated to the dead past when Ed Gein was not alone in the world.

Someone else visited the Gein home on Tuesday—William Belter, a thirty-year-old former state assemblyman from Wautoma who had accepted Gein's request to serve as his defense attorney. A Wood County deputy sheriff gave Belter a guided tour of the house, complete with a graphic description of Eddie's death-mask collection, which Belter later shared with the press.

The officer explained how the masks had been made by separating the faces from the skulls, then stuffing the skins with newspapers. According to the deputy, investigators had found "more noses than faces," which had led them to revise their estimate of the number of Eddie's victims. Originally, the officer explained, the police believed there was a total of ten or eleven women involved—"depending on whether Mrs. Worden's head was counted." The sum now stood at fifteen, a figure based on the recovery of ten masks, Mrs. Worden's severed head, and four "extra noses."

Gein had spent the previous night being questioned by a pair of police officers from the Chicago Homicide Bureau, who had traveled to Wautoma in the hope of shedding light on three highly publicized unsolved murder cases: the butchering of a woman named Judith Anderson, the mysterious deaths of two sisters named Grimes, and the slaying of three young boys whose mutilated bodies had been discovered in an Illinois forest preserve in 1955.

Gein insisted that he had never been farther away from home than Milwaukee, and then only once, for his army physical in 1942. After an interrogation that lasted until three in the morning, the Chicago detectives announced to the press that they believed Gein was telling the truth.

Still, there were those who felt that Gein, for all his apparent meekness and simplicity, was actually a shrewd and calculating individual—a "smart cookie," in the words of one observer—whose cagey replies to his questioners revealed the workings of a diabolically cunning mind. The best way to check the validity of his claims, Kileen and others felt, was to administer a lie detector test. Plans had been made to transport Eddie to Madison on Tuesday morning, where he would be questioned by the crime lab's polygraph expert, Joe Wilimovsky.

There was, of course, another, though far more controversial, way of checking out at least one of Gein's assertions—namely by digging up some of the graves he claimed to have violated. The issue of exhumation was already generating heated arguments in the village of Plainfield and would give rise to many more before it was finally settled. The matter was first raised publicly on Tuesday morning, when reporters asked both Sheriff Schley and Crime Lab Director Charles Wilson if plans were afoot to open any burial plots in the local cemeteries.

Schley had intended to drive Gein to Madison early that morning, but the snow and icy roads forced him to delay the trip. Reporters spoke to him at the country jailhouse, where Gein was now the sole occupant, the other prisoners having been summarily released for "good behavior." Even now that his news blackout had been lifted, Schley continued to be wary of reporters and extremely tight-lipped in his comments to the press. When the newsmen asked him if he and Kileen had visited any cemeteries on Monday, the sheriff replied with a sardonic "I don't remember." Was he aware of any plans to check the grave sites today? Schley stared out a window at the falling snow and shrugged. "I wouldn't know about that."

Wilson, who was interviewed in Madison where he was making preparations for the impending polygraph test, was more forthcoming. "There's no sense going out with a pick and shovel to check the graveyards near Plainfield until we have exhausted the possibilities of evidence we already have," he explained. He acknowledged that some of the body parts recovered from Gein's house contained formaldehyde—"Our noses tell us," he said. But he insisted that the presence of embalming fluid did not in itself prove that Gein was a grave robber. After all, Wilson told the reporters, Gein could have put the fluid there himself. "We don't know. Maybe he's an amateur taxidermist."

Like so many speculations regarding Gein, Wilson's off-the-cuff conjecture was soon widely reported as fact. It didn't matter that not a single stuffed animal had been found on Eddie's farm. From that moment on, amateur taxidermy became a permanent feature of the Gein legend. Eventually, it would find its way into pop mythology, as the hobby of Eddie's most famous fictional descendant.

Back in Plainfield, the search of Eddie's farmhouse was nearing its conclusion. "Our case is pretty well cleaned up," Kileen told reporters. "We have no missing persons in our county. The only thing here is the murder rap."

There were still some loose ends to be tied up in the Worden case, and, early on Tuesday, the investigation moved to the hardware store, where crime lab technicians spent the morning shooting photographs of the murder scene. Barred from entering the building, newsmen clustered around the windows. There wasn't much to see inside—just a neatly organized, well-stocked country establishment, offering a wide selection of merchandise, from housewares to farming tools, small appliances to sporting goods. One detail, however, did catch the newsmen's attention. A gun rack stood against one wall of the store, and, peering through the windows, reporters could clearly see that one of the rifles was missing.

Schley had told the reporters gathered at the jailhouse that the trip to Madison might have to be put off for a day, but late in the morning, the snow let up enough for him to reconsider. At eleven thirty-five A.M., with Schley on one side and Deputy Leon Murty on the other, Gein was escorted through a jostling crowd of journalists and cameramen and led into a waiting police car. Several hours later, at around one-thirty P.M., he arrived at the capital and was immediately taken to the State Crime Laboratory at 917 University Avenue for the first of several lie detector tests—tests that would extend into the following day and would end up confirming that in the case of Eddie Gein, no fantasy, fiction, or fabrication could possibly be as unbelievable as the truth.

While Eddie was being prepped for his polygraph test, Herbert Wanerski, the Portage County sheriff involved in the investigation of Mary Hogan's murder, dropped a bombshell that would explode across the front pages of the evening papers.

Wanerski, along with the Portage County DA, John Haka, had driven to Madison that morning in a car behind the one carrying Gein. While he waited for Eddie's lie test to begin, Wanerski was asked by reporters if the Hogan investigation was "a case of divided jurisdiction."

"Yes, definitely," Wanerski said. Then, wholly unexpectedly, he made a startling announcement. Referring to the missing tavern keeper, Wanerski said, "We've got a head and face that is hers without question." As the newsmen scribbled excitedly in their notepads, Wanerski explained that the head in question was actually a woman's "facial skin and hair peeled back from the skull." There was no doubt, he asserted, that it was Mary Hogan's.

Though rumors regarding Hogan—including one that her skull was part of Gein's private collection—had been buzzing around Plainfield for the past few days, this was a sensational disclosure. But Wanerski wasn't through. The sheriff said that he had "strong doubts" that Gein could have spent much time in the house where Mrs. Worden's carcass and the other human-flesh trophies had been found. There was too much undisturbed dust in the place—not just in the boarded-off rooms that had belonged to Eddie's mother but throughout the house. "You couldn't walk by without knocking the dust off," Wanerski said.

He then told the newsmen that authorities were checking into stories that Gein had a habit of sleeping in barns and abandoned houses throughout the countryside. If that were the case, then Eddie's farm might not be the only body-part storehouse in the area. As one newspaper later put it, "the grim thought behind the rumor was that more heads or bodies might be discovered."

Wanerski had one last shocker in store. Referring back to the Hogan death mask, he insisted that it smelled unmistakably of embalming fluid. Since Mary Hogan had been very much alive at the time of her disappearance, the implication was clear, though the sheriff took the trouble to spell it out anyway.

"Eddie Gein never robbed a grave in his life," Wanerski said bitterly.

That evening, something else arrived in Madison from Plainfield: the State Crime Laboratory's Mobile Field Unit van containing the mountain of items collected from Eddie's home. The crime lab was located directly across from the University of Wisconsin campus, and as Jan Beck and James Halligan—the two technicians who had brought the truck down from Plainfield—began to unload the piles of evidence, a crowd of students joined newsmen on the sidewalk to gawk.

As the two topcoated technicians moved back and forth between the van and the crime lab building, reporters kept a painstaking inventory of the items, while the undergraduates craned their necks in the hope of catching a glimpse of something truly gruesome.

Most of the evidence, however, was packed in cardboard boxes; the rest seemed disappointingly mundane. As a result, the onlookers were forced to rely heavily on wishful thinking in order to satisfy their morbid curiosity.

Spotting a bunch of "cellophane wrapped objects" inside a cardboard box, for instance, one reporter concluded that they "may have been human heads." A few moments later, after several straightbacked chairs with "saffron colored seats" had been removed from the van, the same reporter was accosted by a coed—"a cute little brunette with an Italian haircut," in the words of the writer. "Did those chairs have skin bottoms?" she asked hopefully.

The sheer quantity of stuff was staggering. There were firearms and an old oak barrel, quart jars full of thick brown liquid, a metal tub, a bunch of wood-handled tools, a bucksaw, a strongbox, an old medical volume, a cash register (presumably the one taken from Bernice Worden's store), and countless cardboard boxes and brown paper grocery bags, whose contents were hidden from view. One of the last items removed from the van was a three-foot length of barbed wire.

It took the two officials thirty trips and a full half-hour to empty the truck. When the job was finished at ten that night, crime lab director Charles Wilson met with a mob of newspaper, radio, and television reporters. The newsmen had been begging for precise information about the contents of Eddie Gein's home. Indicating the "avalanche" of evidence that had just been unloaded, Wilson told the reporters that they could now see for themselves "what an impossible question that was." One of the technicians who helped empty the van elaborated on Wilson's remark. "Even Eddie Gein doesn't know what's all here," he said.

# 21

For the good folk of Plainfield, the horrible murder of one of their most respected citizens was, of course, an unpardonable crime. But even more unforgivable, perhaps—at least to the townspeople at large—was the offense Eddie Gein had committed against the community. For the hundred-odd years since its founding, the minuscule farming town was a place that enjoyed the peacefulness of absolute obscurity. Even within Wisconsin, few people had ever heard of Plainfield. All at once, their quiet little community was the focus of nationwide attention—and for the most dismaying of reasons. Other small towns across the U.S.A. could boast of being the birthplace of politicians, athletes, and movie stars. Plainfield suddenly found itself famous as the home of America's most demented murderer.

If Gein was ultimately responsible for all the unwanted attention, it was the news media that, at least in the eyes of some local residents, had turned their hometown into the societal equivalent of a sideshow freak, an object of morbid fascination and curiosity. Plainfield was overrun by reporters, so avid for lurid tidbits that they would print the most flagrant kinds of hearsay as unimpeachable truth. And the reporters had no trouble finding local sources to supply them with juicy quotes. For every person like Sheriff Schley or Frank Worden who refused to cooperate with the press, there were a half-dozen who couldn't resist the temptation of seeing their names in the papers or, even better, their pictures in *Life* magazine. And some of those people were willing to tell the newsmen just what they wanted to hear.

One early and wholly erroneous story, for example—widely reported in newspapers, over the radio, and on TV—was that lynch mobs were forming in the streets of Plainfield. "We're all at a real pitch here," one unnamed townsman was quoted as saying. "There's no use monkeying around. If the town got a hold of that guy, the town'd know what to do about him, all right." Ed Marolla, editor of the local weekly the *Plainfield Sun*, found himself expending a good deal of ink in an effort to refute this and similar rumors of mounting vigilantism—rumors whose spread he blamed directly on "big city reporters," who didn't hesitate to exaggerate the truth for the sake of a more sensational story.

Of course, members of the news media weren't the only ones prone to exaggeration. Though Gein was a notoriously reclusive individual, he suddenly seemed to have acquired a wide circle of intimates, who were only too eager to share their knowledge of the killer with the press.

A former Plainfield resident named Turner, for example, told newsmen that he "knew Ed Gein better than any living man." Turner explained that he had grown up on a farm a half-mile south of the Gein place and, though he had moved to Milwaukee many years before, had remained in close touch with his childhood buddy.

"Ed was the best friend I had," Turner said. "As a boy, the Gein farm was my second home. I stopped there practically every day after school. And I ate as many meals there as I did at my own home. Ed taught me to hunt, fish, and play the accordion and the flute. We went hunting together lots of times. Ed was a very nice fellow. He would do anything for you."

Turner allowed that there was one aspect of the Gein affair that puzzled him: Eddie's claim that he had been in a "daze" while performing his gruesome deeds. In all the years he had known the man, Turner said, Eddie "never suffered from dazes."

"When I first found out about the murder," Turner told his interviewer, "I was shocked. At first I figured they had the wrong man. Later the sheriff told me the whole story. I just couldn't understand what came into that man's mind."

An even more remarkable testimonial to Ed's character came from a Plainfield woman named Adeline Watkins, who achieved instant, if exceptionally short-lived, celebrity by announcing that she was Ed Gein's sweetheart.

Described in the papers as a "severely plain woman" (in fact, she bore an uncanny resemblance to actress Margaret Hamilton in the role of Miss Gulch in *The Wizard of Oz*), Watkins revealed her twenty-year romance with Gein in an interview that appeared on the front page of the *Minneapolis Tribune* under the headline "I LOVED KIND, SWEET MAN, STILL DO, SAYS CONFESSED KILLER'S 'FIANCEE.'"

The fifty-year-old spinster, who shared a small apartment in Plainfield with her widowed mother, described her "last date" with Eddie on February 6, 1955. "That night, he proposed to me," Watkins told the reporter. "Not in so many words, but I knew what he meant. I turned him down, but not because there was anything wrong with him. It was something wrong with me. I guess I was afraid I wouldn't be able to live up to what he expected of me."

When asked about the specifics of their relationship, Watkins described the activities she and her suitor enjoyed. "Eddie and I discussed books," Watkins replied. "We never read the same ones, but we liked to talk about them anyway. Eddie liked books about lions and tigers and Africa and India. I never read that kind of books."

During the six-month period leading up to Eddie's proposal, the couple went out "an average of twice a week," usually to a movie theater in Wautoma. Watkins's mother, who sat quietly in a nearby rocker during her daughter's interview, confirmed that Gein was the soul of politeness, always having her daughter home by ten P.M.

Occasionally, Watkins said, the couple would stop off at a tavern. "I liked to drink beer sometimes," she confessed, "but I would almost have to drag Eddie into a tavern. He would much rather have gone into a drugstore for a milkshake."

Watkins concluded the interview by indicating once again that the failure of their relationship reflected her own shortcomings, not Gein's. "Eddie was so nice about doing things I wanted to do," said Watkins, "that sometimes I felt I was taking advantage of him."

Adeline Watkins's revelations made quite a splash, particularly in Plainfield, where no one could remember Eddie Gein's ever having been involved with a woman. And indeed, within days of the interview's appearance, Watkins contacted Ed Marolla of the *Sun* to offer a radically different version of her relationship to Gein.

According to Marolla, Watkins had fallen victim to the wiles of the big-city press. "The city papers," he claimed, "hungry for 'human interest' news, played up the innocent enough relations," and Watkins—much to her distress—found herself "in the national spotlight," her "photo on the front pages of every daily in the country."

Watkins's revised account of her friendship with Gein amounted to a complete retraction. She declared that she was not Ed Gein's "sweetheart" and had never used that word in the presence of reporters.

Moreover, she insisted that—although Eddie had "called on her" every now and again, stopping by her apartment and occasionally accompanying her to the Plainfield Theatre—"there was no twenty-year romance."

Though Miss Watkins conceded that she had described Gein as "quiet and polite," she denied ever having referred to him as "sweet." And she was "quite emphatic in stating that she had never 'practically dragged him into a tavern,' as was reported."

In short, Adeline Watkins wanted the public to know that there was not a shred of truth to the highly sensationalized account of her love affair with the little man who stood accused of the grisliest crimes in Wisconsin history. "She says that she kind of felt sorry for him," Marolla explained, "and that mostly they just sat at her house."

To the editor of the *Sun*, the Watkins case was yet another illustration of the media's flagrant manipulation of the facts. Marolla accused the reporters of "plying people for interviews," then "putting words in their mouths" or seriously misrepresenting what they had actually said. Whatever the truth of this allegation, it was certainly the case that in the days immediately following Eddie's arrest, newsmen roamed the streets of Plainfield, pouncing on anyone who was willing to speak for the record.

Given the tininess and tightly knit character of the town, most of its citizens had at least a passing acquaintance with Gein. Some of them, like Eddie's neighbor Stanley Gerlovic, had kindly words to say about the accused, describing Gein as "always happy, smiling, congenial—a good worker," who "never said a dirty word or cussed." Others emphasized Eddie's social backwardness—his "shyness," "meekness," and awkwardness around women. And a few prided themselves on having been sharp enough to detect all along that there was something distinctly unsettling—even creepy—about the man. "He had a sly sort of grin when he would talk to you," one of Ed's neighbors told reporters, and a local storekeeper who preferred to remain anonymous admitted that whenever he gave change to Gein, "I put it on the counter rather than touch his hand."

No one, however, not even the people who claimed to have sensed that the little bachelor wasn't as harmless as he seemed, imagined that Eddie Gein was actually a murderer (let alone a defiler of the dead). The general reaction to Gein's arrest among the populace of Plainfield was bewilderment and disbelief. "When I first heard what they were saying he had done," one of Eddie's neighbors told reporters, "I couldn't believe it. Now, of course, I know it's true—but I still can't believe it. You know what I mean? I mean, I believe it, but at the same time I don't believe it—it's just too fantastic." Another of Gein's acquaintances concurred. "Before this happened, if you asked me who could be capable of something like this, the last man in the world I'd have named would've been Eddie Gein."

Robert Wells—the *Milwaukee Journal* reporter who had described the lunatic interior of Eddie's farmhouse in such graphic detail— provided an equally vivid look at the local reaction to the crimes. In light of what had happened, Eddie's oddball behavior—which had been dismissed as harmless, even amusing eccentricity—had taken on a terrible new significance. Eddie's neighbors recalled his various quirks—his refusal, "with rare exceptions," to "allow anyone in his house"; the way he would smile and nod in agreement "when people kidded him about what a dangerous fellow he was—a joke that was only funny because he seemed so harmless."

"And did not the children, half believing it while they laughed, say his old house was haunted?" asked Wells. "And were there not tales, which seemed to have been fairly common knowledge among the youngsters, that he had a collection of 'shrunken heads'? Did he not read detective stories avidly and exhibit more than the ordinary interest in talk of crimes and violence?"

There seemed to be some vaguely guilty sense among many of the townsfolk that the community should have taken these things more seriously. Looking back at Ed's behavior—and at the strange stories and rumors that had clustered around him for so many years—his neighbors could see the warning signs, the symptoms of Gein's growing derangement. But that perception was purely retrospective. At the time, there seemed no real cause for alarm. After all, as Wells pointed out, "every child knows of a haunted house, and you can buy shrunken heads made of plastic for $2.50, and every man, especially every little man, must learn to go along with a joke when he's the butt of it."

To be sure, many of Eddie's neighbors regarded him as peculiar, but no more so than "any of dozens of other people they knew. Every small town knows a few lonely bachelors living out their bleak lives on remote farms, the objects of occasional pity and a little good-natured ridicule." For all his adult life, Eddie was perceived as one of these poor, pathetic, slightly ludicrous souls—until the night, that is, when Bernice Worden's headless body was found hanging by its heels in his summer kitchen.

Though the press may have had an enormous appetite for rumor, it was the townspeople themselves who kept that appetite fed, dishing up gossip as fast as the news media could gobble it down. "To reporters who spent the last week in the neighborhood," Wells wrote, "it has sometimes seemed that everyone they met had a tale to tell of how Eddie peered in their bedroom window on some bygone night or how he sneaked around on tennis shoes, startling women."

Not surprisingly, perhaps, it was the female population of Waushara that had the most spine-tingling stories to tell. The county suddenly seemed to be populated by women who had just barely escaped death (or worse) at the hands of the mad butcher of Plainfield. Effie Banks, the wife of one of Eddie's neighbors, told a reporter for *Life* magazine about the time, shortly after Eddie's mother died, when her "daughter kept hearing rustling noises outside the house at night." Her parents "thought she was imagining things." One afternoon, "Gein knocked on the door and asked if he could come in." He "said he might want to build a house and wanted to get a look at ours," Mrs. Banks explained. "Nobody else was here and for some reason I decided not to let him in. I guess I can thank my lucky stars for that."

Another neighbor of Eddie's recollected the time when the little man had dropped by her house for a visit late in the afternoon, before her husband and sons had returned from work. She was in the midst of setting the table for dinner. All of a sudden, she had a funny feeling, and when she turned around, there was Eddie, standing right behind her with a big kitchen knife in his hand. Naturally, she "about jumped sky high," but Eddie hastily explained that he had noticed a string hanging down from her apron and had just meant to cut it off. Fortunately, the menfolk showed up about then, but Eddie was never allowed inside the house again.

And then there was the young girl who worked in the bakery in Wautoma. Eddie had come by the shop on a Friday, just the day before he murdered Mrs. Worden, as it turned out. The two were alone. Suddenly, Eddie stepped behind the counter, touched her hair, and said, "You look like my mother." Just then, some other customers entered the store, and Eddie left in a hurry. At the time, the girl didn't know what to make of the incident, but when she later realized who the weird little man had been, she broke down into hysterics.

There were plenty of other stories like these, many of which were clearly the products of overheated imaginations. One of the few women who may, indeed, have found herself in a ticklish situation with Gein was Irene Hill, who also had a story to tell about a time she and Ed were alone. They were standing in her grocery store when the little man suddenly picked up a butcher knife. "He run his finger along the top of the thing," Mrs. Hill recounted, "and he looked at me kind of strange, and I said, 'Ed, put that darned thing down before you get cut! That's sharp!' And he dropped it, just like that. But what he had in mind, I don't know." There is good reason to believe that this story is true, since, besides spending a fair amount of time in Gein's company, Mrs. Hill possessed two important characteristics shared by the other murder victims: she was middle-aged and the proprietor of her own business.

Referring to the spate of rumors circulating through Plainfield in the days immediately following Gein's arrest, Robert Wells opined that "it is probable not even the tellers of some of these anecdotes are sure any more where fact stops and embroidery begins. It hardly seems likely, however, that Gein found time to do one-tenth of the things he is now credited with doing."

Still, the papers couldn't seem to get enough of these stories. The *Madison Capital Times* ran a front-page article about an Oregon man who, while hunting near Gein's farm years before, had been told, "We don't want any snooping around here" and then "run off the property." The most remarkable thing about this story— considering its prominent position on page one—was that it had nothing at all to do with Eddie. As it turned out, the person who had ordered the trespassers off his premises was Gein's older brother, Henry.

But even this bit of trivia seemed less inconsequential than some of the "news" items the papers were willing to print. Still, it wasn't until an article headlined "300 POUND MAN RECALLS PINCH AND REMARK BY GEIN" appeared in the *Milwaukee Journal* that the press's greed for any Gein-related material reached its ludicrous extreme. According to this hard-hitting story, "A 300-pound Neenah barber who owns a farm near slayer Ed Gein's house, said the recluse pinched him on the belly once and said he'd be 'just about right for roasting.'" The barber also revealed that, though he "didn't think too much of the remark at the time," he definitely noticed that "Gein had a peculiar look in his eye" when he said it.

Undoubtedly, there were those in Plainfield who enjoyed all the journalistic attention, who basked in the media spotlight and were excited to find themselves, as one observer put it, "part of an event which the whole nation was watching." But in general, the towns-people felt increasingly exploited, even victimized, by the press. And not just by what Ed Marolla continued to refer to as the "big city" press. Indeed, the single most outrageous news item, from the point of view of the Plainfield citizenry, was one that appeared in a small-town weekly, the *New London Press* ("The Only Newspaper," in the words of its motto, "That Gives a Hoot about New London").

Written by editor Gordon Culver, a one-time resident of Wau-shara County, the article strove to make sense of Gein's atrocities in the context of their social and geographical setting. Culver offered a haunting portrait of a place ideally suited for the breeding of madness and crime, an area he referred to as the "great dead heart" of Wisconsin.

Like the rest of that "dead heart" region, Culver wrote, the western edge of Waushara County is marked by a "peculiar, lonely, wild feeling. A feeling of people struggling just for subsistence. A feeling that an honest living is hard to come by in this throbbingly poor area. Western Waushara County has some farms, but almost all show no signs of prosperity. Almost all look run down. And as the line is crossed into Adams County, the wildness takes over into desolation."

Culver recalled his childhood in the nearby town of Almond and how, even as a young boy, he "could feel the mystery of that wild marsh and woods country. We knew the rule there was to disregard game laws. We knew that big fights at dances always took place back in the marsh country in the shacky dance halls that sprang up there. We knew that moonshiners worked that desolate area. . . . And always and down through the years that area has been burned into our memories as wild, willingly not law abiding, and poor.

"And so, when this murder took place on the border of that netherland, it was something we'd suspect would take place. Could take place. People seemed to have a disconcern about what other people, even their neighbors, do. Their own struggles are sufficient for their capacities. And if something strange or odd takes place, it is much more likely to be accepted as their business and nobody else's."

Culver acknowledged the existence of "law abiding citizens" in the area, of "successful farmers," "huge acreage used for potato and onion farming," and a certain "aura of civilization." But "always coming out of the 'dead heart' area," he insisted, "is the everlasting mood of wildness and mystery. And we suspect the lonely, fifty-one-year-old bachelor now being held in the Waushara County jail at Wautoma was held to that spell of wildness. Where he was alone. Would be left alone. Where the laws of man were obliterated by the constant and encroaching frontier of wilderness. Where a man would kill a person and clean it like he would a deer.

"Having known this area all our lifetime," Culver concluded. "Hunted in it. Fished in it. Planted trees in it. Driven cattle in it. Investigated mysterious disappearances in it. This is where murder like Edward Gein carried out would be most likely to spawn."

Bad publicity wasn't the only unpleasantness that Plainfield had to contend with in the wake of Gein's crimes. The community was wracked with deep, if irrational, fears. Doors and windows were bolted shut by people who had never known the need for a lock. Parents reported an outbreak of bad dreams among their children—the first manifestation of a mythicizing process that would eventually see Gein transformed into a creature of nightmare, a semilegendary bogeyman.

The stories of Ed's cannibalism generated even ghastlier rumors—that the little man had handed out packages of human flesh to his neighbors, passing the meat off as venison—and local clinics suddenly found themselves trying to cope with an epidemic of gastrointestinal complaints. Every newspaper in Wisconsin, it seemed, published a map pinpointing the exact location of Gein's farm, and hordes of curiosity seekers swarmed into Plainfield to gawk at the notorious "house of horrors."

As the publisher of the *Sun*, Marolla found himself acting as the town's unofficial spokesman, writing a lengthy defense of his community for the *Milwaukee Journal*. He urged the "outside world" to "take the time to notice and remember some of the nicer things" about Plainfield, "a village where farm and townspeople work and play together, without distinction of any kind, for the good of the schools, the churches, and the little civic things that go toward making a town a pleasant place in which to live." That congenial little town, Marolla maintained, is "Plainfield as it was, as it is, and how we hope it will continue to be."

And, indeed, the people of Plainfield did their best to restore a sense of normalcy to their lives. They went about their business. The dairy farmers did their chores, the women their shopping and housework. Merchants shoveled the sidewalks in front of their stores and hung their windows with Thanksgiving decorations. Children went off to school and deer hunters headed into the woods. Even Frank Worden reopened his mother's hardware store less than two weeks after her murder. "We'll try to carry on as before," he said.

But, of course, things would never be quite the same as they were before. Plainfield would never free itself of its reputation as the hometown of Edward Gein. And its citizens would not find it easy to shake off those questions that even Ed Marolla—for all his boosterism—found so intensely troubling that he posed them on the front page of his paper, for all the world to see.

"Why didn't the neighbors suspect Edward Gein," he asked, "when it was known he had human heads in the house?

"Why didn't the authorities check after Mary Hogan disappeared and it was known Gein had a truck similar to the one suspected?

"As the story of the awful crimes still unfolds, people around Plainfield find it hard to believe. They know it happened, they know it happened here. But why . . . and how . . . and how the series of crimes could have so long gone undiscovered is beyond comprehension."

Bernice Worden, Eddie Gein's last victim. (Wide World)

The Gein farmhouse. (Wide World)

The summer kitchen, attached to the rear of the farmhouse, where Bernice Worden's body was found. (UPI/Bettmann Newsphotos)

A Wautoma police officer points his flashlight at the spot inside the summer kitchen where Bernice Worden's dressed-out body was discovered hanging by its heels from the rafters. (Wide World)

Eddie Gein's kitchen. (Frank Scherschel, *Life* magazine © 1957 Time Inc.)

One of the rooms belonging to Augusta Gein, which her son had sealed off from the squalor of the rest of the house. (Frank Scherschel, *Life* magazine © 1957 Time Inc.)

Sheriff Arthur Shley escorts Gein into the Waushara County Courthouse.
(UPI/Bettmann Archive)

Gein at his preliminary
hearing. (Wide World)

The hearse bearing Bernice Worden's casket drives past her hardware store on
the morning of her funeral. (Wide World)

The entrance to the Plainfield cemetery, one of three local graveyards plundered by Gein. (UPI/Bettmann Newsphotos)

Plainfield sexton Pat Danna stands by the looted grave of Mrs. Eleanor Adams. Directly behind the Adams' plot are the graves of Eddie Gein's mother and father. (Wide World)

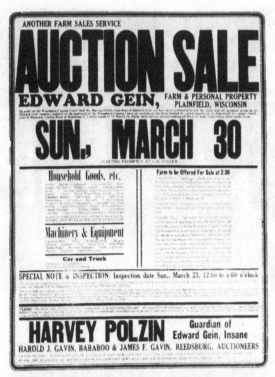

Poster advertising the auction of Eddie Gein's
property. (State Historical Society of Wisconsin)

Aerial view of the crowd roaming over the Gein property on the day of the
auction. Visible in the right foreground are the charred remains of Gein's
farmhouse, burned to the ground by a suspicious fire ten days earlier.
(Wide World)

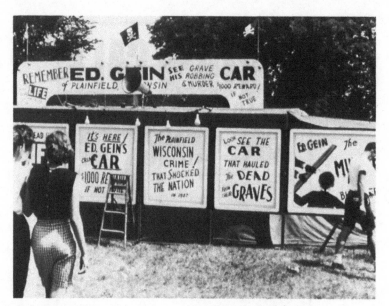

The Ed Gein "death car" display. *(Milwaukee Journal)*

An older—and stouter—Eddie Gein is surrounded by reporters as he is led into the Waushara County Courthouse for the start of his 1968 trial. (Wide World)

# 22

Q. *"It seems this item is from a leg, or probably from two. Is that sewed in two places?"*

A. *"That's from a person from the grave."*

Q. *"What about the face masks?"*

A. *"When I made those masks, you see, I stuffed them all out with paper so that they would dry. On the vagina I did, you know, sprinkle a little salt. . . ."*

Q. *"Was there a resemblance in some of these faces to that of your mother?"*

A. *"I believe there was some."*

From Edward Gein's confession

Altogether, Gein was questioned for just under nine hours. The first part of the interrogation, conducted at the Crime Lab headquarters, commenced at one-forty on Tuesday afternoon and continued until seven-twenty-five P.M., when Eddie was removed to the Madison city jail. There he spent the night under double guard in a special seventh-floor detention cell. At eight-forty-five the next morning, the questioning resumed.

Various investigators were present during these sessions, though the interrogation itself was conducted by the Crime Lab's polygraph specialist, Joe Wilimovsky. The actual testing time was brief—Eddie was hooked up to the "lie box" for only nineteen minutes on Tuesday and eleven more on Wednesday. The rest of the time, Wilimovsky alternately conversed with and quizzed the prisoner, delving into those details of the crimes that Eddie was able, or willing, to recall.

Though Gein displayed no signs of remorse or, indeed, any awareness at all of the enormity of his deeds, he did not come across as a cold-blooded killer. On the contrary, he seemed so friendly and cooperative—so childishly eager to please—that Wilimovsky had to be careful not to put words into his mouth. Eddie would cheerfully admit to the most extreme perversions.

> Q. Do you have any recollection, Eddie, of taking any of those female parts, the vagina specifically, and holding it over your penis to cover the penis?
> A. I believe that's true.
> Q. You recall doing that with the vaginas of the bodies of other women?
> A. That I believe I do remember; that's right. . . .
> Q. Would you ever put on a pair of women's panties over your body and then put some of these vaginas over your penis?
> A. That could be.

On the other hand, Eddie was much less forthcoming about the murders he had committed, a sign to some observers that he was not as crazy as he seemed. Clearly, looting graves and violating corpses are mad and odious crimes—abominations in the eyes of God and man. But from a legal point of view, they are not exceptionally serious ones compared to first-degree murder. Eddie did finally confess to Mary Hogan's killing, though the evidence against him was so overwhelming that he had very little choice. And though he acknowledged once again his responsibility for Bernice Worden's death, he continued to maintain—as he would throughout his life—that the shooting was accidental.

To some of those present at Gein's interrogation, the prisoner seemed like an obedient, if hopelessly demented, little boy. But others saw in his answers the signs of a cunning criminal intelligence. For the rest of Gein's life, people who met him would come away with the same paradoxical impression, struck by both his childlike simplicity and his monstrous criminality. One person who got to know Eddie in later years probably captured this contradiction best when he said that Gein seemed to be a kind of "idiot savant" of the macabre, "a genius at the ghoulish things he did but, in anything else, an innocent."

Patiently, methodically, Wilimovsky ran through the details again and again, until he had obtained a complete, step-by-step account of Eddie's insane procedures. Throughout his testimony, Eddie's tone remained perfectly matter-of-fact, as though he were explaining the mechanics of the most ordinary of hobbies—furniture refinishing, say, or leathercraft.

Eddie explained how he would test the freshness of a grave by inserting a metal rod into the soil. After digging up the casket, he would work the cover open with a pry bar.

"Would you open the entire casket or just one of the halves?" Wilimovsky asked.

"Just the half," Eddie said.

"And slip 'em out?"

"That's right."

On some occasions, Eddie would spirit his prize back home and busy himself with it at leisure. At other times, working hurriedly by moonlight in the fetor of the open grave, he would remove only the anatomical parts he wanted, then return the mutilated cadaver to the coffin.

"What section of the flesh would you remove?" Wilimovsky wanted to know.

"The head."

"The head?" asked Wilimovsky. "How about the vagina?"

Eddie seemed a little flustered. "Well, that—not always."

"In removing the head, did you first cut through and then snap the bone?"

"I guess that would be snapping."

Wilimovsky wanted further clarification. "Would you work the head back and forth in the same fashion as you would when you attempt to break a piece of wire in two?"

"That's a good description of it," said Eddie. "I never took a saw to the cemetery."

Once again, Eddie explained his technique for collecting and preserving human faces and scalps. "You just peeled the skin off the skull and disposed of the bone and other material that was in the head, is that it?" asked Wilimovsky.

Eddie nodded. "That's right."

Wilimovsky wanted to know if the skins had been prepared in any particular way.

"I probably put some oil on, that's all," Eddie replied. "To keep it soft, you know."

Then, for the first time, Eddie revealed shocking new details about the uses to which the face skins had been put. They were not, as the investigators had originally thought, simply ghastly souvenirs or ghoulish decorations. The whole truth turned out to be even worse.

Following a hunch, Wilimovsky asked Eddie if he had ever used the skins as masks, placing them over his own face.

"That I did," Eddie replied without hesitation.

When Wilimovsky asked how he secured the faces to his own head, Eddie's answer was simple. With a cord, he explained.

And would Eddie "wear the faces over a prolonged time?" Wilimovsky inquired.

Eddie shook his head. "Not too long," he said. "I had other things to do."

But there was worse to come. The skin masks weren't the only articles fashioned from human flesh that Eddie Gein enjoyed wearing. He also admitted to slipping on the mammary vest, wrapping his legs in the crudely stitched-together skin stockings, and covering his penis with a preserved vulva. Then, decked out from top to bottom in his corpse costume—a cross-dresser who derived his pleasure not from donning women's clothes but from wearing their skin and hair—he would parade about the cob-webbed rooms of his house or, on warmer nights, strut about in the moonlight.

Eddie casually related other details. He described how he had sawed off the skullcaps and used them as bowls (an idea that came, he said, from reading about the "old Norwegian style" of drinking mead from human skulls). He told how he had sprinkled salt on the vulvas in an effort to preserve them, though one of them began to go green anyway. He explained that he had touched that one up with silver paint to see if that would stop it from decaying further.

From time to time during the interrogation, Eddie complained of hunger and asked for something to eat. At one point, he was presented with a slice of apple pie, topped with a chunk of Wisconsin cheddar. Eddie munched on his snack while continuing to answer Wilimovsky's questions. Apparently, however, the food did not come up to Eddie's finicky standards. Interrupting his tale of body snatching and corpse flaying and flesh wearing, the little man who ate his soup from skullcaps and kept a shoebox full of salted vaginas, turned to his interrogator and began to fuss about the dryness of the cheese.

*"The thief cometh not, but for to steal, and to kill, and to destroy."*

*John* 10:10

**W**hile Eddie sat in Madison, casually confessing to a string of unparalleled perversions, the funeral rites for his final victim were taking place back in his hometown.

The stores were closed and the streets hushed as more than two hundred of Bernice Worden's relatives, friends, and neighbors filled Plainfield's First Methodist Church, a handsome brick building located on Main Street, two blocks north of her hardware store. An anteroom that served as the church's Sunday school had to be opened to accommodate the crowd.

The predictable pack of reporters was there, mingling with the townsfolk, and a photographer from *Life* magazine shot pictures of the mourners as they filed past the open bronze casket, resting among a mass of bouquets. Mrs. Worden's body—mended and restored by all the art at mortician Ray Goult's disposal—showed no visible signs of the ravages inflicted on it by her killer.

Following a solo rendition of "Abide by Me" sung by Mrs. Clifford Tubbs, the church's young pastor, Rev. Gerald Tanquist, spoke. "We ask ourselves," said Rev. Tanquist, "why does God let these things come about?" For an answer, he turned to both the Old Testament and the New, citing Psalm 23—"The Lord is my shepherd"—as well as John 10:11—"I am the good shepherd; the good shepherd giveth his life for the sheep."

It might appear to some, said the pastor, "that our Shepherd has abandoned us here in Plainfield. But the psalmist didn't promise to keep us from all the dark days of our lives, but only that the

Shepherd will be with us, comforting us. He is still the guardian of our souls and our lives."

Rev. Tanquist went on to urge the community to reaffirm its faith in God and to remember that even "in the face of this horrible incident," the "Lord has not abandoned us."

Following rites by the Order of the Eastern Star, of which Mrs. Worden had been a member, the casket was carried outside to a waiting hearse and driven slowly down Main Street, past the Worden hardware store, and out to the village cemetery, west of town.

There Bernice Worden was interred beside her husband—dead since 1931—in a snow-covered family plot sheltered by cedars and pines.

# 24

*"He's got a good appetite and never talks back to anyone."*

SHERIFF ART SCHLEY

At around two P.M. on Wednesday, just twenty-four hours after his arrival in Madison, Eddie was taken from the Crime Lab headquarters by Sheriff Schley and Deputy Murty and placed in a police car for the trip back to Wautoma.

Though the "Plainfield head collector," as some of the local tabloids had taken to calling Gein, looked a bit wan, he was clean-shaven for the first time since his arrest and smiled broadly for the cameras as he was led through the throng of newsmen eagerly awaiting the results of his tests. In fact, he seemed so relaxed and cheerful that the reporters wondered whether he was simply enjoying some attention for the first time in his life or experiencing the cathartic aftereffects of confessing. As one observer put it, perhaps Gein "had gained mental release by unburdening his mind of his long-hoarded fiendish activities."

Immediately after Gein's departure, Charles Wilson met with the press to release a short, highly selective summary of the polygraph findings. "The lie detector tests of Edward Gein have now been completed," read the statement, "and after consultation with the several interested district attorneys we are able at this time to state that the results of the tests referred to eliminate the subject, Edward, 51 years, as the person responsible for and/or involved in the disappearance of Evelyn Hartley in La Crosse County on Oct. 24, 1953; the disappearance of Georgia Jean Weckler in Jefferson County May 1, 1947; and Victor Travis in Adams County Nov. 1, 1952.

"Mr. Gein has now admitted that he is responsible for the deaths of Mary Hogan in Portage County on Dec. 8, 1954, and Bernice Worden in Waushara County Nov. 16, 1957. This release jointly concurred in by the interested local officials is being made to eliminate Mr. Gein from unnecessary suspicion and conjecture."

Gein had also been questioned about another, more recent missing-persons case, that of a thirty-year-old Fort Atkinson woman named Irene Keating, who had vanished the previous August, but though the lie detector tests were inconclusive, he never seemed to be a serious suspect.

As for Gein's other crimes, Wilson would only say that "an avalanche of evidence has been recovered which will take weeks, and possibly months to completely evaluate and process. When this is done the results will be made known to the proper local officials."

After trying unsuccessfully to pump the Crime Lab director for additional details, the reporters hurried off to file the news of Gein's confession in time for the evening headlines.

So many stories linking Eddie to the Hogan murder had already been circulated—including, most sensationally, Sheriff Wanerski's identification of the murdered woman's head as one of Eddie's "trophies"—that Wilson's announcement was almost anticlimactic. It did, however, produce one immediate and dramatic result. A thirty-seven-year-old woman from Carlinville, Illinois, Mrs. Christine Selvo, revealed that she was Mary Hogan's daughter, abandoned by her mother twenty-seven years earlier and raised by foster parents. For several years, Mrs. Selvo had been trying to locate her natural mother's whereabouts. With Wilson's official confirmation of Gein's guilt, her search was over. She had managed to trace her mother's movements from Springfield to Joliet to Chicago to Pine Grove, Wisconsin—a wayward path that had come to an abrupt and appalling end in the blackness of Eddie Gein's charnel house.

Back in Wautoma, District Attorney Kileen told a group of reporters that he hoped to file a first-degree murder charge against Gein on the following day. He was only awaiting the results of a ballistics test that the Crime Lab was conducting on a .22-caliber rifle recovered from the display rack of the Worden hardware store. An expended cartridge had been found in the chamber of the rifle, and Crime Lab technicians were checking it against the bullet extracted from Bernice Worden's severed head.

Kileen added that he intended to ask the court to order a sanity hearing for Gein. Then he broke the bad news.

According to Kileen, whom reporters had come to rely on as their primary source of information, he had been given "a spanking" by Attorney General Honeck, who had advised him not to release any further information that "would tend to inflame potential jurors." Kileen was a bit defensive, insisting that "the only things I have divulged are what everybody knew anyway." But he told the newsmen that he had no intention of disregarding the attorney general's "advice."

From the press's point of view, Kileen's announcement was undoubtedly the single most upsetting development in the case. When they approached Honeck to protest his directive, the attorney general brushed their objections aside, explaining that he was simply acting in the interests of justice. "With the widespread statements being made, some ill-founded, contradictory, and groundless on things that are supposed to have happened," Honeck said, "people might reach conclusions which might affect their ability to sit as jurors. In some places, confessed murderers are walking the streets, turned loose on the grounds that they couldn't get a fair trial. That's what we're trying to avoid in this case."

Honeck insisted that a news blackout was the "farthest thing from our minds." But he made it clear that his order to withhold information would remain in force until Gein was brought to trial. "I think the public will know the whole story at the proper time," he said.

There wasn't much the press could do about Honeck's position except grumble. In spite of the attorney general's disclaimer, it looked, one reporter complained, as if the news blackout that had "confused the details surrounding Edward Gein's butchery" was about to "become even blacker."

By this time, Eddie was back in his cell in the Waushara County jailhouse, wolfing down a dinner of roasted lamb, mashed potatoes, canned corn, lettuce salad, apple pie, and coffee.

After disposing of his meal, Gein was visited by his attorney, William Belter, who informed Eddie of his intention to enter a plea of not guilty by reason of insanity. Eddie nodded agreeably— happy, as always, to go along with a good suggestion.

He assured his attorney that he had been treated fairly in Madison. In fact, he expressed only the warmest feelings for his interrogator, Joseph Wilimovsky. "Joe," as Eddie called him, had never once tricked him into saying anything he didn't mean. His questions had actually helped Eddie "clear his mind."

Still, as Belter told newsmen after conferring with Gein, there were lots of things that Eddie was "still hazy" about. And it was obvious to everyone who came into contact with Eddie, his defense attorney included, that one of the things Gein was most glaringly "hazy" about was the sheer magnitude of his crimes. Gein exhibited no awareness at all of their enormity. He couldn't have been any more nonchalant about them if they had consisted of a string of parking violations. As Belter, displaying a real skill for understatement, later said of his client, "I don't think he has a full appreciation of what he has done."

By late Wednesday afternoon, it was evident to the reporters who were still staking out Eddie's farm that the investigation was drawing to a close. Police had boarded up the first-floor doors and windows and nailed a "No Trespassing" sign to the house. The only significant activity at all was taking place outside, where several Wood County deputies were busily digging up some holes around the property. At one location—the spot near the outhouse where Eddie had dumped Mrs. Worden's blood—the searchers found nothing. At another site, they turned up a small bone. Unable to determine if it had come from an animal or a human finger, they dispatched it at once to the Crime Lab.

At the jailhouse in Wautoma, Sheriff Schley confirmed that, from his point of view at least, the investigation was over. Whatever remained to be done was "up to the State Crime Lab." "They've got the skulls," Schley told reporters in an uncharacteristic burst of communicativeness. "Let them find out if they're embalmed. That's what they're for."

Kileen seconded Schley's statement, adding, "There aren't any more facts left."

Kileen had no way of knowing it, of course, but in less than a day, his pronouncement would be belied, for the Gein case was nothing if not a seemingly never-ending source of lurid revelations. And blackout or no blackout, a new and particularly sensational one was about to come to light.

# 25

*"Gein was a sexually normal man."*
COLIN WILSON, *A Casebook of Murder*

Under the sponsorship of Joseph E. Seagram & Sons, the whiskey concern, which was celebrating its centennial in 1957, a symposium entitled "The Next Hundred Years" was held in New York City on January 21. Eight prominent scientists, including two Nobel prize winners and rocket pioneer Wernher von Braun, took part in the conference, and their rosy predictions were reported on the front pages of papers across the United States.

The panelists foresaw a world transformed into an earthly paradise by the wonders of science and technology, a world where savory synthetic foods would eliminate hunger; where deserts, irrigated by purified sea water, would blossom with vegetation; where advanced automation would lead to a four-hour work week; and where, thanks to miraculous psychoactive drugs, no one would ever be "mentally or emotionally sick."

But this hypothetical wonderworld, according to the experts, was still a century away. And to anyone following the unfolding of the Gein case—and that would have included most of the population of Wisconsin—the gap between the marvels of this imagined future and the much bleaker realities of the present couldn't have been clearer. For on the very day that Wisconsin newspapers were reporting on the Seagram symposium and its vision of a twenty-first-century utopia free of labor, hunger, and mental disease, their front pages were dominated by the latest revelation regarding Gein's own mental condition, a condition that more than one psychiatrist would come to describe as "unparalleled in modern history."

It is remarkable that in the four days since the Gein atrocities became known to the public, no one involved in the investigation—not Sheriff Schley or District Attorney Kileen or any of the Crime Lab personnel—had said a word about a motive. It was as if Gein's behavior was so incomprehensibly monstrous that it was simply beyond explanation. But on Thursday, November 21, all that began to change.

Generally speaking, identifying a cause for even the most heinous of acts can offer a degree of comfort. Crimes that seem completely unmotivated—the casual slaughter of a family by a serial killer who selects his victims at whim, for example—terrify because of their very randomness. They strike at one of our most fundamental human impulses—the urge to believe in a universe governed by forces other than sheer accident and chance. It was typical of the Gein case, however, that the motives put forth for his actions only added to their horror. Though nothing could be more appalling than the crimes themselves, the explanations that began to emerge on the twenty-first conjured up a whole new set of nightmares.

The story broke in the *Chicago Tribune* and spread quickly to the front pages of every newspaper in Wisconsin. But it was the headline in the late edition of that day's *Milwaukee Journal* that best summed up the newest Gein-related shocker. The headline read:

OBSESSIVE LOVE FOR HIS MOTHER DROVE GEIN TO
SLAY, ROB GRAVES
GHOULISH ACTS WERE STIRRED BY HER DEATH
He Thought Victims Resembled Parent,
Authorities Learn During Quizzing

The source of the story was an "unidentified investigator" who had been present during Gein's interrogation at the Crime Lab on Tuesday and Wednesday. From this informant, the public learned for the first time the ghastly details of Gein's unspeakable practices—how he would carry the freshly disinterred corpses home and "cut them up," keeping only the heads, strips of skin, and what the papers euphemistically referred to as "some other parts" and disposing of the rest by "burning it in small pieces in his kitchen cook stove." They learned how he "gave particular attention" to the faces, which he would peel from the skulls, "leaving a human mask," and how he preserved these masks by keeping them "as cold as possible" and rubbing "oil on them whenever they became stiff."

Then came the revelation about the skin vest stripped "from the upper part of one woman's body." The public read the appalling particulars of Eddie's grotesque masquerade—how he would, on occasion, "don one of the masks, slip into the torso skin vest, and attach to himself other parts he had removed from a woman's body and parade around by himself in his lonely farm house," a ritual that "gave him great satisfaction."

Almost as shocking as these deranged acts, however, was the motive which, according to the anonymous informant, had driven Gein to perform them. Gein, the investigator explained, suffered from an Oedipus complex which accounted for all his criminal behavior, including the murder of two women "who resembled his mother."

In the course of his interrogation at the crime lab, Gein had revealed an "unnatural attachment" to his dead mother, Augusta, an attachment that had caused him to acquire perverse "feminine attitudes." Even before her death, the investigator revealed, Gein "wished that he had been a woman instead of a man. He bought medical books and studied anatomy. He wondered whether it would be possible to change his sex. He considered inquiring about an operation to change him into a woman and even thought of trying the operation upon himself, but did nothing about such plans."

Following his mother's death in 1945, Gein "brooded for a long time. From this disconsolate mood emerged his compulsion to visit cemeteries. After a few nocturnal trips to graveyards, he began digging into fresh graves."

After a while, however, the gratifications of his grave-robbing and corpse-collecting activities did not, apparently, suffice. One afternoon, Gein stopped for coffee at Mary Hogan's tavern with a neighbor who had employed Eddie to help out with an odd job. As soon as Eddie laid eyes on the proprietress, "it struck him that she resembled his mother." Later that day, Eddie returned to the tavern, shot Mrs. Hogan through the back of the head with a .32-caliber Mauser, loaded her two-hundred-pound body into his truck, drove home, hoisted her up by her heels with a pulley arrangement in the summer kitchen where his parents had once slaughtered hogs, and butchered her body with a homemade knife fashioned from a file.

Several years later, he repeated this atrocity with Bernice Worden, another local businesswoman who strongly reminded Eddie Gein of his own hefty, strong-willed, dear departed mommy.

Public reaction to these sensational disclosures (characterized by the *Chicago Tribune* as "the appalling denouement of the entire case") was explosive, particularly among members of the psychiatric community, who, as one observer put it, had a "field day" with the findings. Though some psychiatrists refused to engage in idle speculation—as one Milwaukee doctor sensibly pointed out, "without questioning Gein at length, it would be difficult to explain his aggressive acts toward women whom he thought resembled his mother"—others lost no time in describing Gein as the most unique case of psychosis "in modern psychiatric history" and "one of the most dramatic human beings ever to confront society."

Opinions regarding the precise nature of Gein's madness varied somewhat. One psychiatrist theorized that Gein was "a sexual psychopath, somewhat mentally defective, and possibly schizophrenic." Dr. Edward J. Kelleher, on the other hand, chief of the Chicago Municipal Court's Psychiatric Institute, was unequivocal in his diagnosis. Gein, he asserted, was "obviously schizophrenic," a condition "created by a conflict set up by his mother." Couching his explanations (insofar as possible) in layman's terms, Kelleher explained that Gein's behavior demonstrated a high degree of ambivalence—"two conflicting types of feelings." The "biggest example of ambivalence," said Kelleher, "is that love and hate are possible toward the same individual. It is possible to have this dual set of feelings toward women."

Gein "probably began this whole set of feelings with his relationship toward his mother," Kelleher continued. Thus, "it would be more likely that these feelings would be there in acute form with women who resembled his mother."

Why Gein should have developed such violently divided feelings for his mother—with murderous hatred coexisting alongside worshipful love—had something to do, Kelleher suggested, with the sexual attitudes instilled by Augusta. Gein had told his questioners about his mother's view of modern women, her belief that all of them (besides herself) had "the devil in them." And "we know," said Kelleher, "that whenever a mother hammers away at an abnormal attitude toward other women, it affects her children."

The result of Gein's abnormally conflicted feelings for his mother, according to Kelleher, was a cluster of symptoms "unparalleled" in the annals of sexual psychopathology, a sickness combining acute forms of transvestism, fetishism (the "disordered love" of nonliving objects), and, ghastliest of all, necrophilia (the "love of the dead"). 

When Kelleher was asked if Gein's behavior might somehow be "an extreme form of voyeurism," the psychiatrist didn't discount the presence of this aberration as a component of Gein's personality but denied that it could account for the crimes. Voyeurs, he said, "are not any closer to murder than you or I."

Professional psychiatrists like Dr. Kelleher weren't the only ones to engage in the long-distance diagnosis of Gein. Armchair psychoanalysis suddenly became a popular pastime in Wisconsin, and subjects that were not exactly the stuff of everyday conversation in 1950s Middle America—sexual deviance, transvestism, fetishism, necrophilia—were being tossed around as casually as the daily deer-hunting statistics. Even Crime Lab director Charles Wilson, a man not given to offhand pronouncements, agreed that "an oedipus complex" was probably involved in Gein's case, though he denied knowing anything about Eddie's purported desire to be a woman. "It's news to me," Wilson told reporters. In any event, Wilson went on, it would be up to the psychiatrists who examined Gein to figure out precisely what was wrong with him. "This is something that the boys in the short white coats will have to decide," the Crime Lab director declared.

And it was indeed true that, as of yet, Gein had not been examined by a single psychiatrist, though, as one commentator put it, that hadn't "slowed up the torrent of words and explanations."

While the newspaper-reading public was being treated to a crash course in sexual psychopathology, the object of all this attention was being arraigned at Wautoma. Flanked by Attorney Belter and Sheriff Schley, the stoop-shouldered little man stood in the courtroom of Waushara County Judge Boyd Clark and heard himself formally charged with first-degree murder.

Anyone laying eyes on Eddie for the first time would have found it hard to believe that he was the infamous "ghoul-slayer" of Plainfield. With his work clothes and pleasant mien, he looked more like a furnace repairman, there to service the courthouse's heating system, than Wisconsin's most notorious criminal. But even Eddie seemed to have finally comprehended the seriousness of his position. Though he had fortified himself that morning with his usual hearty breakfast—corn flakes, pork links, toast, and coffee—he trembled slightly as he listened to Judge Clark.

The charge said that Edward Gein, "did on the 16th day of November, 1957, at the village of Plainfield in said county [Waushara] feloniously and with intent to kill, murder Bernice Worden, a human being, contrary to section 940.01 of the Wisconsin statutes against the peace and dignity of the state of Wisconsin."

The arraignment was over quickly. Eddie spoke only two words, acknowledging his identity and answering "Yes" when the judge asked if he was represented by an attorney. Belter then entered his pleas—not guilty and not guilty by reason of insanity—and waived a preliminary hearing. After accepting the pleas, Judge Clark found "probable cause" that the crime had been committed, bound Gein over to the circuit court for trial, and ordered him held without bail. Three minutes after it began, the arraignment was over, and Eddie was escorted back to his cell.

Eddie had two visitors that day. Adams County Sheriff Frank Searles—the officer who had found Mrs. Worden's abandoned panel truck in the pine grove just outside Plainfield—arrived at the jailhouse to question Gein about the mysterious disappearance of the forty-three-year-old Friendship man, Victor "Bunk" Travis, who had last been seen leaving a Plainfield tavern in the company of a stranger named Burgess on the evening of November 1 five years before.

After spending an hour in Gein's cell questioning the prisoner, however, Searles came away unsatisfied. "I couldn't get anything out of him," he told a crowd of reporters afterward. "The only answers he would make were 'I don't remember' and 'I don't know' and others like that." Still, Searles strongly suspected that Gein might "know something" about the disappearance of the two hunters along with their car. According to the sheriff, Gein had been heard to comment on Travis's disappearance in the same joking way he had spoken about Mary Hogan's. "And if this happened with the Hogan case," said Sheriff Searles, "the same could be true with the Travis case."

Shortly after Searles's departure, someone else showed up at the jailhouse, asking to see Gein: Rev. Kenneth Engleman, the boyish-looking, thirty-three-year-old pastor of Wautoma's Methodist Church.

Though Eddie had previously told Schley that he would like to talk to a minister, the harried and overstressed sheriff hadn't gotten around to summoning one. On Thursday afternoon, Rev. Engleman showed up without notice at the jailhouse, explaining that he felt Gein was in need of spiritual counsel. Eddie, of course, had been raised as a strict Lutheran. Nevertheless, he eagerly accepted the Methodist's offer, welcoming the young minister into his cell.

Afterwards, Rev. Engleman held a press conference to describe his meeting with Gein and set the record straight about the widely circulated reports of the killer's "cold and unresponsive" nature.

As far as he was concerned, Rev. Engleman told the reporters, those stories were completely inaccurate. Indeed, no sooner had he walked into Gein's cell than the prisoner broke into uncontrollable sobs. Gein, said the minister, was "sorry for himself for having gotten involved in trouble" and full of remorse for the "pain he had inflicted on other people." The two of them spent some time discussing Eddie's parents, whose deaths, Gein told the minister, had left an "empty spot in his life." Later, when the two men knelt on the cold floor of the cell to pray for "comfort, help, and strength," Eddie began sobbing again.

When one of the reporters asked the minister what had prompted his visit, Rev. Engleman answered without hesitation. "I'm a Christian minister and Mr. Gein is a child of God," he said. Indeed, "God may be nearer to Mr. Gein than the rest of us because God comes closer to people in dealings with life and death." And when it came to matters of life and death, the minister concluded, making an observation that would have been hard to dispute, "Mr. Gein is closer to such things than the rest of us."

Rev. Engleman's interview with Gein was deeply envied by the reporters, none of whom had been allowed to exchange a single word with the prisoner, a situation they regarded as profoundly unjust. Now that the search of the Gein farm was complete and Eddie, for the present at least, was installed at Wautoma, the media spotlight had been turned on the county seat, where at least three dozen reporters could be seen roaming around the downtown streets at most times of the day.

As had been true in Plainfield, feelings about all this media attention were mixed. Some residents wished that the reporters would simply go somewhere—anywhere—else. Others, particularly the local restaurant owners and the folks who ran Brock's Motel on the east side of town where most of the press corps was lodged, couldn't have been happier.

One man, however, was unequivocal in his negative feelings for the newsmen. Sheriff Schley's wariness and distaste remained as powerful as ever. Six weeks on the job, struggling to handle the most sensational murder case in Wisconsin history with a full-time staff of only two deputies and an annual budget of $11,500, Schley had been trying his best to perform his duties while dealing with the demands and importunities of the press. Schley's dislike of the reporters wasn't anything personal. But it was simply impossible, he said, "to try to conduct an investigation with about sixty newsmen following you everywhere you go." Only recently, Gein had volunteered to take Schley back to his farm and show him something. By the time the two men arrived there, however, the place was so overrun with newsmen and photographers that Eddie got spooked and changed his mind. Schley still didn't know what Gein had intended to show him. For all he knew, it might have been another body.

Schley's respect for the newsmen's methods—not high to begin with—dropped even lower when a reporter approached him on the sly and offered him a considerable sum of money for the opportunity to spend just ten minutes talking with the Plainfield "butcher-ghoul," a bribe Schley angrily rejected, telling the reporter "what he could do with his money."

On the evening of Thursday, November 21, the simmering tensions between Schley and the newsmen—who for days had been hounding the sheriff for access to Gein—finally boiled over.

Eddie's lawyer had responded to the reporters' increasingly clamorous appeals by promising to arrange for an interview between the newsmen and Gein. Thursday had been set as the tentative time, and in the early afternoon, immediately after Eddie's return from his arraignment, about two dozen reporters crammed themselves into the small reception area at the front of the county jailhouse and waited. And waited. As more and more time passed without a sign of either Belter or Schley, the newsmen grew increasingly disgruntled. The suspicion arose that the whole thing was a setup, a ploy to keep the reporters occupied while Eddie took Schley back to his farm to show him where more bones and body parts were buried.

As it turned out, Schley was in the jailhouse all along, down in the basement, where he was helping to repair some leaky hot-water pipes. Belter, meanwhile, who also served as justice of the peace, was busy hearing game-law violations.

It was well into the evening—a good eight hours since the newsmen first began their frustrating wait—before Belter finally spoke to Gein and obtained his consent. Eddie would speak to six reporters, who would then pool the information with the rest of the journalists.

The lucky six—three representatives from the major wire services plus reporters from *Time* magazine, the *Milwaukee Journal*, and the *Oshkosh Daily Northwestern*—were chosen by Belter. Only one reporter—the *Chicago Tribune* man—kicked up a fuss about being excluded, but even he was placated after a while.

Belter and the chosen six left the building and walked around to the jail entrance at the rear. The rest of the reporters followed close at their heels, hoping for a chance to eavesdrop.

Sheriff Schley had positioned himself at the entrance to the jail, and when he saw the jostling mob of reporters coming toward him instead of the agreed-upon six, he became furious. He would only allow three reporters inside his jail, he shouted. The newsmen began objecting loudly, denouncing Schley and pleading with Belter to intervene. The whole scene was becoming increasingly chaotic.

Caught between Schley and the newsmen, Belter had little choice but to go along with the sheriff's decree. As soon as he made the new cut, however—picking the reporters from the Associated Press, the United Press, and *Time*—the man from the International News Service howled in protest. An argument between Schley and the newsman ensued, which because increasingly bitter, until Schley leveled a few final swear words at the journalist, announced that the whole affair was off, and stepped inside the jail, slamming the door behind him.

The reporters were devastated. They had spent the better part of the day packed inside the jailhouse, only to be denied, at the very last moment, their long-awaited interview with Gein. Their outrage and disappointment were amplified by their sense of helplessness. As long as Eddie was locked in Schley's jail, they were left with no recourse.

At least one of them, however—Robert Wells of the *Milwaukee Journal*—was capable of seeing some irony in the situation. "A week ago," wrote Wells, "there wasn't a person in the entire world who would have gone far out of his way to have a word with the little handy man with the twisted smile." And yet here were the "representatives of the nation's press" crying out in despair "over being unable to hear a few syllables from Gein's own lips."

There could be no surer sign of Eddie's new status. In a few short days, he had gone from being a complete nonentity—even in his humble hometown—to being a bona fide sensation. He had achieved the kind of phenomenal overnight fame that only the media can offer.

Eddie Gein was a celebrity.

# 26

*"Somewhere along about the time they finished with the swamp, the men who knocked over the bank at Fulton were captured down in Oklahoma. But the story rated less than half a column in the* Fairvale Weekly Herald. *Almost the entire front page was given over to the Bates case. AP and UP picked it up right away, and there was quite a bit about it on television. Some of the write-ups compared it to the Gein affair up north, a few years back. They worked up a sweat over the 'house of horror' and tried their damndest to make out that Norman Bates had been murdering motel visitors for years."*

ROBERT BLOCH, *Psycho*

The Gein story was everywhere. It dominated not just the news media but daily discourse as well. For several weeks, wherever Wisconsinites congregated—in stores and schoolyards, in cafés or at the dinner table—it was all people could talk about. Such was the magnitude of the story that if you lived in Wisconsin in the fall of 1957, you simply couldn't help knowing every detail of the case, even if you never picked up a paper or turned on the TV.

One individual who first heard about the Gein affair from local gossip was a forty-year-old writer named Robert Bloch. A longtime resident of Milwaukee, Bloch had been publishing mystery and horror fiction since adolescence, having received his earliest encouragement from the celebrated fantasist H. P. Lovecraft. After a successful career as an advertising copywriter for the Gustav Marx Agency in Milwaukee, Bloch had decided in 1953 to devote himself to full-time freelance writing. His stories—many of them published in pulp magazines—were known for their gruesomely clever twist endings, which often made them read like extended sick jokes. Psychopathic killers featured prominently in his fiction. One of his best-known works was a tale entitled "Yours Truly, Jack the Ripper."

In the fall of 1957, Bloch was residing in Weyauwega, Wisconsin, his wife's hometown, located some ninety miles north of Milwaukee and less than thirty miles east of Plainfield. Marion Bloch had been suffering from tuberculosis of the bones. The disease was in remission, but the couple had moved to Weyauwega so that Marion could be close to her parents in case her condition worsened again.

Listening to the rumors about the nightmarish discoveries in the nearby town of Plainfield and reading the unbelievable facts in the *Weyauwega Chronicle* and the *Milwaukee Journal*, Bloch immediately saw in the Gein case the raw materials for a first-rate tale of terror. Here was a real-life horror story far more grisly than anything ever dreamed up by Lovecraft. A story that featured the darkest acts of depravity, all performed by a shy, bland, completely harmless-looking bachelor driven to his abominations by his pathological attachment to a tyrannizing mother who continued to dominate her son's existence years after her death.

What Bloch found most intriguing about the Gein case, however, was its setting—the notion, as he later put it, "that a ghoulish killer with perverted appetites could flourish almost openly in a small rural community where everybody prides himself on knowing everybody else's business."

As Bloch pondered the outlines of his story, he quickly confronted an important problem: how to furnish his killer with a suitable supply of victims.

Given the shy, retiring nature of the main character, it didn't seem credible to have him actively go out and stalk his prey, like Jack the Ripper. The prey would have to come to him. And what better way to provide a killer with a steady stream of victims than to have him operate some kind of business—say, a small, run-down, out-of-the-way motel?

# PART 4

# Diggings

# 27

*"In the damp and cold November night
on the day of the dead,
our love awakes.
The love of the dead."*

From the diary of a necrophiliac

Gein was in court again on Friday for a brief appearance before Circuit Judge Herbert A. Bunde. Dressed in baggy green work pants and a blue woolen jacket, Eddie, his stubbled face displaying no trace of emotion, was led into the large, high-ceilinged courtroom by Sheriff Schley. About eighty spectators, at least thirty of them newsmen, half filled the courtroom. The crowd was hushed as the fragile-looking "ghoul-slayer" was brought before the bench, though the news photographers present were squirming with frustration. At Eddie's request, they had been barred by Judge Bunde, a stern, no-nonsense jurist, from taking pictures during the proceedings.

Throughout the week, rumors had continued to circulate that certain individuals in Plainfield were outraged at the notion that Gein, by pleading insanity, might evade punishment for his crimes. District Attorney Kileen had sought to reassure the public by stating categorically that "Gein would never walk the streets of Plainfield again." Still, there was a good deal of bitterness at the thought that Gein might end up in a mental hospital, which, as far as certain people were concerned, would be tantamount to his getting away with murder.

Fearing, perhaps, that there might be some sort of outburst among the spectators—an angry, possibly violent display of protest or even an attempt on the prisoner's life—the judge had ordered an unprecedented degree of protection for the defendant. Seven armed men—three city policemen, three deputies (including Leon Murty, who arrived at court dressed in a bright red deer-hunting outfit), and Sheriff Herbert Wanerski—stood with their backs to the bench, keeping a close eye on the spectators. Schley, who never left Eddie's side, wore a revolver on his hip.

As it turned out, these precautions were completely unnecessary. The spectators, many of them courthouse employees, looked on politely, as silent and undemonstrative as the defendant. Even the photographers kept their disgruntlement to themselves and sat watching with quiet interest.

Like the preliminary hearing on Thursday, Friday's arraignment was over quickly. His manacled hands folded in front of him, Eddie stood before Judge Bunde and once again heard himself formally charged with first-degree murder and armed robbery. As on Thursday, he was required only to confirm his identity and point out his lawyer, William Belter (who had been mildly rebuked in a *Milwaukee Journal* editorial that day for having told reporters that he had accepted the distasteful task of defending Gein with "reluctance"). Once more, Belter entered a plea of not guilty by reason of insanity.

What was different this time, however, was the recommendation by Kileen that Gein be committed to the Central State Hospital for a sanity test before a trial date was set. By way of buttressing his request, Kileen described for Judge Bunde the condition Bernice Worden's body had been found in, "hanging by its heels" and "dressed out" like a deer. "I don't know whether a person in his right mind would do that sort of thing or not," Kileen opined.

Belter, who had announced several hours before that he intended to get an independent medical opinion on Gein's sanity from a Milwaukee psychiatrist, concurred with Kileen. He told the judge that Gein had admitted removing entire corpses and various body parts from graves. "Some mental aberration is involved," was Belter's assessment.

The entire arraignment lasted little more than five minutes. After listening to the recommendations of the prosecutor and the defense attorney, Judge Bunde made a statement. "It seems advisable under the circumstances as related by both the counsel for the state and the counsel for the defendant," he said, "that expert determination be had whether he is now competent to stand trial," as well as whether he was sane at the time of Mrs. Worden's murder.

Then Bunde signed an order committing Eddie to the Central State Hospital for the Criminally Insane at Waupun for a thirty-day

examination period and remanded him to the custody of Sheriff
Schley, who led Eddie back to the jailhouse to await transportation
to the mental institution.

Later that afternoon, DA Kileen held a meeting with Judge Bunde
and several other local officials, including Schley, Waushara County
board chairman Earl Simenson, and Harold Collins, village president of Plainfield, to discuss a number of issues in connection with
the Gein case.

One of the questions they considered had to do with the round-
the-clock protection of Gein's home. Ever since the Gein story hit
the front pages, deputy sheriffs from Waushara and Portage counties had been standing guard at the farm to discourage curiosity
seekers, including groups of fraternity boys from the University of
Wisconsin bent on throwing beer parties in the infamous "house of
horror." But the officials didn't know how long the county could
afford to post a twenty-four-hour watch at the crime scene.

Another of their concerns, also based on economics, had to do
with the Travis case. Was it worth the county's while to pursue its
investigation into that and the other disappearances Eddie was
suspected of? Kileen's feeling was that Waushara—"a poor
county"—shouldn't have to "foot the bill" for the investigation of
any crimes that Gein may have committed elsewhere. "Why should
we be the goat?" he argued. As long as Gein was locked away—
either in prison or in a mental hospital, it made no difference to the
district attorney—he would be satisfied. The fact that Gein might
have killed people in other parts of the state was regrettable but not,
in the end, the concern of Waushara County.

Neither of these questions, however, was the main item on the
district attorney's agenda. The primary reason Kileen had called the
meeting was to deal with a far more sensitive, indeed potentially
explosive, issue—the issue of exhumation.

From the moment that Eddie claimed to have procured his
anatomical "trophies" from local cemeteries, the issue had generated a considerable degree of controversy. Sheriff Wanerski—who
had sneered at Eddie's grave-robbing story—was by no means the
only skeptic. In general (no doubt because the notion was too awful
to entertain), the citizens of Plainfield refused to believe that Gein's
hideous collection had been assembled from the town's graveyard,
that the faces, vaginas, and other parts found in the squalor of his
farmhouse were the relics of their own closest relations, the
mummified scraps of their departed sisters, wives, and mothers.

That a person as passive as Eddie could have committed such depredations seemed highly unlikely to most of the townspeople, who viewed the little bachelor as too meek and shiftless for such a deed. "I don't think he ever had ambition enough to open a grave," was the way Gyle Ellis, the owner of a local grocery store, put it. Though Gein was a wiry fellow, it seemed impossible that he could have had the strength to dig up a grave by himself, break open the casket, remove the corpse and perform his grisly operations on it, then rebury the coffin and smooth over the sandy soil so that no trace of his crime remained—all in the space of a few hours.

Moreover, the townspeople didn't see how such an activity could possibly have gone undetected, particularly over the course of several years. Gein, they argued, would have had to perform his nocturnal pillaging by lantern light, and even in an area as isolated and lonely as Plainfield, it hardly seemed credible that no one would have once spotted a suspicious glow coming from the cemetery or noticed Gein's pickup truck parked there in the night and wondered what the strange little recluse was up to.

One person eminently qualified to comment on the situation was the sexton of the Plainfield cemetery, Pat Danna, who completely discounted Gein's story. Danna insisted that during the time he'd been caretaker, no graves had ever been molested. He was out at the cemetery all the time, mowing it once a week during the summer and checking it regularly in the winter, and he had never seen a single sign of disturbance. Moreover, he'd kept a particularly close eye on the place for the past several years, ever since a couple of vandals did about twenty-five hundred dollars' worth of damage to a nearby cemetery during a drunken spree.

Gein's claim just didn't seem credible to Danna. In the summer months, the cemetery was "too busy" for anyone to get away with grave tampering (among other things, local teenagers were known to use it as a trysting place). And in the winter, the ground was just too hard. It would take a strong man half a day of heavy labor to dig up a grave when the cold weather set in. Moreover, in tombs with concrete vaults, a "body snatcher" would need a block and tackle to get at a corpse—and concrete vaults were common in Plainfield because of the area's notoriously sandy soil. Besides, Danna explained, most modern coffins were made of steel, hermetically sealed, and exceptionally hard to pry open.

Danna was firm in his belief. Whatever other kind of monster Eddie Gein might be, he certainly wasn't a grave robber.

Another authority in the matter was a bit less positive than

Danna. This was Ray Goult, Plainfield's only mortician. According to Goult, many caskets were not enclosed in concrete vaults but rather within wooden boxes whose covers were secured with eight or ten easily removable screws. As for the caskets themselves, they were not always sealed tight. This was especially true of wooden coffins. But even ones constructed of steel were often put into the ground with their lids unlocked.

Still, Goult tended to agree with Danna. He confirmed that the digging would be difficult and extremely time-consuming for one man. And because of the sandiness of the soil, it was generally necessary to shore up the sides of a grave with timber to prevent cave-ins. All in all, it seemed highly unlikely that little Eddie Gein could have broken into even one buried coffin, let alone a bunch of them.

But if the human fragments in Gein's collection hadn't come from desecrated corpses, that could mean only one thing: they were the remains of at least ten murder victims. And that explanation was equally hard to accept. As a killer, Gein wasn't known for behaving (in the words of one observer) "with any large degree of cleverness." In the case of both the Hogan and Worden slayings, he had simply strolled into the victims' business places in broad daylight, shot the women in the head, and then dragged their bodies out to a waiting truck, without bothering to remove even the most obvious clues (such as the empty shells from the guns he had used to kill them). Considering this modus operandi, it hardly seemed possible that Gein could have gotten away with eight other killings without being caught.

Still, of the two equally improbable alternatives, most Plainfield residents found it easier to conceive of Eddie Gein as a mass murderer than a ghoul. "The people here will have to be shown the dug-up graves before they'll believe it," Ed Marolla told a reporter, summing up the sentiments of his fellow townspeople. And indeed, digging up some graves did seem to be the only way the matter would ever be definitively resolved.

At first, Kileen seemed strongly opposed to the idea of disinterment. As the district attorney of Waushara County, he was concerned only about the slaying of Mrs. Worden, to which Gein had already confessed. As for the other remains uncovered in Gein's charnel house, Kileen seemed willing to take the prisoner at his word.

During a meeting with reporters on Wednesday, Kileen had announced that Waushara County was not about to conduct any exhumations. "I want no part in opening any graves to prove anything," he told the newsmen. "Just think how the poor relatives would feel."

He repeated that his county had no unsolved missing-persons cases. From his point of view, therefore, a check of the cemeteries wasn't necessary. "If other counties want to get court orders to open graves," Kileen said, "it's up to them," though he added that if the survivors "don't like it, I'll do everything possible to stop it."

For a while, it seemed as if the Crime Lab might offer the best solution to the problem. Charles Wilson had nine of his men working full-time on the case, analyzing the evidence and employing the most up-to-date techniques for identifying the victims from their remains. By comparing dirt particles gathered at the crime scene with soil samples from local cemeteries, the technicians hoped to determine the validity of Gein's claim.

But the sheer quantity of evidence—by far, the largest amount ever handled by the ten-year-old Crime Lab—made it hard for Wilson to promise a quick resolution. Though Kileen urged the director to give the soil analysis top priority, it was clear that a final answer might take weeks, even months.

In the meantime, Kileen was under growing pressure from the Plainfield citizenry to determine the truth of Gein's assertion. It was becoming increasingly obvious that the townsfolk would never be able to rest without knowing whether their loved ones had, in fact, been ravaged in their graves.

On Friday afternoon, therefore, following his meeting with Judge Bunde and the other officials, Kileen called a press conference to make an electrifying announcement.

Early the next week, he told the reporters, and contingent on the permission of the next-of-kin, two graves would be opened in the Plainfield cemetery.

Kileen's change of mind regarding the exhumations wasn't his only about-face. He also seemed to have become suddenly dubious about the whole grave-robbing story. When one of the reporters asked him if he still believed Gein's claim, Kileen snorted. "Do you?" he asked in a heavily sarcastic tone that made his skepticism clear.

For the first time, the district attorney revealed that Gein had supplied authorities with a list of "eight or nine" people whose corpses he had presumably violated. Kileen's intention was to dig up two of these graves, "unless the ground freezes." If nothing was found, he explained, no other bodies would be exhumed. On the other hand, if Gein turned out to be telling the truth, Kileen might go ahead and order the opening of "the other graves named by Gein."

When the reporters asked Kileen how he reconciled the "eight or nine" names with the significantly larger number of masks and skulls recovered at the farm, the DA only shrugged. "That's a question I can't answer and nobody can answer," he said. "Only Gein can."

Kileen refused to disclose the names on Eddie's list, with one exception. He told the newsmen that the first body he intended to disinter was that of Mrs. Eleanor Adams, a fifty-two-year-old woman who had died six years before and been buried in a coffin enclosed in a wooden box. Mrs. Adams's grave, the district attorney revealed, was right next to the burial plot of Eddie Gein's parents.

When a reporter asked Kileen if Augusta Gein was one of the women on the list, the DA shook his head. According to Kileen, Gein had denied opening his mother's coffin.

Of course, his mother's coffin, added Kileen, was encased in a concrete vault. Whether Eddie had tried—and failed—to reach Augusta's body was something that the district attorney could not, or would not, say.

# 28

*"What we are dealing with here, in a large number of cases, and what is probably one of the main functions of folk-humor, is an interesting folklore mechanism of great importance and relative frequency. . . . It is the* rationalization—*the attempt to make understandable, or at least believable, even endurable, if only as a 'joke'—of some highly charged situation into which the original folk-teller of the tale has stumbled or has found himself forced to live. . . . This is certainly the principal function of the creation of humor, and certainly of the accepting of things as humorous, such as cuckoldry, seduction, impotence, homosexuality, castration, death, disease, and the Devil, which are obviously not humorous at all. [Such] humor is a sort of whistling in the dark, like Beaumarchais' Figaro, who 'laughs so that he may not cry.'"*

GERSHOM LEGMAN, *Rationale of the Dirty Joke*

It has been said that in the midst of tragedy, time seems to drag, that every moment becomes an eternity. But it is equally true that tragedy can make time spin by with a terrifying swiftness. Nothing causes life to change more quickly than a tragedy.

Saturday, November 23, was a somber anniversary for the people of Plainfield. It had been a week ago exactly that one of their most beloved neighbors had met an unspeakably awful end. But in the short time since Eddie Gein had shambled into Worden's Hardware Store with a glass jug in one hand and a couple of .22 shells in his overalls pocket, the world had changed forever, not only for the slain woman's family and the deranged little bachelor who had slaughtered her like a game animal but for every member of their stunned and beleaguered hometown.

Though its citizens were doing their best to get back to the ordinary business of life, Plainfield remained a community in crisis, still reeling from the sheer monstrousness of the Gein revelations, mortified by the media attention that had turned it into a back-country sideshow, and deeply riven by conflict over Kileen's plan to dig up the graves. For, while most of the townspeople were eager to see the grave-robbing question settled once and for all, others remained fiercely opposed to the idea of violating the hallowed soil of their little cemetery.

Added to this tension were the unabating rumors that continued to send shocks through the town. Stories had spread, for example, that the grisly remains found in Gein's bedroom and kitchen weren't the worst of what the farmhouse contained, that its basement was full of horrors so dreadful that the police had deemed it best to conceal them from the public. There were also reports, which occasioned more than a few sleepless nights for the matrons of Plainfield, that investigators had turned up a "death list" in Eddie's house, a roster of local farm wives slated to take their places on the walls, shelves, and ceiling beams of Eddie's private death museum. Most unsettling of all, however, was the persistent rumor that Eddie had not worked alone, that another man had accompanied him on his grave-looting forays and even taken part in the depraved operations Gein had performed on his newly unearthed treasures.

The citizens of the town had begun to feel like pariahs or freaks. According to one source, when the postmaster of Plainfield, Harry P. Walker, was introduced to his colleagues at a statewide convention in Milwaukee, he was "greeted first by audible gasps and then by a horrified silence."

Perhaps as a result of this distressing experience, Walker concocted a plan which he proposed in a letter to Senator William Proxmire, a plan he hoped would correct the poor impression of his town created by the press. "You are no doubt well aware of the intense national publicity Plainfield has received in connection with the Gein murders," Walker wrote to Proxmire. "While Plainfield, of course, had nothing to do with the Gein affair, except to be unfortunate enough to be the locale, we have been damaged greatly by the horrible publicity."

What Walker proposed as a way of generating some positive feelings for his hometown was the printing of a commemorative postage stamp honoring the prairie chicken, which would be "introduced on its first day of issue" through the Plainfield post office. By designating Plainfield as the place of issue for the prairie chicken stamp, the government would create favorable publicity for the town, not only among the country's millions of philatelists but also in the national press.

Just how seriously Walker's proposal was taken is a matter of conjecture. In any event, nothing ever came of it. Walker and his neighbors had no choice but to learn to live with their hometown's new (and, as it would turn out, permanent) reputation—to resign themselves to seeing the "fair name of Plainfield" (as one observer put it) forever "muddied as the home of murder-ghoul Ed Gein."

Elsewhere in Wisconsin, the reaction to the Gein atrocities was markedly different, if no less intense. In fact, the statewide response to the Plainfield horrors was so striking that it immediately attracted the interest of various psychologists, who had never witnessed a mass phenomenon quite like it. Besides the extreme fascination with every detail of the case, from the precise number of masks found inside Eddie's house to the menus of his jailhouse dinners, the crimes had generated an unprecedented outbreak of black humor, a craze for Gein-related sick jokes (dubbed "Geiners") that quickly swept the state.

Within days of the discovery of the crimes, every youngster in Wisconsin, it seemed, was swapping "Geiners" not only with schoolmates but with parents as well. Gein jokes became the latest rage, repeated with near-obsessive frequency wherever people gathered. As early as Friday, November 22, Dr. Rudolf Mathias, chief psychologist at the Wisconsin Diagnostic Center in Madison, was theorizing about the significance of Gein humor, which he likened to "the jokes exchanged among soldiers who are going into battle."

But it was a psychiatrist named George D. Arndt who undertook the most extensive study of the phenomenon. After making a field trip to central Wisconsin, where he gathered scores of examples, Arndt published the results of his research in the *Bulletin of the Menninger Clinic*. Titled "Community Reactions to a Horrifying Event," Dr. Arndt's piece argued that the compulsive joking about the Plainfield killer was a collective coping mechanism, a way of dealing with the deep anxieties stirred up by the crime, of exorcising the nightmare with laughter.

Arndt classified the jokes according to the taboos they dealt with—cannibalism, sexual perversion, and so on. But, in essence, all the jokes were the same—grisly quips of varying degrees of cleverness and wit whose purpose was to ward off terror with levity, in the way that children will whistle a cheerful tune while walking past a graveyard.

> Why did they have to keep the heat on in Ed Gein's house?
> So the furniture wouldn't get goose bumps.

> Why did Ed Gein's girlfriend stop going out with him?
> Because he was such a cut-up.

> Why won't anyone play cards with Ed Gein?
> He might come up with a good hand.

> What did Ed Gein say to the sheriff who arrested him?
> Have a heart.

> Why did they let Ed Gein out of jail on New Year's Eve?
> So he could dig up a date.

The most remarkable sample collected by Arndt, however, was not a joke but a poem, a macabre reworking of Clement Moore's "A Visit from St. Nicholas":

> 'Twas the night before Christmas, when all through the shed,
> All creatures were stirring, even old Ed.
>
> The bodies were hung from the rafters above,
> While Eddie was searching for another new love.
>
> He went to Wautoma for a Plainfield deal,
> Looking for love and also a meal.
>
> When what to his hungry eyes should appear,
> But old Mary Hogan in her new red brassiere.
>
> Her eyes how they twinkled, ever so gay,
> And her dimples, oh how merry were they.
>
> Her cheeks were like roses when kissed by the sun.
> And she let out a scream at the sight of Ed's gun.

Old Ed pulled the trigger and Mary fell dead,
He took his old axe and cut off her head.

He then took his hacksaw and cut her in two,
One half for hamburger, the other for stew.

And laying a hand aside of her heel,
Up to the rafters went his next meal.

He sprang to his truck, to the graveyard he flew,
The hours were short and much work must he do.

He looked for the grave where the fattest one laid,
And started in digging with shovel and spade.

He shoveled and shoveled and shoveled some more,
Till finally he reached the old coffin door.

He took out a crowbar and pried open the box,
He was not only clever, but sly as a fox.

As he picked up the body and cut off her head,
He could tell by the smell that the old girl was dead.

He filled in the grave by the moonlight above,
And once more old Ed had found a new love.

He let out a yell as he drove out of sight,
"If I don't get caught, I'll be back tomorrow night!"

For all its crudeness, this raw parody reveals something important, a significant transformation in the popular perception of the
Plainfield killer. It reveals Gein's metamorphosis, in the imagination of the public, from a homicidal madman into a creature of
folklore—a night-demon swooping down from his lair after sunset
in search of new victims to gratify his unholy lusts.

And so, the people of Wisconsin, faced with a horror too awful to
absorb, found refuge in laughter. But if, on Saturday, November 23,
jokes about "old Ed" were generating chuckles in playgrounds and
taverns, truck stops and beauty parlors throughout the state, there

was one place, at least, where the quip about the contents of Ed Gein's cookie jar ("lady fingers") or the one about his favorite beer ("lots of body but no head") was likelier to provoke a sharp word or an angry scowl. That place, of course, was Eddie's hometown.

To the residents of Plainfield, the Gein affair was definitely not— and never would be—a laughing matter.

# 29

*"We all go a little mad sometimes."*
NORMAN BATES

Eddie was supposed to have been transferred to the state mental hospital at Waupun late on Friday. On Saturday morning, however, he was still sitting in the county lockup in Wautoma, under the watchful eye of Sheriff Schley. At the request of investigators from another jurisdiction who wanted to question Gein about yet another missing-persons case, Kileen had agreed to postpone the move.

The customary crowd of newsmen was gathered at the jailhouse early Saturday morning to cover Eddie's removal to Central State Hospital. When they caught sight of Schley, they began shouting questions at him, trying to pin down the intended time of Gein's departure. The sheriff—whose few remaining traces of civility toward the press had completely evaporated since the shoving episode on Thursday—virtually snarled his reply. He had no idea when he would take Gein to the hospital. For all he knew, the transfer might not take place for weeks. "I have the right to hold him here a month if I feel like it," he said, his tone compounded equally of bitterness and contempt.

A short time later, however, Schley approached the reporters to offer a deal. Though his proposal seemed uncharacteristically conciliatory, it did not, in fact, reflect a shift in Schley's attitude. He continued to regard the newsmen as a pack of predators. But there was something important he needed to do, and to keep them off his back for a while, he was willing to throw them a sop.

Eddie, said Schley, had something to show the sheriff back at his farm, and Schley wanted the newsmen's word that they would stay put in Wautoma. He didn't want a replay of Eddie's last aborted outing, when so many reporters and photographers had descended on the farm that the shy little killer had gotten cold feet. In return for their cooperation, Schley promised the reporters that he would not spirit Eddie off to Waupun without informing them in advance.

Having secured the grudging agreement of his journalistic nemeses, Schley, accompanied by Deputy Arnie Fritz, led Eddie out of his cell and into a police car, then headed off in the direction of Plainfield.

The trip consumed the rest of the morning. Eddie remained seated inside the squad car for most of the time, getting out only once at his boarded-up home, where he led Schley, Fritz, and authorities from Portage County (who, by prearrangement, were awaiting Gein's arrival at the farmstead) to a large ash heap in a remote corner of his property. It was there, Eddie informed the lawmen, that they would find the residue of Mary Hogan's body, which he had carved up in his summer kitchen and then, after saving the sections he coveted, cremated in his pot-bellied stove.

Afterward, the two parties got back into their cars and, following Eddie's directions, retraced the route he had taken on the day he had slain the tavern keeper. By noon, Eddie was back in his cell in Wautoma.

True to his word, Schley informed the press that the prisoner would be transported to the maximum-security hospital at approximately two P.M. His announcement set off an instant mass exodus as the newsmen immediately decamped for the town of Waupun, located about fifty miles southeast of the county seat.

After the nonstop media hoopla of the preceding week, the sudden silence that descended on Wautoma seemed slightly jarring. An air of abandonment, almost desolation, hung over the town's two hostelries—Brock's Motel and the Sheldon Hotel—after their noisy week-long occupation by the forces of the nation's press. Still, as far as most of Wautoma's citizens were concerned, the journalists' departure couldn't have been more of a relief.

Only two newsmen stayed behind in Wautoma to cover the start of Gein's journey: a reporter and a cameraman from the *Milwaukee Journal*. At two-fifteen P.M., Eddie emerged from the jailhouse, dressed in the outfit—woolen jacket, work pants, high-topped rubber boots, and plaid peaked cap sitting askew on his head—that was by this point so inseparable from his public identity that he would have seemed unrecognizable in anything else. All that was missing, as he paused for a picture at the entranceway, was his simpleton's smile. Hollow-cheeked and unshaven, he stared vacantly at the camera, like a nocturnal thing dazed by the sunlight.

Schley ushered Eddie into the back seat of the squad car and got in beside him, while Arnie Fritz took the wheel.

Precisely sixty-five minutes later, the car pulled up before the walls of Central State Hospital, the prisonlike institution that would be home to America's most famous psychotic for some time to come.

Central State Hospital for the Criminally Insane has since been converted into a "correctional reception center," a way station to which all of Wisconsin's convicted felons are sent for evaluation before being moved on to prison. Its name has been changed, too, to Dodge Correctional Institute. In 1957, however, it was, and had been since its founding in 1913, a maximum-security mental institution with an all-male population of dangerously—and, for the most part, incurably—deranged inmates. Constructed on a seventy-two-acre site close to but separate from the state prison, the hospital consisted of a central administrative area with eight wards that housed, at the time of Eddie's arrival, just over three hundred inmates.

Though special precautions were taken to ensure that the inmates stayed put, many of them enjoyed a fair amount of freedom within the institution. During the day, they were permitted to move about the hospital at will, to watch TV, read magazines, play cards, take part in sports (there was a baseball diamond on the grounds), and participate in various occupational pursuits such as gardening, ceramics, and farm work (the hospital maintained a one-hundred-fifty-acre stock farm, complete with hogs and chickens).

At night, the inmates were immured in rooms with locked doors and barred windows. The rooms—some of which held as many as five men—had been painted in pastel colors in an effort to soften their distinct prison feel.

New admissions to the hospital were not permitted to participate in the normal round of hospital activities until they had undergone a prolonged observation period, during which their behavior and attitudes were evaluated by the staff. Given the extraordinary nature of the Gein case, additional tests and procedures would be employed, which were outlined for the press on Saturday by Dr. Edward F. Schubert, head psychiatrist and superintendent of the hospital.

Besides a thorough physical exam "to determine if he is physically ill and if such illness had a bearing on his acts," Gein would receive a "full battery" of psychological tests, including the Minnesota Multiphasic Personality Inventory, the Wechsler-Bellevue Intelligence Test, the Rorschach (or "inkblot") test, and "many, many other tests" to determine his psychological and, more specifically, his sexual attitudes. Gein would also undergo "exhaustive" interviews by the staff. His family background, meanwhile, would be researched by Kenneth Colwell, head of the hospital's social service department, who intended to seek out and question Gein's relatives and friends, assuming any existed.

The main purpose of this elaborate evaluation process, Schubert explained, was to determine "the legal question of Gein's sanity," whether he "understands the nature of his acts, can cooperate in his defense, and knows the difference between right and wrong." If, at the end of the thirty-day observation period, the psychiatrists deemed Gein to be sane, he would be tried for first-degree murder in the slaying of Bernice Worden.

On the other hand, if his examiners judged him mentally incompetent, Gein could expect to spend the rest of his days inside the walls of Central State.

While Schubert and his staff were preparing to begin their examination of the most significant case ever consigned to their care, Eddie's attorney, William Belter, was back in Wautoma, making a most surprising disclosure. According to Belter, Eddie's week of confinement in jail had allowed him to engage in some deep introspection—"amateur psychological probing," as Belter put it—which had led him to nothing less than the ultimate source of his troubles. All by himself, Gein had solved the mystery of his madness. The news story that appeared in the next day's issue of the *Madison Capital Times* summed up the results of Gein's self-analysis in its headline: "GEIN DIAGNOSES OWN CASE: BLAMES DOG."

What Gein had described to his attorney was the distressing incident he and his mother had witnessed back in 1945, when, having gone to a neighboring farm to purchase some straw, they had come upon the owner in the process of beating a puppy to death. Gein told Belter about the woman who had come rushing out of the farmhouse, screaming at the man to stop, and how upset his mother had been by the incident, primarily because the woman "wasn't married to the farmer" and "shouldn't have been at his house."

As a result of this unfortunate episode, Gein was convinced, Augusta had suffered her second stroke, the one that had killed her. And it was the unbearable loneliness caused by his mother's death which had, he felt, driven him to dreadful extremes.

The headline of the *Capital Times* story, however, turned out to be misleading in one important respect, because it wasn't the dog that Eddie blamed for his downfall. Nor was it the farmer who had brutalized the pup. "Oddly," Belter commented, "he blames the woman. If she hadn't been there, his mother wouldn't have had the stroke, and he wouldn't have been left alone."

Eddie's habit of blaming life's troubles on the wickedness of women was, as Dr. Schubert and his staff were about to find out, a hallmark of his derangement. Certainly, his identification of the unmarried farm woman—whose greatest crime was her frantic attempt to prevent the brutal slaughter of a puppy—was patently insane.

Still, his self-diagnosis, his powerful, if dimly defined, sense that a baneful woman was at the root of his problems, was not, in itself, inaccurate.

Eddie was simply too far gone to recognize the real culprit, the one who had truly driven him insane.

# 30

*"We're all human and make mistakes. We could have made the same mistakes."*

From a sermon on the Gein crimes delivered by Rev. John Schmitt of St. Paul's Church in Plainfield, Sunday, November 24, 1957

Sunday, November 23, was a piercingly cold but brilliant day, with a cloudless, crystalline sky. The sunlight glaring off the snow-crusted ground was sharp enough to hurt. It was the final day of the 1957 deer season, and hunters hoping for a last crack at a buck headed out to the woods in droves.

But the hunters weren't the only ones to hit the road early that morning. Beginning just after daybreak, the highways cutting through central Wisconsin were filled with vehicles that carried, not groups of men geared up for a day in the woods, but parties of sightseers from around the state, all of them headed in the same direction.

Throughout the day, a seemingly endless procession of cars—as many as four thousand by one estimate, most of them carrying entire families—crawled through the tiny community of Plainfield. Many of the passengers stopped for a bite to eat in local taverns and cafés; others pulled up at one of the town's filling stations, looking for fuel and directions. One local merchant grew so weary of answering the identical question again and again that he simply drew the same little map on every sheet of a hundred-page notepad and, as soon as a car pulled up to his store, tore off a copy and handed it to the driver, without exchanging a word.

It was a perfect day for a family outing, and all these eager sightseers had driven for hours just to take a peek at Wisconsin's latest and hottest roadside attraction—the dilapidated building that served as residence and slaughterhouse for the "mad butcher of Plainfield."

Not that there was much for them to see—just a forlorn old farmhouse with a buckled porch, boarded-up windows, and rusted bits of farming equipment littering the snow. Deputies were posted on the property to keep traffic moving and turn away any curiosity seekers who tried approaching the house. The pilgrims had to content themselves with the view from the road. Still, a glimpse was all it took to get the feel of the place. Even in radiant sunlight, Eddie's home was unbearably bleak and dispiriting. It wasn't hard to imagine it as a breeding ground for madness.

Apart from the sentries, the farm seemed utterly deserted. But though the sightseers had no way of knowing it, there was, in fact some important activity going on there that day. Seven men—Sheriff Herbert Wanerski and six other law officers from Portage County—were digging up and transferring into two-foot-high cardboard barrels the enormous ash pile that Gein had pointed out to them the day before. By the time they were done, they had filled up nine of the containers, which would be transported to the crime lab for analysis.

Other items would be forwarded to the crime lab, too, for the pile contained more than ashes. In the course of the dig, Wanerski and his men came upon a number of charred teeth and blackened bits of bone. It was clear to the investigators that Mary Hogan wasn't the only person whose incinerated remains had ended up in Eddie's ash heap. Even at a glance, they could see that there were far more fragments than could have possibly come from a single human being.

With hundreds of cars making their way down Main Street on that bright Sabbath morning (many of them slowing to a virtual halt as they passed the Worden hardware store), it would have been impossible for any of Plainfield's citizens to put the Gein horrors out of their thoughts. The nightmare was simply inescapable. Even in their houses of worship, the townspeople couldn't shut it out.

In the Methodist Episcopal Church, the memory of Bernice Worden's funeral was still fresh in the minds of her fellow parishioners, who had set up a special fund to purchase a new stained-glass window in honor of the murdered woman. In other churches, the pastors attempted to come to terms with the Gein crimes in the course of their Sunday sermons. "Everybody has been wondering how such a great sin could take place in our very midst," said Rev. David Wisthols of the First Baptist Church. "But everybody has sinned, even if he is not guilty of murder." Father John Schmitt of St. Paul's Catholic Church also urged his congregation to keep the inevitable moral shortfalls of humanity in mind. Every person is liable to error, he insisted, and any of us "could have made the same mistakes" as Ed Gein did. Both clergymen urged their parishioners to look upon their fallen neighbor, Edward Gein, with as much compassion and understanding as they could muster.

But however much they might have agreed with such sentiments in principle, the townsfolk of Plainfield weren't about to forgive and forget.

Elsewhere in the Midwest, a criminologist named Lois Higgens, president of the International Association of Policewomen, was drawing a very different moral from the Gein case. To Officer Higgens, the case was an object lesson, not in the innate sinfulness of human nature, but in the evils of modern-day American culture. Noting that any highly publicized murder is likely to set off a cycle of copycat killings, Higgens predicted that the Gein case would lead to "a rampage of bizarre crimes" throughout the country.

What Higgens found most alarming, however, was not the prospect of a nationwide Gein-inspired orgy of violence but rather the widely reported fact that Eddie had been an avid reader of crime magazines and similarly lurid publications. To Higgens, the Gein atrocities could be traced directly to the harmful influence of such material on a dangerously impressionable mind, and her plan was to travel to Plainfield in order to collect firsthand information for a series of lectures on the dangers of crime magazines and horror comics—publications which, she maintained, offered their readers nothing less than "short courses in murder, cannibalism, necrophilia, and sadism."

In the meantime, while the clergymen were praying, the criminologists predicting, and the sightseers craning their necks for a better view of Eddie's house, preparations were under way to carry out the next and most emotionally charged phase of the Gein investigation: the digging up of caskets to check out Eddie's grave-robbing claim.

Throughout Sunday, District Attorney Kileen and officials from both Waushara and Portage counties continued to review the list of graves Gein had provided. Kileen revealed to reporters that Gein's nocturnal forays had been conducted not only in the Plainfield cemetery but in Spiritland cemetery in the nearby town of Almond as well and that over the course of several years, Gein had made, by his own reckoning, a total of more than forty visits to the two graveyards. On all but nine of those occasions, according to Eddie, he had turned back without attempting to get at a corpse. The question now confronting the authorities was which of the nine supposedly violated graves to check.

The decision to disinter the coffin of Mrs. Eleanor Adams seemed firm, but as of Sunday afternoon, Kileen and his colleagues were still undecided about the other names on Eddie's list. But if the DA was unable to say precisely which caskets would be dug up, he was unequivocal about the exhumation itself.

On Tuesday morning, graves would be opened in the Plainfield cemetery—with or without the permission of the relatives.

# 31

*"The twelvemonth and a day being up*
*The dead began to speak:*
*'Oh who sits weeping on my grave,*
*And will not let me sleep?'"*

"The Unquiet Grave"

Something was happening at the cemetery.

In spite of Kileen's announcement that the graves would be examined on Tuesday, Ed Marolla, editor of the *Plainfield Sun*, decided to drive out to the cemetery first thing Monday morning, having heard rumors that the exhumations might, in fact, be carried out earlier as a way of circumventing the press. Sure enough, when he arrived at the graveyard entrance—a wrought-iron gateway topped with a filigreed sign—he was stopped by law officers.

What, Marolla asked, was going on? The officers refused to say. But as the newspaperman stood there, trying to assess the situation, a pickup truck drove up and entered the cemetery, followed closely by two workmen carrying shovels and spades.

It didn't take long for word to spread. Within an hour or so, a crowd of newsmen had descended on the graveyard, only to find it ringed by a contingent of law-enforcement officials posted there for the sole purpose of keeping the media away. Three of the five roads leading into the pine-studded cemetery had been chained. The remaining two were guarded by deputy sheriffs.

One enterprising reporter had come equipped with a tall ladder, which he leaned against the cemetery fence and mounted to its highest rung. But even from that elevated vantage point, he couldn't make out very much. A knot of men was gathered around a grave site, but the plot they were examining was too far inside the cemetery to be clearly perceived from the perimeter.

The newsmen, however, were not so easily deterred. By mid-morning, a single-engine airplane carrying a cameraman from the *Milwaukee Journal* was circling the cemetery. But the authorities had anticipated just such a stratagem and had come prepared to counter it. By ten A.M., when the digging began, a tentlike canopy had been erected over the burial plot of Mrs. Eleanor Adams, so that the work of removing her casket from what was supposed to have been its final resting place could proceed in as much privacy as possible.

The gathering at the grave site consisted of District Attorney Earl Kileen, Sheriff Art Schley, Deputy Arnie Fritz, Plainfield village president Harold Collins, mortician and cemetery director Ray Goult, Floyd Adams (the deceased woman's widower) along with his son and son-in-law, Allan Wilimovsky of the State Crime Lab accompanied by a pair of colleagues, and two experienced gravediggers, sexton Pat Danna and an assistant named Don Wallner.

Standing there on that bleak wintry morning, more than one member of that somber company was struck by two details in regard to Eleanor Adams's grave: its proximity to the burial place of Augusta Gein and Mrs. Adams's simple headstone inscription, which consisted of her name, the dates of her birth and death, and then, at the very top of the marker, a single word which must have resonated with a special meaning to a man like Eddie Gein—"Mother."

A cold wind blew that morning, and the frozen crust of snow that covered the ground made the digging hard going for Danna and his assistant. Even so, the job didn't take long. The skeptics who had scoffed at the notion that a little man like Eddie Gein could, in the course of a few hours, dig down to a coffin buried six feet in the soil had failed to take account of a crucial fact. It was true that the coffins themselves lay fairly deep underground. But the coffins were enclosed in either concrete vaults or wooden boxes. And the tops of those containers lay little more than two feet below the surface.

As a result, it took Danna and Wallner only an hour of digging before their shovels scraped the top of the rough wooden box that contained the casket of Mrs. Adams. It was immediately apparent to the observers that a determined grave robber could have easily reached his goal in a fairly short time, particularly if the job had been done when the grave was fresh and the ground wasn't frozen.

Gein had already divulged to his attorney that he had plundered Mrs. Adams's coffin on the very night of its interment, before the grave had even been completely filled in. And Eleanor Adams had died in the summer, on August 26, 1951.

As the diggers began to remove the last few inches of sandy soil from the cover boards of the crude wooden box, Kileen braced himself. He still entertained serious doubts about Gein's claim and fully expected to be confronted that morning with the awful sight and fetor of a long-buried cadaver. But the instant the box cover came into view, he, along with the other witnesses staring into the dankness of the newly opened grave, saw that something was amiss.

The cover had clearly been tampered with. It was split lengthwise in two.

It was the work of a moment for Danna and Wallner to remove the two rotting pieces of cover. Inside the box lay Mrs. Adams's wooden coffin. Dirt was scattered across its top. The workmen reached in and lifted the lid.

The huddling group stared wordlessly into the coffin.

The coffin was empty. Except, that is, for one object that lay on the spotted satin lining.

That object was a twelve-inch crowbar.

As Floyd Adams, Eleanor's widower, would later remark to a crowd of reporters, "Everything was there but the body."

The plundered grave was photographed. The crime lab people took possession of the crowbar. Then the diggers refilled the grave, and the group moved thirty yards across the cemetery to the second of the selected sites.

It was the burial place of Mrs. Mabel Everson, who had died of a lingering illness at the age of sixty-nine on April 15, 1951, just a few months before the death of Eleanor Adams.

Once again, Danna and Wallner set about their task. Once again, the job took about an hour. This time, however, Kileen and the others had their answer even before the diggers got down to the top of the rough wooden box in which the coffin was encased.

Fifteen inches or so below the surface lay a pile of eroded human bones—a jaw, a section of skull, part of a leg, and a scattering of smaller fragments. The diggers also turned up an upper and a lower dental plate, a scrap of clothing with a store label still attached, and a gold wedding band.

As soon as the officials laid eyes on this grim collection of remnants, they knew that it was all they would find of Mrs. Mabel Everson.

The digging resumed. Another foot down, and the workmen had reached the crude wooden box cover. This time, none of the men was the least bit surprised to see that it had been chiseled in two, crossways.

Nor were they surprised when the coffin lid was removed to reveal nothing inside but the moldering lining.

Several of the men did wonder about the bones they had found. What were Mrs. Everson's remains doing there, outside her casket? But Eddie had already confessed that he had been troubled from time to time by "pangs of conscience" following his nocturnal forays and, on several occasions, had journeyed back to the cemetery to return the stolen bodies—or at least those parts he had no further use for—to their graves. The grisly odds and ends uncovered in Mrs. Everson's plot only served to confirm Eddie's story.

The entire operation took only two and a half hours. At twelve-thirty P.M., the chilled and somber crew of investigators left the graveyard to meet with the mob of reporters, clamoring for the results of the exhumations. To a certain extent, Kileen could only have been relieved. The awful experience he had steeled himself for had not materialized. He had been spared the spectacle and stink of human decay. But the discoveries he and the others had made that morning were, in their own way, every bit as dreadful.

"I won't open any more graves if I can help it," Kileen told the newsmen. "As far as I'm concerned, this verifies Gein's story."

There could be no more doubt about it. For years following his mother's passing, Eddie Gein had tried to slake his unbearable loneliness by seeking companionship in the community of the dead.

# 32

*" 'Tis I, my love, sits on your grave*
*And will not let you sleep,*
*For I crave one kiss of your clay-cold lips,*
*And that is all I seek."*

"The Unquiet Grave"

Though Eddie freely admitted to grave robbing and didn't hesitate to supply the authorities with information—a complete list of his victims, the dates of his raids, and a detailed account of his methods—he never spoke about any sexual activity with the dead, except to deny that he had made use of the bodies in that way. Indeed, when asked whether he had ever performed sex on a corpse, he reacted indignantly—not, however, because the notion of copulating with the cadaver of a sixty-nine-year-old invalid seemed monstrous to him but rather because it seemed so unhygienic. He had avoided sexual relations with the unearthed bodies, he told authorities, because "they smelled too bad."

No one can say for certain exactly what Eddie did to the bodies once he had them in the privacy of his home—besides, that is, dissecting them, preserving their parts, and, on occasion, arraying himself in their skin. But it is possible to draw some inferences by examining his crimes in light of similar cases. Gein would go to his own grave insisting that, besides masturbation, he had never had a sexual experience of any kind in his life. Nevertheless, his cravings and compulsions clearly fall under the category of necrophilia, that perversion which Richard von Krafft-Ebing, in his classic study *Psychopathia Sexualis*, calls the most horrible of all the "aberrations of the sexual instinct."

The most thoroughly documented instance of this aberration—
"the classic case of necrophiliac perversion," as one authority calls
it—is that of a young French soldier known as "Sergeant Bertrand,"
who was born in 1822 and commenced his ghoulish career at the
age of twenty-three. Out for a stroll near his garrison one afternoon
in 1846, Bertrand was passing by a cemetery when he happened to
notice a half-filled grave. A physician who later studied him, a man
by the name of Epaulard, describes what happened next: "In the
most horrible excitement, without thinking that he might be seen, it
was in broad daylight, he tore open the grave with the shovel and
began in a frenzy, for want of another instrument, to strike into the
dead body with the shovel. He made such a noise that a workman
who was busy near the graveyard came in curiosity to the entrance.
When B. saw him, he laid himself close to the dead body in the
grave and remained quiet for a short time. While the workman was
bringing the authorities, he covered the corpse again and left by the
cemetery wall. . . . Two days later, he dug out the grave once more
with his hands, but now on a rainy night. His hands were bleeding,
but he dug until he had the lower part of the body exposed. He rent
it in pieces and then closed the grave once more."

Shortly afterward, Bertrand began digging up the corpses of
women and cutting out their genitals, an act that provided him with
the "greatest satisfaction."

He also began to perform coitus on the cadavers. At the Douai
cemetery, he dug up the corpse of an adolescent girl and there, as he
later described the experience, "gave myself up for the first time to
the mad embrace of a dead body. I cannot describe my sensations,
but all the joy procured by possession of a living woman was as
nothing in comparison with the pleasure I felt. I showered kisses
upon all parts of her body, pressed her to my heart with a
madman's frenzy. I overwhelmed her with the most passionate
caresses. After having regaled myself with this pleasure for a quarter
of an hour, I started to cut the body open and pulled out the entrails.
Then I replaced the body in the grave, covered it lightly with earth,
and returned to the barracks by the same road I had come."

Still, as intense as it was, the pleasure Bertrand derived from
having coitus with a corpse "was as nothing," he explained, to the
delight he felt in cutting it to pieces. "The urge to dismember the
bodies," he declared, "was incomparably more violent in me than
the urge to violate them."

Much of Eddie's behavior matches the insane actions of Sergeant
Bertrand and others of his kind. Even Gein's attitude toward his

corpse collecting—which, in spite of occasional twinges of guilt, he didn't regard as a particularly serious crime—fits the pattern. According to one authority, the necrophile is "likely to feel, when he attempts to analyze his own behavior, that he could not have done otherwise, that he was driven by forces quite beyond his control, and that there is, therefore, no basis for remorse or guilt; also, he 'didn't hurt anybody.'"

There is the case, for example, of the infamous French necrophile, Henri Blot, a pleasant-looking fellow of twenty-six who was in the habit of falling into a "profound sleep, or coma, or trance state" after digging up and performing coitus on the cadavers of young women in the Saint-Ouen cemetery. On one of these occasions, Blot passed out so completely following his ghoulish act that the next morning, cemetery workers discovered him lying fast asleep beside a ravished corpse. Brought to trial, Blot displayed an astonishing nonchalance about his behavior and (in the words of one commentator) "won a certain immortality for himself" in the annals of psychopathology when, after being rebuked by the judge for the "depravity of his offense," he responded loftily, "How would you have it? Every man to his own tastes. Mine is for corpses."

Eddie, too, as it turned out, felt that he was driven to his ghoulish activities by an irresistible force, which he experienced and described to his interrogators as an "evil spirit" invading his mind from someplace outside himself. He also confessed to another motive for his graveyard expeditions. Eddie had first been impelled to the Plainfield cemetery by a conviction that he possessed the power to raise the dead.

In this belief, he was similar to another notorious deviant, a young man named Viktor Ardisson, who was born in 1872 and, at the age of twenty-eight, after having pursued his perverse activities for more than nine years, was caught and convicted when his neighbors complained to the police of a terrible stench emanating from his house. The source of this odor turned out to be the cadaver of a three-and-a-half-year-old girl that Ardisson had brought home from the graveyard a week before and (until the body had reached such an advanced state of decay that he "no longer ventured to touch it") performed cunnilingus on, believing, in the words of the physician who examined him, that "this sort of caress could wake the dead."

Other features of Eddie's behavior can be found in the case histories of "classic" necrophiles. Like Eddie, many of these deviants derive intense, fetishistic satisfaction from possessing specific parts of their victims. Before Ardisson was arrested, for example, he had dug up and decapitated the corpse of a thirteen-year-old girl and carried home her head, which he kept for so long that it eventually "underwent a kind of mummification." Ardisson would speak to this prized possession in the tenderest tones, smother it with kisses, and call it "my little bride."

Another necrophile, a middle-aged laborer, "first gratified himself sexually upon a corpse, then in a fury, hacked the body in pieces and took away with him the severed breasts and genital portions of the body, including the anus." In another, very similar case, a forty-three-year-old man named Albert Beyerlin "used a dead woman for sexual intercourse, then slit open the abdomen, cut out the breasts and sexual parts of the corpse, and still carried them in his pocket the next day."

Cases have been reported of necrophiles who were particularly attracted to the hair of the dead and collected their scalps (as did Eddie Gein). In another case, described by R.E.L. Masters, the individual "derived his gratification from eating the nail trimmings of corpses."

There is one last but all-important trait which Eddie shared with many other necrophiles. Almost without exception, writes Masters, the necrophile is a man who is "quite incapable of making an effective sexual approach to a living woman."

Lodged in Central State Hospital, Eddie Gein was about to undergo a monthlong battery of tests to determine the question of his sanity. But Dr. Schubert and his staff could have resolved that issue simply by consulting Krafft-Ebing, who, in speaking of necrophilia, writes that "this horrible kind of sexual indulgence is so monstrous that the presumption of a psychopathic state is, under all circumstances, justified." The discovery of the empty graves in the Plainfield cemetery had not only substantiated Eddie's story but earned him a permanent place in the standard histories of sexual psychopathology. The list that included some of mankind's most deranged sex criminals—Bertrand, Ardisson, Beyerlin, and their fellow necrosadists—had just been augmented with the name of Edward Gein.

# 33

*"Halloween came a little late this year."*
JIM MCBRIAR, Plainfield resident

To most of those following the unfolding of the Gein story, Monday's graveyard revelations represented the shocking denouement. To be sure, further developments in the case continued to make headlines throughout the Midwest. But as far as the public could tell, the true climax had occurred when Mrs. Adams's coffin had been opened to reveal nothing inside but Eddie Gein's twelve-inch pinchbar. What resolution could be more dramatic? And for a while, at least, it looked as though the public might be right.

Indeed, it looked for a while as though the Gein investigation might come to a complete halt with the exhumations. Under the state law of the time, any county requesting the assistance of the Crime Lab in a murder case was obligated to pay fifty percent of the lab's expenses. It was costing the Crime Lab about one thousand dollars a day to analyze the truckload of evidence that had been gathered at Gein's farm. Thus, a heavy financial burden had suddenly fallen on Waushara, a sparsely populated and unprosperous county.

Earl Kileen had already made it clear that Waushara couldn't afford to foot the bill for a prolonged investigation into every crime Gein may have committed. Assuming Gein was found sane by the experts, the district attorney had more than enough evidence to convict him of Bernice Worden's murder. The doubts about Gein's grave-robbing claims had been definitively resolved. As far as Kileen was concerned, there was no need to continue a probe that was proving so costly to his county.

Other officials, however—particularly Crime Lab director Charles

175

Wilson—took a very different position. To Wilson, the fact that some of Eddie's body-part collection had been acquired at the local graveyard did not rule out the possibility that other of his "trophies" were the remnants of murder victims. Arguing that "bookkeeping considerations" should not interfere with a matter that was "of concern to all the citizens of the state," Wilson appealed to Governor Vernon Thompson. Thompson's response was prompt and decisive. On Monday afternoon, directly following the disinterments at the Plainfield cemetery, the governor announced that he was ordering Attorney General Stewart Honeck to take immediate charge of the Gein investigation.

"Developments in the case now indicate a state-wide concern in ascertaining the facts," Thompson said. His order—which also ensured that the state would provide all the necessary funds for the Crime Lab to complete its work on the case—guaranteed that the investigation would continue until, in the governor's words, "the possibilities of additional homicides" committed by Gein had been thoroughly "exhausted."

Honeck's first act as the new head of the Gein investigation was to announce that at the suggestion of Charles Wilson, Gein would be taken back to Madison for another lie detector test.

Honeck's announcement was made to the press early Wednesday morning, November 27, following a closed-door meeting with Wilson, Kileen, and John Haka, district attorney of Portage County. The authorities wanted to question Gein about the bones and other objects unearthed during the exhumation—"valuable evidence," according to Honeck, which might shed more light on the crimes. At present, the attorney general couldn't say whether more coffins would be opened. But if Gein's role in any other homicides could only be "determined by digging up more graves," he declared, "rest assured that they will be dug."

The state, Honeck continued, was "proceeding on the assumption that Gein would be found sane and would have to stand trial," first for the slaying of Bernice Worden and then for that of Mary Hogan (although Gein had yet to be charged with the second crime).

There was another assumption that the state was operating under: that those two murders were not the only ones Eddie was responsible for, that Gein, as Honeck put it, "may have been involved in more deaths."

Accompanied by attendants from the state mental hospital, Eddie arrived at the crime lab headquarters in Madison later that morning for a polygraph test. Though it lasted well into the afternoon, the examination failed to produce any startling revelations. The authorities did learn that one of the nine graves Eddie had pillaged was located in yet another rural cemetery, the one belonging to the little town of Hancock, several miles south of Plainfield in Waushara County. They also confirmed that, in the words of the statement released later that day by Attorney General Honeck, "the subject's activities which involved the disturbance of graves and murder, did not involve any male victims."

Much of the questioning focused on the matter of a possible accomplice, but, in spite of persistent rumors that Eddie had been assisted by a shadowy figure named "Gus," the lie test seemed to substantiate Gein's claim that he had performed his ghoulish activities alone.

Gein was also interrogated one more time about the disappearances of Evelyn Hartley, Georgia Weckler, and Victor Travis. Again, the polygraph results excluded him as a suspect.

At four-thirty P.M., after seven and a half hours of questioning, Gein began complaining of a headache. The examination was halted, and the prisoner was transported back to his room in Central State Hospital.

On Thursday, November 28, families all across America sat down to their turkey dinners and pumpkin pies, but to most of Plainfield's citizens, it didn't feel much like Thanksgiving. As more than one of them remarked, it felt more like Halloween.

Perhaps people were simply glutted on horror. Perhaps, after the nonstop nightmare of the previous two weeks, the ghastly had come to seem run-of-the-mill. Whatever the reason, the news that still more skeletal remains had been uncovered on the Gein farm no longer seemed very sensational. Certainly, it wasn't shocking enough to unsettle a public that had grown used to reading daily descriptions of butchered grandmothers, human-face wall decorations, flesh-upholstered furniture, and abducted cadavers.

The new discovery was made on Friday, November 29. Herbert Wanerski, sheriff of Portage County, and his deputy, George Cummings, had learned about the location of a garbage trench in a wooded area on Gein's property, about a quarter-mile from the farmhouse. According to some of Eddie's neighbors, the strange little recluse was in the habit of going out there with a shovel at all hours of the day and night to bury things. Up until two weeks ago, the neighbors had assumed he was burying garbage.

Equipped with shovels, Wanerski and his deputy drove out to the farm on Friday afternoon and hiked to the spot pointed out by Gein's neighbors. It didn't take long to locate the forty-foot trench. They began at one end, digging up the trench to a depth of two feet. Thirty minutes later, they came upon the bones, scattered in the dirt among rusted tin cans and decomposing clumps of household rubbish.

Even at a glance, it was clear that—though some pieces were missing (there was no rib cage, for example, and only one foot)—the remains they had unearthed constituted a nearly complete human skeleton. When the two men bent to examine its skull, they were struck almost immediately by two things. The first was the condition of the teeth or, more precisely, of one particular tooth. It was a molar, and it was crowned with gold. The second was the skull's size. It seemed noticeably larger than the other heads found inside Eddie's farmhouse.

Further digging turned up a three-by-five-inch patch of denim with a brass button attached to it and several stiffened pieces of leathery material that appeared upon inspection to be dried-up chunks of human flesh. At three-forty P.M., the officers abandoned their excavations but returned the next morning with a party of fifteen men, including Sheriff Frank Searles of Adams County and Sheriff Schley. This time, however, though the digging was conducted at various places around the farm, nothing was found but a few additional bones lying close to the spot where the remains had been discovered on Friday.

News of Friday's find set off widespread speculation that the bones had belonged to one of the men who had disappeared from the area in 1952—the mysterious stranger known as Ray Burgess, the last person to be seen in the company of the missing Adams County farmer Victor "Bunk" Travis.

To some of the investigators, the dimensions of the skull suggested that, unlike the others in Eddie's collection, it was that of an adult male. And Burgess was known to have had a gold tooth. Indeed, a week before the ill-fated hunting trip (during which the pair had simply vanished from sight after setting off to hunt the property of Gein's neighbor Lars Thompson), Burgess had drawn considerable attention to himself at a local tavern by flashing a broad gold-toothed grin and a wad of hundred-dollar bills.

The discovery of a skull with a gold-crowned molar in Eddie Gein's garbage trench lent weight to the suspicion that in spite of the results of the polygraph tests, which seemed to exonerate Gein, the "killer ghoul" had been responsible for the disappearance of the two hunters. By early Saturday, rumors had begun to spread through Plainfield that the missing men's car, which had vanished along with them, was hidden somewhere on Gein's land. A search party, led by Sheriff Schley and comprising officers from Waushara, Portage, and Adams counties, spent the better part of the day covering Gein's one-hundred-sixty-acre property on foot. But no car was ever found.

In the meantime, Attorney General Honeck met with the press to announce that in the opinion of the technicians at the crime lab, it was highly unlikely that the gold-toothed skull was Burgess's. Their belief—based on information Gein had supplied during his recent polygraph examination—was that the latest remains were those of still another cadaver taken from the Plainfield cemetery. Moreover, state authorities remained convinced that, as Honeck repeated, Gein's crimes did "not involve males."

And, indeed, once the new remains were conveyed to the crime lab, it took technicians only a day or two to confirm that they were the bones of an adult woman, thirty to fifty years old, whose corpse—like those of eleven other wives and mothers who had died in the Plainfield vicinity between 1947 and 1952—had been snatched from its grave.

The first of December was a Sunday very much like the previous one in Plainfield, with thousands of sightseers passing through town on their way out to the Gein farmstead. Throughout the afternoon, traffic was bumper to bumper on Main Street. Once again, however, rubberneckers hoping for a close look at the crime scene were severely disappointed. Indeed, security measures had been tightened up at the farm since Friday's discovery. Even Eddie's lawyer, William Belter, was turned away when he drove out to his client's home to examine the site of the latest find.

Belter had become the subject of a good deal of speculation in Plainfield. Rumor had it that as payment for his legal services, he would eventually come into possession of the Gein farm. Besides its inherent value, the property—and particularly the house itself— had suddenly acquired a new and possibly incalculable worth. It was known that various entrepreneurs had already inquired about purchasing the place, and the citizens of Plainfield were of the belief that the eventual owner, whoever that turned out to be, was likely to convert Eddie Gein's "house of horrors" into a tourist attraction. Some people pointed to the case of the Little Bohemia tavern, where John Dillinger had shot his way out of a police trap years before. The owner of the bar had reportedly gotten rich by charging curiosity seekers an admission fee. Needless to say, the prospect of having their little town become the home of a permanent Eddie Gein horror museum did not fill the good people of Plainfield with enthusiasm.

If there were still places in America that hadn't heard of the Gein crimes, that situation changed on Monday, December 2, when that week's issue of *Life* magazine hit the stands. The Gein case was the lead story, covered in a nine-page spread headlined "House of Horror Stuns the Nation." The text conveyed the gruesome substance of the case, and the accompanying illustrations—somber photographs of the hollow-cheeked killer, his grim decaying home, and the insanely cluttered rooms in which he dwelt—powerfully caught its American Gothic essence.

In the same week, the case also received detailed coverage in another major weekly, *Time* magazine, which—in contrast to the horror-stricken tones of the *Life* piece—adopted a distinctly sneering attitude toward Gein. The article described the killer ghoul (whose last name, the writer explained, "rhymes with wean") as an extreme case of "arrested development," a middle-aged "mamma's boy" whose fanatical, domineering mother had taught him to shun all women but herself.

After recounting the details of Bernice Worden's slaying and the appalling discoveries made inside his farm, the article cited the diagnoses of anonymous psychiatrists, who saw Gein "as the victim of a common conflict: while consciously he loved his mother and hated other women, unconsciously he hated her and loved others. She had subjected him to deep frustration. . . . For Gein, cutting up women who reminded him of his mother and preserving parts of them satisfied two contradictory urges: to bring her back to life and to destroy her as the source of his frustration."

The *Time* story concluded by noting that at the end of the previous week, Gein had been committed to Wisconsin's Central State Hospital for the Criminally Insane. There, according to the article, the experts hoped to solve what was perhaps the deepest of all the mysteries connected to the Gein case: "why Eddie Gein's childhood experiences, unfortunate but far from unique, exploded in his case into such horrendous crime."

# 34

*"The overall picture is not that of a well person."*
From the psychological profile of Edward Gein

Between November 25—two days after his admission to Central State Hospital—and December 18, Eddie underwent an exhaustive series of physical and psychological tests. The results of these examinations were compiled into a lengthy report, which was submitted to Judge Bunde the week before Christmas. This report is a fascinating document, containing the first truly substantial information about Gein, whose life and behavior had been the subject of so much ungrounded speculation.

The physical exams he was given were far more complete than any he had experienced in his life, certainly more thoroughgoing than the army physical he had received fifteen years earlier in Milwaukee during his only trip away from home. He was gone over from head to foot, every part of him weighed, measured, prodded, poked, X-rayed, and analyzed. His scalp was checked for vermin, his tonsils for inflammation, his rectum for hemorrhoids. A small lesion on his tongue was detected and duly recorded, and his testicles were palpated by hand ("pain elicited by pressure," the physician noted). Samples of his blood, urine, and spinal fluid were collected and analyzed.

On the whole—and in spite of the existence of a suspiciously enlarged lymph gland "in the left supraclavicular area" which the physician wanted biopsied—Eddie appeared to be in good health. His muscle tone was not what it had once been (indeed, the wiry little man was beginning to go to flab). Still, his weight—one hundred forty-one pounds—was only slightly above the ideal for a man of his height (sixty inches). His posture was poor (Eddie had been stoop-shouldered all his life), but his temperature, pulse, blood pressure, and respiration rates were normal. All in all, for a fifty-one-year-old man who had led what was in many ways a bitterly deprived life, he was in decent shape.

There were a few things the report took special note of. One was the soft, fleshy growth on Eddie's left eyelid, which, though nonmalignant, caused the eyelid to droop and contributed to the slightly quizzical simpleton's expression that Eddie so often wore. The physician was also struck by Eddie's constant and apparently psychosomatic complaints of headaches and nausea. Often during his examinations, he would begin to whine like a sickly old woman, insisting that his head hurt or that he was feeling sick to his stomach and needed a wheelchair to take him back to his ward.

And then there was the matter of the smells.

Eddie was always complaining of smelling "bad odors." When the doctor asked him to describe exactly what it was he smelled, Eddie thought for a while and then came up with the closest analogy.

"It smells," he said, "like flesh."

Following his physical exams, Eddie was put through a full battery of standardized psychological tests, beginning with the Wechsler Adult Intelligence Scale. His Verbal IQ was computed at 106, his Performance IQ at 89, and his Full Scale IQ at 99—a score that placed him in the "low average" category. According to Eddie's examiner, however—a psychologist named Robert Ellsworth—Gein possessed "a fair amount of information, a good vocabulary, and an ability to reason abstractly," all of which pointed "toward a higher intellectual potential, near the 'bright normal' level." The great discrepancy between his verbal and performance levels suggested to Ellsworth that Gein's functioning was impaired by a "strong emotional disturbance" which was probably "psychotic in nature."

Ellsworth's assessment of Eddie's intelligence seemed confirmed by the results of the Rorschach (or "inkblot") test, which indicated, again, that the subject was of "better than average intelligence" but functioning at an "inefficient" level. "The overall picture" that emerged from this test was, in Ellsworth's words, "not that of a well person but of one with insufficient ego, immaturity, conflict concerning identification, and possibly the presence of illogical thought processes."

Other tests administered by Ellsworth—Bender-Gestalt Designs, the Thematic Apperception Test, the Minnesota Multiphasic Personality Inventory, and more—brought to light other traits: a strong "feminine identification," "bizarre religious beliefs," a tendency to "project the blame for evil on some other person," and a strikingly immature level of sexuality characterized by "strong feelings of guilt."

All in all, Ellsworth concluded, the tests showed the patient to be "a very suggestible person who appears emotionally dull. Beneath that lies aggressiveness that may be expressed by inappropriate reactions that are followed by remorse and mild-manneredness. He is an immature person who withdraws and finds forming relationships with others difficult. He has rather rigid moral concepts which he expects others to follow. He is suspicious of others and tends to project blame for his own inadequacies onto others. His fantasy life is immature in nature, possibly he pictures himself as a much more adequate and bigger man than he is.

"Sexually he is a conflicted individual and is functioning on an immature level. Guilt feelings are great and repression is put to use quite frequently in this area.

"In general, it appears that this is basically a schizophrenic personality with several neurotic manifestations. At the present time, he is confused and has difficulty in looking at his situation realistically."

The report also included a "social history" of the patient, put together by hospital social worker Kenneth Colwell, who obtained most of his information from Gein, though he also drew on interviews he had conducted with some of Eddie's neighbors in Plainfield. Eddie, as always, was extremely cooperative. Indeed, he seemed deeply—almost touchingly—appreciative of all the attention he was receiving at the hospital. As Colwell put it, Gein seemed to "view the staff's professional approach as an acceptance of him personally that he has not experienced in his home community in many years." Colwell noted that Eddie talked "freely in a low voice, frequently with his head in his hands." Occasionally, however, Gein "professed confusion, partial loss of memory, as well as trouble distinguishing between what he remembers and what he was told."

The bulk of Colwell's report consisted of a brief review of Eddie's life—his family background, his schooling, the deaths of his parents and older brother, his relationship to the community. In terms of Eddie's psychological condition, however, the most illuminating part of Colwell's report is the section labeled "Sexual History":

Patient's early sexual information was given by the mother who impressed upon him the need for sexual abstinence prior to marriage. He indicated that she was not as strict in her admonitions against masturbation. He obtained additional information in a more uncouth manner from his classmates. He views not marrying, in part, as a family trait, saying that his brother did not marry, nor did two of his mother's brothers.

The patient gave more thought to marriage after the death of the mother and felt he would have married if he could only have found "the right girl." He rejected one girl after he learned that she could not get along with her mother and "I couldn't straighten her out on that. I almost fell in love with another girl, but found out that she had many affairs with other men. Morality is pretty low in Plainfield."

The patient also described the moral standards of his two victims. The first "was a dirty talker, operated a tavern, and people said she was in some crooked business." He states that the second victim wooed her husband away from another girl and married him shortly after the other girl committed suicide. (He became tearful when describing his sorrow for the other girl.) He went on to describe the husband's death as his just punishment and then relates that his victim broke up another marriage. His comments have a strong religious connotation. . . .

He indicated that he would not have gotten into his present difficulty if he had married, if the neighbors had treated him better, or if he had been able to sell his farm and travel. He stated that prior to the first grave robbing incident, he had been reading adventure stories of head hunters and cannibals. He related in detail one story of a man who had murdered a man, acquired his yacht and was later captured and killed by head hunters. He learned about shrunken heads, death masks, etc., from other similar stories.

He admitted to feelings of excitement during the grave robberies and describes periods when he felt he should return the bodies. There were also feelings that the bodies should be preserved and that he should care for them. When asked about the sexual aspects of this activity he commented on the great variations in age of the bodies. When it was pointed out that he was interested only in the bodies of women, he stated that the articles he read indicated that these heads were more valuable because of their longer hair.

The heart of the Central State document, however, consisted of three lengthy reports. The first was written by Schubert, who interviewed Gein on two occasions. Their first meeting took place on December 9, and, almost immediately, Schubert later wrote, Gein began speaking "about the difficulty which had brought him to the institution":

He rather vehemently stated that none of this would have happened if his neighbors had shown some interest in him and would have visited him. He stated that the only time the neighbors came to his home was when they wanted to borrow things. He complained about the neighbors playing "dirty deals." He applied this phrase to business dealings that he had had with one particular neighbor who had rented a field from him some years ago for $10.00 a year. This neighbor paid the rent for the first year but neglected to pay the rent for subsequent years. He claims that about five of his neighbors were constantly taking advantage of him and that they all owed him money. He denied that he had any difficulty with the people in Plainfield, although he said that many of them didn't appreciate the things that he did for them.

He complained of memory deficits and more specifically with regard to the crimes he is accused of committing. He stated that he is unable to recall any of the details of the murder of Mrs. Hogan and . . . is not clear on many of the details involved in the murder of Mrs. Worden. He vaguely remembers putting a cartridge, which he found in his pocket, in a rifle which he took from a rack in the Worden store, but he feels that her death was an accident because the gun must have discharged accidentally. He states that he does not remember putting the body in his truck and driving it to his home, although he admits that he must have been the one who did this.

His opinion of Mrs. Worden is that she was a rather disreputable woman who was known to have a bad reputation. To illustrate this opinion, he stated that, prior to the marriage of Mr. and Mrs. Worden, Mr. Worden was keeping company with the daughter of a dentist and that Mrs. Worden stole her future husband from this other woman, and that this woman subsequently killed herself with chloroform because of this. He denies that he blames Mrs. Worden for the girl's death, but he also stated that he feels Mrs. Worden received her just desert when her husband died of some blood dyscrasia and feels that this was in the nature of a punishment for her.

Much of the interview was spent in discussing his feelings about his mother. His mother was a very religious woman and his only description of her was that "she was good in every way." His mother suffered two strokes, and much of his time was spent in caring for her after the first stroke. He began to cry when he described his mother's infirmities and stated that "she didn't deserve all of her suffering."

His feelings for his father are completely negative. He stated that his father drank excessively and would abuse both him and his brother. . . .

With respect to his claims of memory deficits, he says that his lapses of memory started after the death of his mother. When asked specifically about his interests since the death of his mother, his only answer was that he wished he could have had more contact with other people. He stated that since the death of his mother he has had feelings that things around him were unreal and at one time, shortly after the death of the mother, he felt that he could raise the dead by will power. He also stated that he heard his mother talking to him on several occasions for about a year after she died. His mother's voice was heard while he was falling asleep.

He mentioned one unusual experience occurring two or three years ago in which he saw a forest with the tops of the trees missing and vultures sitting in the trees.

He feels that the death of Mrs. Worden was justified because she deserved to die, and he goes on to explain that he is actually fatalistic and that this whole sequence of events was ordained to happen.

Three days later, on December 12, Schubert concluded his examination of Gein.

He again denied any knowledge about the death of Mrs. Hogan and stated that he admitted this crime because this was what the investigators wished him to do. It was impossible to obtain a chronological series of events with regard to the death of Mrs. Worden. He specifically denied remembering the evisceration of the body.

He stated that he had violated nine graves and when questioned as to his reasons for doing this, he stated he thought it was because he wanted a remembrance of his mother. He denied any sexual relations with any of these bodies and gave as his reason for this that "they smelled too bad." He again admitted that, for a period of time after his mother's death, he felt he could arouse the dead by an act of will power. He claimed to have tried to arouse his dead mother by an act of will power and was disappointed when he was unsuccessful. He also admitted this sort of thing with some of the bodies which he had exhumed. . . .

There is ample reason to believe that his violation of the graves was in response to the demands of his fantasy life, which was motivated by his abnormally magnified attachment to his mother.

On December 13, the day after Schubert's second interview, Eddie was examined by the hospital's chief of medical services, Dr. R. Warmington. The record of that meeting sheds additional light on the bizarre operations of Gein's profoundly disordered mind.

After a brief review of the patient's family background, Dr. Warmington's report goes on to consider three major aspects of Gein's psychological condition—his personality makeup, mental status, and criminal motivation:

The subject is an introverted, odd, withdrawn personality that has had difficulty relating closely to other people. He also has shown some paranoid trends but on the other hand may have been duped and unfairly used on some occasions as he speaks of doing work for other farmers and failing to be paid for his labor. He is passive, inhibited, and somewhat evasive when questioned about the offense and may harbor deep-seated feelings of hostility.

He denies ever having had sexual experience and declares that in this connection he was taught the moral code by his mother that sexual experience before marriage was wrong— "If a woman is good enough for intercourse, she is good enough for marriage." . . .

Since coming here, the patient has been very tractable, cooperative and readily abides by the institution rules. Consciousness is clear, there is no history of epileptic seizures, orientation is correct in all fields and the train of thought is coherent and relevant but sometimes somewhat illogical. Faces have been seen by him in leaves and he spoke of hearing his mother's voice while in a twilight sleep, but it is uncertain if these should be designated as overt hallucinations.

No delusional material has been elicited but his behavior has been very unusual as he admits to excavating several bodies. During interviews he talked of using a rod to determine the nature of the rough box by its sound upon tapping and he also knew some of the exhumed people in life. They were all women of varying ages. The bodies were removed from three cemeteries—Plainfield, Spiritland, and Hancock—but some were returned after a short time because he became remorseful.

In other instances, he made the so-called masks from the head by removing the skin and separating it from the bones. The tissue in the back of the neck was cut and the cavity stuffed with papers or sawdust. One of these was placed in a cellophane bag but others were kept throughout the house. The unused parts of bodies were burned or buried and eating is denied. He also denied having sex relations with the bodies or parts of them as he declares the odor was offensive.

His memory is intact for most subjects but when emotionally charged situations are encountered there is a suggestion of a self-serving amnesia or vagueness. At times the remark was made—"It seems like a dream, impossible."

Mrs. Worden, in one interview, was described as being short, inconsiderate, and brusque, but during a later interview was declared to be a friendly, pleasant woman. Physical attraction for either woman was not admitted and he denied seriously attempting to escort Mrs. Worden to a roller skating rink. Mrs. Hogan was a tavern operator. It is gathered that she was regarded by the patient as being a rather poor representative of womankind and that he could have felt justified in shooting her because of his self-righteous, rigid attitude.

The motivation is elusive and uncertain but several factors

come to mind—hostility, sex, and a desire for a substitute for his mother in the form of a replica or body that could be kept indefinitely. He has spoken of the bodies as being like dolls and a certain comfort was received from their presence, although ambivalent feelings in this regard probably occurred. When questioned regarding the reasons for his bizarre conduct, no explanation is given but sex relations with the bodies has been denied several times. This does not seem to check with hearsay in which he admitted having sex activities with the cadavers.

He has been a lonely man, particularly since the death of his mother, and some drive, uncertain at this time, may have arisen in this area to account for his misconduct.

By December 18, Eddie's term at Central State was drawing to a close. On that date, Gein was brought before a board of specialists for a final round of questioning. Six doctors took part in the session—Schubert, Warmington, a psychiatrist named Larimore, a physician named Goetsch, Dr. Leonard Ganser of the Department of Health and Social Services, and Dr. H. J. Colgan, clinical director of the Winnebago State Hospital. Also present were the hospital's psychologist, Robert Ellsworth, and Kenneth Colwell, the social worker who had researched Gein's family background.

The purpose of the meeting, which lasted several hours, was to arrive at a consensus regarding Gein's mental condition. As a result, the record of this session represents perhaps the single most significant feature of the Central State psychiatric report, since the highly charged issue of Gein's legal sanity would largely be determined on the basis of the board's diagnosis.

A lengthy period of questioning was conducted in which each of the staff members took part. It was determined through this questioning that the patient had been living a withdrawn and solitary existence for a number of years and, since the death of his mother in 1945, has had little social contact with the people in his community. His description of his mother was that she was as good a woman as it was possible for anyone to be, and through her teachings he developed a rigid moralistic attitude regarding women and the use of alcoholic beverages. He claimed that women in general were tainted with evil and should be shunned as much as possible. . . .

There was a very marked sexual preoccupation through-out most of his answers to questions. When asked what was responsible for his activities, he stated that it was all due to "a force built up in me." He feels that this force was in the nature of an evil spirit which influenced him to dig up graves.

With respect to the charge which brought him to the institution, namely, the death of Mrs. Worden, he stated that he had been chosen as an instrument of God in carrying out what fate had ordained should happen to this woman. . . .

There were numerous complaints of physical illness. He complained of headaches, sore throat, chest pains, abdominal distress, and constipation. It was felt by the staff that this symptomatology could best be classified as a pseudoneurotic schizophrenic process.

He readily admitted that he had heard his mother's voice telling him to be good several years after her death and that, on one occasion, he had experienced what was probably an olfactory hallucination, in that he smelled what he thought was decaying flesh in the surrounding environment of his property. Upon occasion, he stated that he has seen faces in piles of leaves.

It was the consensus of the staff's opinion that this man is best diagnosed as a "schizophrenic reaction of the chronic undifferentiated type." Because his judgment is so influenced by his envelopment in a world of fantasy, he is not considered to know the difference between right and wrong. His concept of the nature of his acts is markedly influenced by the existence of the delusional material concerned in particular with the idea that outside forces are responsible for what occurred. Because of his extreme suggestibility, he is not completely or fully capable of acting in his own behalf or in consultation with his attorney.

This man, in the opinion of the staff, is legally insane and not competent to stand trial at this time.

Eddie's thirty-day observation period was officially over on December 22, but, for all practical purposes, the staff meeting on the eighteenth marked the real end of the examination and evaluation process. On December 19, Eddie's medical and psychiatric records were assembled into a package and forwarded to the Honorable

Herbert A. Bunde with a cover letter by Schubert, which summed up the final opinion of the staff.

"Mr. Gein," Schubert wrote, "has been suffering from a schizophrenic process for an undetermined number of years." As a result, "although Mr. Gein might voice knowledge of the difference between right and wrong, his ability to make such judgment would always be influenced by the existent mental illness. He would not be capable of fully realizing the consequence of any act because he would not be a free agent to determine either the nature or the consequence of acts which resulted from disturbed and abnormal thinking."

"Because of these findings," Schubert concluded, "I must recommend his commitment to Central State Hospital as insane."

# 35

*"In many ways, this patient has lived a psychotic life for many years. He has substituted human parts for the companionship of human beings and at the same time has gone through the superficial existence so that in the eyes of people around him he appeared quite rational. This can happen with chronic schizophrenic people."*

DR. MILTON MILLER

Voyeurism, fetishism, transvestism, and necrophilia weren't the only concepts from the field of psychopathology that the Gein case introduced to a wider public. Another was schizophrenia. For the most part, however, that term tended to be used very loosely in various press accounts of Gein's mental condition. As a result, the public received an extremely oversimplified, even distorted, idea of the nature of Eddie's disorder.

As early as November 22, in quoting the views of the Chicago psychiatrist Edward Kelleher, the *Milwaukee Journal* defined schizophrenia as a "split personality"—a popular misconception perpetuated by the work that ensured the Gein crimes a permanent place in American popular mythology, *Psycho.* (In Robert Bloch's original novel, the protagonist actually possesses three separate personalities; Norman, "the little boy who needed his mother"; Norma, "the mother who could not be allowed to die"; and Normal, "the adult Norman Bates.")

Though certain psychotics do, in fact, suffer from what is known as "multiple personality disorder," the schizophrenic personality isn't so much split as shattered. Among the main symptoms of this disorder (all of which were manifested by Gein) are hallucinations and delusions (such as the sense that one's impulses and actions "are not one's own but are imposed by some external force"); bizarre beliefs (such as the conviction that one can raise the dead through willpower); extreme social isolation; "marked impairment" of functioning in "such areas as work, social relations, and self-care"; and gender confusion, uncertainty about one's sexual identity.

There is one way, however, in which schizophrenics often do experience a pathologically severe "split," and that is in relation to their parents, most often their mothers. According to psychoanalytic theory, people who are raised by severely disturbed, unloving mothers often deal with that situation by removing from their consciousness the memory of their painful childhood experiences. Dr. Silvano Arieti, one of the leading authorities on schizophrenia, has written: "The child who suffers on account of his contacts with the rejecting parent, generally the mother, tries desperately to preserve a good image of the parent. He wants to feel that the parent is good. If the parent is punitive and anxiety-arousing, it is not because she is malevolent but because he, the child, is bad: Mother is right in being harsh and strict with him and showing how bad he is. . . . The preservation of the good image of the parent is made possible by the removal from consciousness of the most unpleasant traits of the parent. Thus, the child will have two images of the parent: the good image, which is conscious, and the bad image, which will remain unconscious."

To a certain extent, of course, all people experience a certain amount of ambivalence—of both love and anger—toward their mothers. But the schizophrenic is often someone who experiences these mixed feelings in a particularly acute form—who, even as a grownup, possesses the radically split perception of a little child. Consciously, he views his mother as "all-gratifying, supreme, sublime, and perfect." But at a much deeper level of his mind, he sees her as the exact opposite—a figure of utter evil.

Eddie Gein represents a classic case of such a split. In his conscious mind, Augusta was a paragon of maternal virtue—"as good a woman as it was possible for a person to be." All the hatred he felt for her—all the fury at the terrible mistreatment he had suffered at her hands—he shoved away from his awareness, projecting it onto other women who reminded him of his mother. (It is significant that both Mary Hogan and Bernice Worden not only bore a vague physical likeness to Augusta Gein but also resembled her in another crucial respect: they were no-nonsense businesswomen, as

Augusta had been during Eddie's childhood in La Crosse.) And on those two women—the innocent, unwitting surrogates for Eddie's malevolent mother—the little man wreaked his revenge.

Even his grave-robbing activities were prompted to a large extent by this deeply psychotic split. On the one hand, digging up the corpses of middle-aged mother-substitutes represented Gein's demented effort to rescue Augusta from death. At the same time, the atrocities he performed on the bodies of his victims was a deranged form of retribution, a crazed attempt to get back at his mother for the lifetime's worth of torture she had inflicted on him.

# 36

*"If anybody was ever crazy, it was him."*

ROBERT E. SUTTON

His mental tests completed, Eddie was set to be returned to the Waushara County jailhouse on Monday, December 23—a depressing prospect to Arthur Schley, who wasn't eager to regain custody of Gein until the holidays were over. "I'd rather they keep him past next week," the sheriff explained to reporters. "After all, I've got a family, and I like to put a little Christmas into my family. But still, I'll do what they tell me to do."

Hoping to postpone Gein's return, Schley contacted Dr. Schubert, requesting an extension of the killer's commitment period until December 26. Schubert had no objections. Gein, Schubert told newsmen, had been a model patient—"cooperative, no source of difficulty." During Gein's free hours at the institution, when he wasn't undergoing one examination or another, he had been "permitted out in the rear yard and allowed to walk around." He had adjusted nicely to institutional life and "been accepted very well by the other patients."

Still, Schubert explained, it would require an official order from Judge Bunde to keep Gein at the mental hospital beyond December 22. As it turned out, the judge had no objections to prolonging Eddie's stay at Central State, either. In fact, after reviewing Schubert's report, he issued an order extending Gein's commitment for an indefinite period. He also released a statement which—though withholding any details of the psychiatric findings—summed up the major recommendations of the psychiatric staff.

"The court has received the report relative to Edward Gein from the Central State Hospital," the judge's statement began, "and has given it careful reading and study.

"There exists, based upon the report of experts at the Central State Hospital, definite opinion to the effect that Edward Gein is not mentally competent to stand trial. . . . Further summary hearings will be held at a date suitable to all parties when the defendant is available for such hearings. At that time, both the defense and the prosecution will have opportunity to produce expert testimony to aid the court in arriving at a determination. The court has no alternative but to depend upon the testimony of such experts, and such opinions must be the basis of the court's finding. Mental competency is a matter on which we require the opinions of experts to make a finding.

"Notice of the time and place of such further summary inquiry will be made in the near future, perhaps within a week or ten days. Setting of a trial date must necessarily await the outcome of the inquiry."

The announcement that Gein had been deemed mentally incompetent provoked renewed outcries of anger and protest in his home community. From the very beginning, the townsfolk of Plainfield had been afraid that Eddie would evade punishment by pleading insanity, a legal defense they regarded as especially outrageous in Gein's case. They had known Eddie nearly all his life—gone to school with him, labored alongside him at threshing time, shot the breeze with him at local cafés, teased him about women, listened to his latest crime stories from *Startling Detective* magazine, approached him for favors, hired him for assorted odd jobs—house painting, snowplowing, and even, on occasion, babysitting. Gein might have been an oddball—someone, as Ed Marolla put it, with "a quirk in his mind." But as far as his neighbors were concerned, he certainly wasn't crazy. And he wasn't nearly as simpleminded as he sometimes seemed, either. In the eyes of many of those who knew Eddie Gein, that little "Night Before Christmas" poem all the school kids were reciting said it best. "He took out his crowbar and pried open the box/He was not only clever, but sly as a fox."

Sly enough, anyway, to fool the so-called experts into thinking he was insane.

December 25 turned out to be a happy day for Sheriff Schley. His Christmas wish had come true. The two-story brick building that served as both his living quarters and the county jailhouse was empty of everyone except himself and his family. Eddie Gein remained locked up in Central State, fifty long miles away.

As the year died away, the Associated Press conducted its annual poll of Wisconsin newspaper editors to determine the state's top ten news stories of 1957. The results of the poll were published on Saturday, December 28.

By unanimous vote, the Edward Gein case was selected as "Story of the Year," beating out (in descending order of significance) the Milwaukee Braves pennant win and World Series championship, the death of Senator Joseph McCarthy, the election of William Proxmire (the first Democrat in twenty-five years to represent Wisconsin in the senate) to complete McCarthy's unexpired term, and various instances of tragic fires, traffic fatalities, and local corruption.

Runners-up included the adoption of daylight savings time, an outbreak of Asian flu, and federal court action in which seven leading food companies sought an order to prevent the return of windfall profits on cheese sales to the government.

# 37

*"I think you have to look at what Gein did as a mark that he was mentally disturbed. The fact that he killed one person or perhaps two or more persons, in itself, I do not think is anything of great import regarding Gein's mental disorder. But . . . how he lived, how he thought, how he wanted to return to being a child in his mother's arms, and how he tried to recreate his mother with the bodies that he dug up—these are signs of mental disorder. Very unusual signs of mental disorder."*

DR. EDWARD F. SCHUBERT

The courtroom was filled to capacity, mostly with the grim-faced neighbors of the accused. Journalists and photographers from the major news services were there, and television cameramen milled in the corridors outside the packed courtroom.

It was the morning of Monday, January 6, and Eddie Gein's sanity hearing, a proceeding that would occupy most of the day, was about to get under way in the city of Wisconsin Rapids.

His hands manacled before him, the prisoner was escorted before the bench by Sheriff Schley and Wood County Sheriff Tom Forsyth. For once, Eddie was not wearing his plaid cap and work clothes. Indeed, in keeping with the importance of the occasion, all three men were formally dressed—Eddie in brown trousers, a white shirt, and a tie and the two lawmen in business suits.

As the officers led Gein to the front of the courtroom, most of the spectators rose slightly from their seats, craning their necks for a better view of their former neighbor, the little nonentity who had, virtually overnight, become a figure of near-legendary proportions—their homegrown Jack the Ripper or Lizzie Borden. Staring at him, they couldn't help but notice another, far less remarkable but still

198

striking change that, in the few months since they had last laid eyes on him, had taken place in Eddie Gein. He had put on weight. In fact, the once frail and hollow-cheeked little man was beginning to look distinctly pudgy. Clearly, institutional living—"three hots and a cot," as one of Eddie's attendants put it—agreed with him.

In the state of Wisconsin, at the time of Gein's hearing, the question of a defendant's legal sanity was decided on the basis of a principle known as the M'Naghton Rule. According to this rule, a medical diagnosis of mental illness was not, in itself, enough to prevent an accused person from standing trial. A defendant could only be ruled legally insane if—as Attorney General Honeck explained in his opening statement at the hearing—"two facts are found by the court: (1) that the accused is incapable of conferring with counsel and assisting in his own defense; and (2) that the accused does not know the difference between right and wrong."

To determine if these criteria applied in Gein's case, the court relied largely on the testimony of three psychiatrists, who were questioned closely by Judge Bunde and cross-examined by Honeck, as well as by Eddie's attorney, William Belter.

Dr. Schubert took the stand first. He summed up the results of the various psychological tests Gein had undergone at Central State. He clarified, in answer to questions posed by Judge Bunde, the precise nature of Gein's mental illness. And he concluded by repeating the "considered opinion" of the hospital's staff, namely that Gein was a chronic schizophrenic who had been lost in "his own little world" of fantasy and delusion since the death of his mother twelve years before.

Schubert was then questioned by Attorney General Honeck, who did his best to raise doubts about the doctor's diagnosis. Honeck, who had made a trip out to Central State Hospital on the previous Thursday to examine Eddie's medical and psychiatric records, began his cross-examination by pointing out that nowhere in the hour-by-hour log of Gein's behavior during his stay at Central State was there any indication of "destructiveness, disturbance, shock, confusion, or other untoward behavior."

"You would say, then, I take it," Honeck asked Schubert, "that his sojourn during that period of time down to the present has been uneventful?"

"That's right," Schubert answered.

"His behavior generally, in the broad sense, is no different than an average person without a mental illness as far as these entries on this record are concerned?"

"Yes," said Schubert.

Honeck then questioned the doctor about Gein's actions immediately after he slew Mrs. Worden in her store, particularly his efforts to get rid of the truck he had used to haul away her body. Didn't such behavior suggest that Gein knew perfectly well that he had done something wrong and that "the law frowned on murder"?

While conceding the point, Schubert remained firm in his insistence that Gein could not be held criminally responsible for his deeds. The fact that he could function rationally for a period of time, even a prolonged one, was not in itself a sign of sanity, since schizophrenics can be actively psychotic at times and in reasonable touch with their environment at others. Judged by the two criteria that Honeck had set forth at the start of the hearing, Gein was legally insane, Schubert asserted, and the chances of his ever recovering from his disorder were "minimal."

It was time to break for lunch. Judge Bunde complimented the spectators—"and particularly the reporters"—for their good behavior, then offered a gentle warning. "You have done very well this morning," he said. "If, however, it should happen that you don't do very well, why I suppose we will find that we will have to ask you to leave. Bear that in mind. Recess until two o'clock."

Throughout the morning, Eddie had sat silently on his bench, chewing gum and gazing on impassively. Shortly after the hearing reconvened, however, a sickly look crossed his face, and he began complaining to Belter that he "couldn't hold out." Another recess was called, this one for fifteen minutes, while Eddie was taken to the bathroom. Then he returned to his seat, shoved a fresh stick of Black Jack into his mouth, and (except for one other occasion, when he told his attorney that he needed to go to the toilet again) sat there with jaws working slowly and his expression a perfect blank.

The first witness of the afternoon was Dr. Milton Miller, an assistant professor of psychiatry at the University of Wisconsin Medical School, who had been retained by Gein's attorney, William Belter. On two occasions, December 14 and 21, Miller had traveled to Central State Hospital, spending a total of six hours examining Gein in Schubert's office.

Miller concurred with Schubert's diagnosis. Gein, he testified, was "suffering from a long standing schizophrenia." He acknowledged that, in certain areas, Gein might well "know right from wrong." "I think," Miller explained, "he would know the right side of a plate on which to put a knife and fork. I think he would know to stand up when the judge comes in. I think he would know to be respectful to an older person." Indeed, if asked about his own criminal activities, Gein might well say that "it is wrong to kill people; it is wrong to uncover graves."

Nevertheless, Miller continued, "to say that he knows these things in the way that a normal person would know them, that they are meaningful to him, is not accurate." The fact that Gein could live such a radically divided life for more than ten years—appearing "superficially normal and rational" to the community while "carrying out grossly insane activities"—was a sign not (as many of Eddie's neighbors believed) of the little man's fiendish cunning but of his extreme madness. In the end, though Miller acknowledged that there was much about the defendant's mind that he didn't understand, he was convinced, like Schubert, that Gein was legally insane. His emotional responses were "grossly inappropriate." His behavior was, in many ways, "beyond comprehension." And "judgment-wise, there were many, many examples of defects in his thinking."

The third and final psychiatrist, Dr. Edward M. Burns, was called to testify by the state. Though Burns agreed that Gein was "chronically mentally ill" and subject to "delusions that his role was predestined," he took issue with the shared opinion of Schubert and Miller regarding Gein's criminal responsibility. According to Burns, Gein was capable of cooperating "with his counsel and is therefore legally sane."

Judge Bunde wanted clarification. "Are you trying to say, Doctor, that you believe he is medically insane but legally sane? Is that what you are trying to say?"

"Yes," Burns answered, though he acknowledged that, in saying so, he was making an extremely tight call—that Gein was very "close to the border" of legal insanity.

In the end, Burns's "borderline" judgment, added to the unequivocal verdicts of both Schubert and Miller, left Bunde little choice. "In a matter of this kind, I must rely on the opinion of experts," he began, his words resounding in the taut silence of the courtroom. "I have no illusions, delusions, or hallucinations of the criticisms of the court's decision, no matter what it would be." The decision now before him, he confessed, was the hardest he had ever faced. Nevertheless, he said, "I can't see how my opinion can be anything other than to find this defendant insane. I so find him and do hereby recommit him to the Central State Hospital in Waupun for an indeterminate term of commitment. From the opinions of various experts, I think it is adequate for me to say that it does not appear that he will ever be at liberty again. Perhaps that is a desirable conclusion.

"That closes the hearing, and the court is adjourned."

# 38

✝

*"I'm glad it came out this way. I think it's better for me."*

ED GEIN

Eddie Gein's connections to normal human society were so tenuous that he hardly seemed to care that he was leaving it behind, perhaps forever. If anything, he seemed relieved, glad to depart from the bitter isolation of the outside world into the sheltering walls of the mental institution.

That departure took place on the night of January 6, just hours after his sanity hearing had ended. It was the last time, for many years, that Gein would be seen outside the walls of Central State.

As soon as Judge Bunde had announced his decision, Gein was hurried out of the courthouse and into Sheriff Schley's waiting car—not his squad car but his own, bright new '57 Plymouth. The choice of the vehicle seemed consistent with Schley's own mood, which was considerably brighter now that he was finally getting free of the burden that had dominated his life since that terrible day back in November when he and Captain Schoephoerster had broken into Gein's summer kitchen. Or perhaps he just wanted the fastest car available to take Gein to the hospital. Certainly, he and his companions couldn't seem to get to Waupun fast enough. Schley, sitting in the passenger seat, let Deputy Virgil "Buck" Batterman do the driving, and though the road conditions were far from ideal, with a powdery snow making visibility poor and icy patches glazing the blacktop, Batterman kept his foot low on the accelerator, maintaining an even speed of eighty miles per hour for most of the ninety-five-mile trip.

Meanwhile, Undersheriff Arthur Schwandt sat in the back beside

Eddie, who remained slumped in the corner, his manacled hands lying slack in his lap and a faraway look in his eyes.

The hospital corridors were jaundice-yellow and reeked of disinfectant. A pack of newsmen—reporters and photographers—waited by the barred doorway that separated the administration area from the wards. At precisely 8:02 P.M., Eddie Gein, still wearing his dress shirt and tie, emerged from one of the admissions offices and approached the doorway. He was flanked by two staff members—hospital supervisor Norman Popham and a khaki-clad guard who held a ring full of big brass keys in one hand.

As Eddie stood there, waiting for the guard to unlock the door, the photographers pointed their cameras at him.

"Oh, not anymore," he said impatiently. The reporters were struck by the sharpness of his tone. They had never heard the mild-mannered little man—the "shy ghoul," as he was sometimes called in the papers—speak that way before.

"Just this one last time, Ed," one of the photographers beseeched.

Eddie smiled slightly. "I just didn't want you to spend any more money," he said, his voice softening a bit. But he remained adamant about the photographs. Turning away from the newsmen, he refused to look at them again, in spite of their entreaties.

The instant the steel door swung open, Popham took Eddie by the elbow and led him briskly down the hallway, leaving the cameramen to snap photos of Eddie's receding back. They were the last glimpses of Gein that the public would have for many years.

After Gein disappeared down the ward, several of the newsmen approached Dr. Schubert to ask what Gein's life would be like in the hospital. Henceforward, said Schubert, there would be "little variety in Gein's existence." His living quarters would consist of a small, Spartan room, containing a cot, dresser, and bedside table. He would be assigned a menial job—"mopping, cleaning, laundry or something similar"—for which he would be paid ten cents a day up to a maximum of fifty cents a week, a sum he would be allowed to spend on candy and chewing gum at the hospital canteen. When he wasn't performing his chores, he would be free to spend time in the day room he would share with a dozen other inmates. There, he could read a newspaper, watch TV, or listen to the radio. Apart from these sources, he would have no contact with the outside world. Only close relatives were allowed to visit inmates. But Gein had no relatives, close or otherwise.

\* \* \*

Gein's commitment to the mental institution seemed to mark the end of the case that had obsessed Wisconsin for months. "The sordid, sad story of Ed Gein closed with the clang of the hospital door," wrote Harry S. Pease, one of the reporters who was there to witness Gein's incarceration. "There can be little doubt that the world will be a better place for his absence."

But though the ghoul himself might be safely shut away, the nightmares he aroused and the furies he provoked weren't so easily laid to rest.

Pease was wrong. Eddie Gein's return to Central State might have ended another chapter in his terrible saga. But the story wasn't over yet.

# 39

*"Resentment ran up and down Main Street."*

ED MAROLLA

In spite of Judge Bunde's assurances that Gein would never walk the streets again, the citizens of Plainfield were deeply embittered by the outcome of the case. There had been no protests at the sanity hearing itself. The townspeople in attendance had remained composed and undemonstrative throughout the proceedings. By the next morning, however, the community's outcries against the judge's decision had grown loud and intense.

Many of the townspeople continued to scoff at the idea that Gein was crazy. In their eyes, Gein had escaped a trial through a combination of his own cunning and the bias of the witnesses, particularly Dr. Miller, whose testimony, they felt, couldn't be trusted because he had been hired by Eddie's attorney. Others, though willing to accept that Gein was insane, nevertheless believed that the issue of his innocence or guilt should have been resolved by a jury, that "the normal path of justice had been detoured," as Village President Harold Collins put it.

And then, of course, there were others, particularly the relatives of Eddie's victims, whose very human desire for vengeance had been thwarted by Judge Bunde's decision. Understandably enough, they wanted to see Gein punished, and punished severely, for the horrors he had perpetrated on their loved ones. Far from suffering for his deeds, however, Gein was actually—in their eyes— benefiting from them. Compared to the conditions he was used to— cut off from the world, subsisting on canned food in an indescribably filthy farmhouse with no electricity or indoor plumbing—his life in Central State, where he would be provided with a clean room, three meals a day, clothes, medical care, even a television set, sounded like a permanent vacation with all expenses paid by the state. To these people, Eddie's incarceration in a mental institution was more than a miscarriage of justice. It was an outrage almost too painful to bear.

Even the passing of the months failed to assuage that sense of outrage. In early March, the citizens of Plainfield held a town meeting to discuss the possibility of appealing Judge Bunde's decision—to the Supreme Court, if necessary. Portage County District Attorney John Haka was prevailed upon to contact Attorney General Honeck to ask if the state was considering an appeal. The residents of Plainfield, Haka informed the attorney general in a letter, were firm in their belief that Gein "should have been found legally sane."

Honeck's response was not encouraging. The fact that Eddie "appeared perfectly sane" to the "people who knew" him did not prove anything about his mental condition. After all, he wrote in his reply to Honeck, "the psychiatrists who examined him and testified at the hearing indicated that the defendant's mental illness was such that it would not be apparent to lay persons in the ordinary transactions and affairs of life." An appeal of Judge Bunde's order, Honeck was convinced, would "quite obviously be futile."

The attorney general did, however, have a bit of reassurance to offer those who believed that Gein should stand trial for his crimes. Bunde's order, he stressed, "did not result in a final disposition of the case. The order merely holds that the defendant Gein is not competent to stand trial at the present time."

Thus, Honeck declared, "upon his recovery, if that should occur, the defendant may still be brought to trial."

The possibility of a trial at some indeterminate point in the future, however, offered little comfort to those who believed that Gein had gotten away with murder. Indeed, the community's anger and bitterness grew more intense as the winter wore on, inflamed by the approach of an event that brought renewed media attention and an enormous influx of sightseers to the traumatized town. That event was the auction of Ed Gein's farm and personal property, scheduled for Sunday, March 30, 1958.

At the request of William Belter, who had been serving as the special guardian of the Gein estate, Judge Boyd Clark appointed Harvey Polzin, a retired district manager for the Wisconsin Power and Light Company, to act as the general guardian of Gein's property. Specifically, Polzin was mandated "to take possession of all the Gein property, prepare an inventory, and sell whatever is necessary to meet any claims against Gein." Eddie was already being sued by Floyd Adams, widower of Eleanor Adams, one of the women whose empty coffin had been exhumed in the Plainfield cemetery and whose remains had subsequently been identified among Gein's ghoulish trophies. Mr. Adams's suit charged Gein with "wantonly disturbing" his wife's grave and causing the plaintiff "mental suffering . . . in the amount of $5,000." Other lawsuits would soon follow, including a $57,800 claim against the Gein estate filed by Frank Worden and his sister, Miriam.

A company named Farm Sales Service of Reedsburg, Wisconsin, was chosen to handle the auction. By early March, a notice had been printed up and distributed around the state, announcing the sale of the farm and personal property of Edward Gein, to begin promptly at noon on Sunday, March 30, 1958. The notice also contained an inventory of Gein's belongings. Without Eddie's graveyard souvenirs, the contents of his household seemed perfectly unexceptional, the kind of goods that might have been offered for sale at almost any country auction.

There were stoves, cupboards, pots and pans, dishes, beds, a sewing machine, a couch, a hand-cranked phonograph, lamps, vases, three battery-operated radios, musical instruments (a violin, zither, harmonica, and accordion), rockers, a family album, a "bookcase and desk combination," a dictionary and a stand, rugs, a carpet sweeper, commodes, and several "antique" pieces of furniture, including a table, love seat, and chest of drawers.

In addition, there were various pieces of farming equipment and machinery—a fanning mill, several plows, a dump rake, a manure spreader, a mower, and more. Eddie's 1949 Ford sedan and 1940 Chevy pickup truck were also being put up for sale.

The farm itself was being offered either in its entirety or in two separate parcels, the first consisting of the buildings (the nine-room house, barn, granary, chicken coop, corn crib, and machine shed) plus forty acres of level land, "nearly all under plow." The second parcel consisted of the remaining one hundred fifty-five acres of land without the buildings.

Prospective bidders were advised that the household goods and property could be inspected the week before the auction, on the afternoon of Sunday, March 23. The notice concluded with the name of the individual under whose authorization the sale was taking place: Harvey Polzin, "Guardian of Edward Gein, Insane."

At a glance, there was nothing at all inflammatory about the notice. On the contrary, it seemed like a perfectly straightforward document, detailing the items that were to be auctioned and the terms of the sale. But like everything else connected with the Gein case, its appearance immediately set off a furor in Eddie's hometown. Two things in particular offended the residents of Plainfield. The first was a statement printed in small type near the bottom of the notice. The line immediately following the information about the inspection date read: "An inspection fee of fifty cents per person will be charged to all persons going through the dwelling."

To the townsfolk of Plainfield, and particularly to the Worden family, the idea of charging a fee for a look inside the Gein house was deeply repugnant. It seemed to confirm their worst fears, that the hated place was being turned into a tourist attraction, a "museum for the morbid" in the words of one outraged local. No sooner had the auction notice been publicized than the town sent a formal protest to Judge Boyd Clark, who had approved guardian Polzin's petition for the March 30 sale. Clark responded without delay. Though Polzin insisted that the only purpose of the fee was to "discourage and limit the number of curiosity seekers," the judge forbade the auction service from charging admission to the house.

Clark's decision clearly pleased the community. But there was something else about the auction that many local people objected to—indeed, that called forth even stronger expressions of protest than the matter of the admission fee. The Reverend Wendell Bennetts, former pastor of the Plainfield Methodist Church, was the first to raise the new issue, pointing out in a letter to the *Plainfield Sun* that March 30, the proposed date of the auction, was Palm Sunday.

Holding the Gein auction on that date, the reverend admonished, "is not very wise." Indeed, such an act, he implied, bordered on the blasphemous. "God has blest our nation above all nations of the earth," Rev. Bennetts wrote, "and if we wish to be blest we ought to honor God and keep his laws. In keeping his laws we honor Him, and to have the State allow an auction is not conducive to good form and rule. Great nations have grown up and disappeared and practically in every case it was because the people ignored the laws of God. This nation would be no exception in the sight of God, for any nation that forgets God, that nation will God destroy."

The moral of Rev. Bennetts's sermon was clear. To conduct the Gein auction on Palm Sunday—"a holy-day, not a holiday," in his words—was to fly in the face of God's laws. It was an open invitation to divine retribution. Disaster was certain to follow.

Other ministers—including Gerald Tanquist of the Methodist Church, David Wisthoff of the Baptist Church, and Irving Bow of the Assembly of God Church, all of Plainfield—joined Rev. Bennetts in voicing an objection to the auction date. Their protests did produce one immediate result. Several community groups, which had intended to sell postcards and sandwiches on the days of the inspection and the auction, abandoned their plans. But according to Judge Clark, there was nothing to be done about the date. The auction had already been too widely advertised around the state.

The sale of Eddie Gein's property and personal belongings would take place as announced on Sunday, March 30, and there was nothing that the community—smoldering with anger and bitterness—could do to stop it.

Or so it seemed.

# 40

*"The house of the wicked shall be overthrown."*
*Proverbs* 14:11

Eddie Gein's nearest neighbors were the Johnson family. On Thursday, March 20, the Johnson's youngest son, Roger, was stirred from his sleep by a brilliant light blazing through his bedroom window. Sunup, Roger thought drowsily as he struggled into full consciousness. But even in his half-awake state, he realized that there was something funny about this particular dawn. For one thing, it didn't seem as if he'd been asleep very long. But there was something else, too, something strange about it . . .

All at once, his head cleared, and he leaped for the window, realizing what was wrong.

The intense brightness was coming from the west. From the direction of Eddie Gein's farmhouse.

It was two-thirty in the morning when Burt Carlson, Plainfield's police chief, spotted the blaze. He immediately notified the town fire marshal, who roused the fifteen members of the volunteer fire department. By the time the men drove the seven miles to the Gein place, however, there was little they could do. The conflagration was out of control. Though they managed to save the outbuildings, they could only look on as the blaze reduced Eddie's two-story white frame house to a blackened heap of smoldering ashes.

Of course, it's doubtful that the destruction they were witnessing could have been anything but a heart-gladdening sight to the growing crowd of onlookers who gathered to watch Gein's home burn. As for the feelings of the fire marshal himself, they can easily be imagined. The fire marshal's name was Frank Worden.

With the coming of daylight, Sheriff Schley—who had headed for the Gein farm the moment he got word of the fire—contacted the state fire marshal in Madison, who immediately dispatched a deputy, John E. Hassler, to Plainfield. The assumption, not only of Hassler and his boss but of most of the townspeople, too, was that the fire had been set. Its timing, three days before the scheduled inspection date, was clearly suspicious. Moreover, for weeks, there had been talk among certain members of the community, talk about doing something drastic to prevent the Palm Sunday auction. And there certainly didn't seem to be any other likely explanation for the blaze. As Gein's trustee, Harvey Polzin, put it, "there was no electrical wiring, and there was no electrical storm, and we know of nothing in the house that could have started a fire. But it did start."

The presumption of arson, however, would remain just that. Neither Hassler's probe nor any subsequent investigation ever turned up a suspect or, indeed, a single shred of evidence that Gein's house had been put to the torch.

However the fire had started, the citizens of Plainfield were delighted to see the abominated dwelling go up in smoke. Even people with less stake in its destruction seemed to derive gratification from the fire, to see it as a perfect climax to the Gein affair—"a fittingly grotesque finish," in the words of one prominent criminologist, "to the most bizarre case in criminal records since medieval times." Indeed, even Gein himself seemed relieved at the burning of his home.

Eddie learned about it from Darold Strege, the psychiatric officer in charge of his unit at Central State, who had heard the news early that morning on the radio as he was getting ready to leave for work. Strege's shift began at six A.M., and Gein was still asleep when Strege arrived at the hospital. Unsure about how the little man would react, Strege waited until Gein had risen, dressed, and finished his breakfast before informing him of the news.

For the rest of his days, Strege would remember Eddie's response. It consisted of only three words, but they suggested to Strege that perhaps there might have been some truth after all to the stories that other, greater horrors had been hidden away in the walls of Eddie's house, horrors that were now forever safe from discovery.

Strege took Gein aside. "Your house has burned down, Eddie," he said as gently as possible.

Eddie paused for a moment and then answered quietly.

"Just as well," he said.

# 41

*"People want to see this kind of thing."*
BUNNY GIBBONS,
exhibitor of the Ed Gein "ghoul car"

Thursday's fire took care of one of Plainfield's concerns. No one was going to make Eddie Gein's home into a "museum for the morbid." But anyone who hoped that the incineration of the house would put a stop to the auction was in for a severe disappointment. That event, Harvey Polzin announced on Friday morning, would go on as scheduled. Indeed, he said, though the loss of Eddie's home and its contents would undoubtedly keep "a lot of souvenir hunters" from attending the sale, he still expected "quite a crowd."

Polzin was right. March 23, the date of the inspection, was a crisp, sunny Sunday, a perfect day for a family outing—and to the residents of Plainfield, it must have seemed as if every family in Wisconsin had decided to take a drive to their little town. Between noon and sunset, an estimated twenty thousand sightseers descended on the village—an astonishing turnout, considering that the entire population of Waushara County at that time numbered just over thirteen thousand people.

On the dirt roads leading to the farm, Sheriff Schley and a handful of deputies did their best to keep the endless procession moving. Eddie's neighbor, Milton Johnson, had posted a sign on his property, offering parking at twenty cents per car, but most of the tourists simply pulled their cars onto Gein's land. A snow fence had been set up around the ruins, and throughout the day, there were never any fewer than three hundred people pressed up against it, straining for a better look at the ash heap that had once been the home of the killer-ghoul, Eddie Gein.

The auction itself—conducted, as scheduled, on Palm Sunday, March 30—brought out a far smaller, though still significant, crowd. Two thousand people showed up on that crisp, brilliantly clear Sunday, although only a few were there to bid. Most were curiosity seekers, come to witness the final disposal of Ed Gein's few remaining possessions.

Walter Golla, a Plainfield junk dealer, bought much of Eddie's rusty old farming equipment, including a plow for fourteen dollars, a disk and mower for nine dollars apiece, and a manure spreader for thirty-five dollars. The remaining pieces of scrap iron went to Chet Scales of Chet's Auto Wreckers, who hauled them away in his other major purchase, Eddie's 1940 Chevy pickup truck, which Scales acquired for two hundred fifteen dollars. Wayne Heinke of Neshkoro bought a pile of lumber for ten dollars, and a man named William Smith picked up two old plowshares for two and a half dollars. Also sold were eight wagon wheels (seven dollars), an old iron range (fifteen-fifty), a keg of nails (seven dollars), and an old violin (seven-fifty).

The farm itself—all one hundred ninety-five acres of scrub pine and sandy soil, plus the charred homestead site and the five tumbledown outbuildings unharmed by the fire—was sold for $3,883 to a Sun Prairie real estate developer named Emden Schey. Within months, Schey would undertake a major reforestation of the property, razing the remaining buildings and planting more than sixty thousand trees on the land.

The only surprise of the afternoon involved the sale of Eddie's 1949 maroon Ford sedan, the car he had been driving on the day of Bernice Worden's murder. It was the single item that set off a bidding war, with fourteen people competing. In the end, the car was sold for the remarkable sum of seven hundred sixty dollars to a mysterious buyer identified variously as "Koch Brothers," "Cook Brothers," or "Kook Brothers" of Rothschild, Wisconsin. Why anyone would pay such a hefty sum for a beaten-up nine-year-old automobile was a puzzling and troubling matter to the townsfolk of Plainfield, who were praying that with Eddie locked away for good and his property disposed of, the lingering morbidity of the Gein affair had finally been purged from their lives.

It didn't take long for the puzzle to be cleared up, and when the answer came, it set off one last firestorm of protest, not only in Eddie's hometown but throughout Wisconsin.

"Koch/Cook/Kook Brothers" turned out to be the fictitious identity of an enterprising fifty-year-old sideshow exhibitor named

Bunny Gibbons of Rockford, Illinois. Though his specialty was trick mice, Gibbons had a friend who, as he put it, "had done pretty good with the Dillinger car. So I got a bright idea when I read about Gein." After acquiring Gein's Ford at the auction, Gibbons had spruced it up a bit, then equipped it with a pair of wax dummies— one in the driver's seat simulating Eddie Gein and another lying in back, representing one of his mutilated, blood-soaked female victims.

The "Ed Gein ghoul car" made its first public appearance in July 1958 at the Outgamie County Fair in Seymour, Wisconsin, where it was displayed for three days inside a large canvas tent covered with blaring signs—"SEE THE CAR THAT HAULED THE DEAD FROM THEIR GRAVES! YOU READ IT IN 'LIFE' MAGAZINE! IT'S HERE! ED GEIN'S CRIME CAR! $1,000 REWARD IF NOT TRUE!" One crudely painted sign showed a man lifting a casket from a grave. Another depicted a woman about to be clobbered on the head with a plank. At the top of the tent, three skull-and-crossbones flags waved in the summer breeze.

Two thousand people paid twenty-five cents each for a peek at the death car. Within days, however, news of the exhibit had spread throughout the state, setting off a major controversy. Plainfield, whose citizens had feared just such a possibility when the car fetched an inordinately high price at auction, was up in arms over the Gein exhibit. In Outgamie County, local parents made angry phone calls to fair officials, charging that their children were being emotionally damaged by the display. And representatives of the Wisconsin Association for Mental Health complained that, while the fair directors had been able to find space for Gibbons's grisly exhibit, their own organization, dedicated to the promotion of public awareness in matters of mental health, had been denied permission to set up a booth because, according to those same directors, there was not enough room.

Gibbons—tickled, no doubt, by all the free publicity—remained unperturbed by the uproar. "People want to see this kind of thing," he cheerfully explained. He even promised that one day he would "play Plainfield." In spite of his vow, however, he decided to skip the Columbia County Fair in neighboring Portage for fear of stirring up the local populace. But even in other parts of the state, Gibbons's exhibit began to run into trouble. At the Washington County 4-H Club Fair in Slinger, Wisconsin, the death car had been on display only a few hours before the sheriff arrived and ordered Gibbons to pack up his tent. Soon, county fairs all across the state were barring the display. Gibbons, grumbling about this unforeseen turn of events, had no choice but to head south for the fairgrounds of Illinois, where the folks, he hoped, would be a little less touchy on the subject of Eddie Gein.

With Gibbons and his "ghoul car" driven from the state, Eddie Gein's story seemed to have run its course. There was, however, one final bit of news still to come. It appeared in the papers toward the end of July, just as the commotion over the car exhibit was dying down. The story, headlined "$300 SET ASIDE FOR GEIN FUNERAL," concerned the distribution of the money that had been netted through the auction of Gein's property. Most of the money— $5,375—was to be distributed on a prorated basis among the people who had filed claims against the Gein estate. Another eight hundred dollars was to go to the state for its care of Gein. That left a total of three hundred dollars, which, by order of Waushara County Judge Boyd Clark, was to "be placed in the county treasury and released only to pay Gein's burial expenses."

Clark's ruling was the final word on the Gein affair that the public would hear for many years. That the word had to do with graveyard matters made it a particularly fitting ending.

# CONCLUSION

# The Psycho

# 42

Truffaut: *I've read the novel from which* Psycho *was taken. . . . I believe [it] was based on a newspaper story.*
Hitchcock: *It was the story of a man who kept his mother's body in his house, somewhere in Wisconsin.*

FRANÇOIS TRUFFAUT, *Hitchcock*

It would be ten years before "Ghastly Gein" (as he had come to be called in the press) was back in the spotlight. But during that decade, something interesting happened to Eddie. He achieved immortality.

An entire generation of Wisconsinites grew up swapping jokes and scary stories about the "Mad Butcher of Plainfield." Eddie became a local legend, a creature who prowled the night, preying on unwary teenage lovers and disobedient children. To the youngsters of Wisconsin, the knowledge that Gein was safely immured in a state mental institution might have been reassuring in daylight. But locked doors and barred windows can't hold the bogeyman, and when darkness fell, all it took was a single threat from an exasperated parent—"If you don't quiet down and get to sleep right now, Eddie Gein will come to get you!"—to subdue the most obstreperous child.

To the kids who came of age exchanging horror stories about him, old Eddie Gein would always be a larger-than-life figure, their homegrown Frankenstein, Dracula, and Mummy. A peculiar fondness for "Crazy Ed" developed among them—similar to the popularity that Alferd Packer, the nineteenth-century cannibal, enjoys in Colorado, where the student cafeteria at the state university is named the "Alferd Packer Grill." (A member of a six-man gold-hunting party that became snowbound in the Uncompaghre Mountains, Packer butchered and lived off the flesh of his companions. The legend goes that at his 1883 trial, the judge who sentenced him to hang declared in indignation, "Packer, there were only seven Democrats in all of Hinsdale County, and you ate five of them, you son-of-a-bitch.") Like the Colorado cannibal, Eddie Gein, the Plainfield ghoul, became a permanent part of the lore of his state.

But the event that truly immortalized Eddie was, of course, the appearance in 1960 of Alfred Hitchcock's consummate terror film, *Psycho*, based on the novel that Robert Bloch had fashioned out of the raw materials of the Gein affair. Though there is no indication that Eddie ever saw—or, indeed, even heard of—the cinematic classic that his crimes had inspired, Hitchcock's film transformed him from a local legend into an undying part of American popular mythology. Thanks to Robert Bloch's initial conception and the cinematic genius of Alfred Hitchcock, who took a clever but minor pulp chiller and transmuted it into a masterwork which left a lasting mark on the dream life of a nation, Eddie Gein had become—and would always be famous as—the original "Psycho" killer, the "real Norman Bates."

Meanwhile, inside the walls of Central State Hospital, Eddie was adjusting nicely to institutional living, completely unaware of the fascination he continued to exert on the outside world. Hospital administrators had instituted a firm policy of forbidding outsiders from interviewing Eddie, so he had no way of knowing that from the moment he had been admitted to Central State, its directors had been bombarded with requests from newspapermen, magazine writers, sociologists, and others seeking permission to talk to Eddie. Bizarrely enough, he did receive an occasional piece of fan mail, but what he made of this macabre correspondence, particularly the letters from certain female admirers, imploring him for a lock of his hair, is anybody's guess.

Over the years, small news items relating to Gein would appear from time to time in the papers. In May 1960, workmen planting trees on Gein's former property spotted several dogs furiously scrabbling at the soil. Curious, the men left their work and traipsed across a field to investigate. In the spot where the dogs had been digging, the men discovered a pile of human bones—ribs, legs, arms, and a pelvis. Though all the buildings on the property had been razed by that time, the bones had been buried near the place where Eddie's barn had stood. These skeletal scraps were immediately shipped off to the Crime Lab to be analyzed and added to the rest of Gein's collection.

The final disposition of that gruesome stockpile was decided on several years later. In December 1962, Crime Lab director Charles Wilson appeared before the State Board of Government Operations to ask for funds to purchase a plot for the burial of Gein's graveyard remains, which, by that time, had been stored in the Crime Lab for five years. The relics, Wilson explained, could simply be cremated, but he had received a request from Bishop William O'Connor of the Madison archdiocese, urging that they be reburied in hallowed ground. The board unhesitatingly approved the request, alloting $125 for a cemetery plot. Shortly thereafter, a decade or more since they had been plucked from their graves, the remains of Eddie Gein's victims were quietly returned to the earth.

It was shortly before the reinterment of the Gein relics that Governor-elect John Reynolds visited the state mental hospital at Waupun to conduct a budget hearing before assuming office. During his tour of the institution, Reynolds, who was accompanied by a crowd of reporters, was taken to the crafts workshop, where a small gray-haired man was hunched over a table, polishing stones for costume jewelry. The governor-elect walked over to the little man, shook hands, and introduced himself, asking the patient what he thought of the hospital.

"I'm happy here," the little man replied pleasantly. "It's a good place." Then, lowering his voice a bit, he added, "Some of the people here are pretty disturbed, though."

The governor-elect nodded understandingly, told the man that it had been nice to meet him, and moved on. It was only then that one of the reporters informed him that he had just shaken hands with Edward Gein.

And, indeed, Eddie *was* happy at the hospital—happier, perhaps, than he'd ever been in his life. He got along well enough with the other patients, though for the most part he kept to himself. He was eating three square meals a day (the newsmen accompanying Reynolds were struck by how much heavier Eddie looked since his arrest five years before). He continued to be an avid reader (though he'd had to turn to new subjects, the hospital library being ill provided with Nazi atrocity stories and books about South Seas headhunters). He liked his regular chats with the staff psychologists and enjoyed the handicraft work he was assigned—stone polishing, rug making, and other forms of occupational therapy. He had even developed an interest in ham radios and had been permitted to use the money he had earned to order an inexpensive receiver from the Sears catalogue.

All in all, he was a perfectly amiable, even docile patient, one of the few in the hospital who had never required tranquilizing medications to keep his craziness under control. Indeed, apart from certain peculiarities—the disconcerting way he would stare fixedly at nurses or any other female staff members who wandered into his line of vision, for example—it was hard to tell that he was particularly crazy at all.

Not that Eddie's underlying condition had improved much. "I doubt if Mr. Gein will ever change," Superintendent Schubert told the reporters at the conclusion of Reynolds's hearing. But, he added, Gein was a model patient. "If all our patients were like him," Schubert said, "we'd have no trouble at all."

Every six months, the doctor explained, Gein's mental condition was evaluated by staff psychiatrists to determine whether he was fit to stand trial. Not that Gein would ever go free, the doctor hastened to add. "If he is brought to trial, he will either be found insane and returned to the hospital or be found guilty and sent to prison." Nevertheless, Judge Bunde had committed Gein to Central State only until such time as he was deemed competent to stand trial, and though there were those who believed that that time would never come (Bunde himself, in a speech to the Elks Club at around this time, announced that there was "less than no possibility" of Gein's ever being brought to trial), Dr. Schubert wasn't so sure.

# 43

*"The court does not accept the defendant's story. It just does not ring true to me."*

JUDGE ROBERT GOLLMAR

In January 1968, precisely ten years after Eddie Gein had been shipped off to Central State, Circuit Judge Robert Gollmar received a letter from Dr. Schubert notifying him that in the opinion of the hospital's psychiatric staff, Gein had recovered sufficiently to understand the charges against him and to aid in his own defense. In short, he was competent to stand trial.

Gollmar, however, could only shake his head at Schubert's concluding sentence. Gein, it said, continued to suffer from a chronic schizophrenic psychosis. From a clinical point of view, he was still insane. Years later, the judge would describe this situation as an example of what he called "the *Alice in Wonderland* labyrinth of American jurisprudence," which could lead, as in this case, to a long and costly legal proceeding with a "predetermined end." Whatever the final outcome of his trial, Gein would end up back in Central State.

Nevertheless, Eddie Gein, who had been put away without ever having stood trial for his crimes, was entitled to his day in court, and a decade after he had disappeared from public view, he would finally get it.

The reopening of the Gein case brought the predictable reactions—feverish excitement in the news media, angry protests in Plainfield. In Eddie's hometown, the question on everyone's lips was the one posed in the headline of a local newspaper editorial: "The Gein Case: Why Dig It Up?" Around Wisconsin, Gein might have evolved into a semilegendary character, a fairy-tale ogre come to life, whose story provided titillating, half-pleasurable chills to children and adolescents. But among Eddie's former townspeople, feelings continued to run high toward the deranged little handyman, who had slaughtered one of their dearest neighbors and, for years, preyed upon their dead.

Sitting in a Wautoma restaurant shortly before Eddie's preliminary hearing was to begin, a reporter for the *Madison Capital Times* overheard a couple of men kibitzing at the bar. "Charley," one of them asked, "are you going to contribute to the Gein defense fund we're getting up? We're buying him a new suit, new shoes, and a shovel."

"Sure," the other man added. "I'll contribute a thirty-aught-six bullet."

The courtroom was jammed to overflowing with spectators (most of them women), as well as newspapermen, photographers, and TV crews—all of them present for the first day of the proceedings, January 22, 1968. While flashbulbs popped and newsreel cameras whirred, Gein, surrounded by deputies, was escorted into the Wautoma County Courthouse and led to the defense table.

The familiar image of Eddie Gein—hollow-cheeked, unshaven, with his lopsided cap and rumpled work clothes—was so deeply imprinted on the popular imagination that his appearance on this day, the first time he had been seen in public in ten years, came as a shock. In spite of his prisoner's pallor, he had clearly thrived in Central State. Everyone was struck by the pounds he had added to his formerly slight frame. Even more remarkable was his style of dress—blue suit, crisp white shirt, red-and-blue-striped tie, and brightly polished black shoes. With his neatly clipped gray hair and his face freshly shaved, he looked positively distinguished.

For all his dapperness, however, he seemed profoundly ill at ease, painfully embarrassed by the stares of the spectators and the clamorings of the press. Judge Gollmar—a courtly, good-humored gentleman whose small white goatee made him look more like a Kentucky colonel than a country judge—permitted the newsmen to remain in the room, seated in the jurors' box, but cautioned them against taking pictures of Gein while court was in session.

As soon as a recess was called, however, the journalists swarmed around the defense table, thrusting microphones and cameras into Eddie's face and bombarding him with questions. Eddie seemed dazed by all the attention. He managed to stammer out an answer when asked about the correct pronunciation of his name—"Some people say 'Gine,' but we—I—always said 'Geen.' It's about half-and-half. I don't know."

When the newsmen continued to assail him with questions, however, his custodian, Sheriff Virgil "Buck" Batterman, half rose from the table and ordered them away. Gein popped a stick of chewing gum into his mouth and began chewing nervously, his gaze fixed straight ahead. Shy, quiet-spoken, and elderly, he seemed so unlike the mad ghoul of legend that, seeing his discomfiture, some of the spectators were astonished to find themselves pitying him. "I don't believe it," one middle-aged woman remarked, turning to a friend. "I actually almost feel sorry for that lonely old guy. But then I start to think back . . ."

In the end, once the initial excitement attending Gein's reemergence had faded, the trial turned out to be, as Judge Gollmar had foreseen, a protracted but rather anticlimactic affair, with a predictable outcome and very little drama. By the time the preliminary matters had been disposed of—appointment of counsel, motions to suppress evidence and dismiss the case, the filing of briefs, a state supreme court ruling on the validity of the original complaint and warrant against Gein, and miscellaneous legal maneuverings—more than nine months had passed. It was early November before the trial itself finally got under way.

It lasted only a week. Eddie's defense team consisted of his 1958 counsel, William Belter (who resigned his position as assistant district attorney of Waushara County in order to represent his former client), a lawyer named Nicholas Catania, and chief defense attorney Dominic Frinzi of Milwaukee. Prosecuting the case were Milwaukee attorney Robert E. Sutton and Waushara County District Attorney Howard Dutcher.

At the request of the defense, which had entered pleas of not guilty and not guilty by reason of insanity, the trial was conducted without a jury before Judge Gollmar. It was to be a "bifurcated" or split trial. First, Gein would be tried for the first-degree murder of Bernice Worden. Then, should he be found guilty, a second trial would be held immediately to determine if he was sane at the time of the killing.

The trial began on Thursday, November 7, 1968. By the next afternoon, the prosecution had rested its case. Altogether, seven witnesses were called to the stand, including Leon "Specks" Murty, the former deputy sheriff who described the trail of blood that had been found in Mrs. Worden's empty store on the night of November 16, 1957; Captain Lloyd Schoephoerster, whose graphic account of his discovery of Mrs. Worden's headless and disembowelled body brought gasps from the spectators; and several crime lab technicians who testified that the bullet extracted from Mrs. Worden's head had been fired from a .22-caliber rifle in her store and that prints found on the weapon matched those of Gein's left middle finger and upper right palm.

One major witness was missing from the trial: former Sheriff Arthur Schley, whose manhandling of Gein on the night of his arrest had been an issue at an earlier stage of the proceedings. In March 1968, just months before the trial was to begin, Schley—by then one of Waushara's most prominent citizens, the owner of numerous lakefront properties in the area and the head of the county highway commission—suffered a fatal heart attack, following a Friday-night fish fry with his wife and some friends. He was forty-three years old at the time, and there were those who felt that anxiety over being subpoenaed to testify at the upcoming trial might have contributed to his early death.

On Friday afternoon, special prosecutor Sutton wound up his case. Arguing that the circumstantial evidence submitted during his two-day presentation constituted "conclusive proof" of the defendant's guilt, Sutton ended with a flourish by quoting from Shakespeare's *Henry VI, Part II*:

Who finds the heifer dead and bleeding fresh,
And sees fast by a butcher with an ax,
But will suspect 'twas he that made the slaughter?

After hearing and rejecting a motion by defense attorney Frinzi that the murder charge against Gein be dismissed on the ground of insufficient evidence, Judge Gollmar recessed the trial until the following Tuesday morning, November 12, when the defense would present its case.

Gein himself was the key defense witness on Tuesday when the trial resumed. Throughout his testimony, he stoutly maintained that he had shot Mrs. Worden inadvertently, when the rifle he was examining accidentally discharged after he had inserted a .22-short bullet into the magazine to make sure that the weapon could accommodate a shell of that caliber. As for subsequent events—the removal of Mrs. Worden's body from the store and the butchering of the corpse—Gein insisted he didn't remember anything about them. He theorized that it was the sight of Mrs. Worden lying dead on the floor of her hardware store that must have caused him to lose his memory. Ever since he was a little boy, he explained, whenever he saw blood he would "either faint or black out. That is why I cannot remember."

One of the few dramatic moments of the day occurred during Eddie's cross-examination by Sutton, when the prosecutor asked Eddie to look at the police photographs of Mrs. Worden's split-open carcass dangling from the roof beams of the shed. Sutton asked Gein if he remembered "what those pictures portray." Once again, Gein denied any knowledge of the butchery. "I know what they portray," he answered. "But I don't remember seeing anything like this." What made the moment so disturbing, however, was not what Gein said but the way he examined the photographs. He held them in his hands for nearly five minutes, gazing at them, Sutton would later say, the way another man might savor a *Playboy* centerfold.

On Thursday, November 14, 1968—just one week after the trial began and eleven years, almost to the day, since Frank Worden returned from a luckless day of deer hunting to find his mother missing from her store—Edward Gein was found guilty of first-degree murder for the shooting of Bernice Worden. In delivering his decision, Judge Gollmar rejected Gein's contention that the killing was accidental, noting, among other things, that Gein's actions "immediately after the shooting" cast a certain degree of doubt on that particular excuse. Instead of behaving the way "most people would have if the shooting were accidental"—by rushing "into the street to seek the immediate aid of a doctor"—Gein, Gollmar explained, "loaded the body into a truck and then into his car. And while he testified that he had no personal recollection of dissecting the body, I think there can be no question that this was done by the defendant, and that he hung her in his woodshed."

"This line of conduct," Gollmar concluded, "does not fit with an accidental shooting."

Immediately after the judge handed down his verdict, the second phase of the trial—to determine if Gein was sane at the time of the killing—began. It took only a few hours to complete this part of the proceeding. Two witnesses were called to the stand: Dr. E. F. Schubert and Dr. William Crowley, director of the north division of the Milwaukee County Mental Health Center. Both psychiatrists reconfirmed that Gein was a long-term schizophrenic. After listening to their testimony, Judge Gollmar delivered his decision: "The court does find that on November 16, 1957, the defendant, Edward

Gein, was suffering from a mental disease. The court does further find that as a result of this mental disease he lacked substantial capacity to conform his conduct to the requirements of the law. The court does therefore find the defendant not guilty by reason of insanity."

Thus, by means of the bifurcated trial procedure, Eddie Gein was both convicted and acquitted—found guilty of first-degree murder for the murder of Bernice Worden and not guilty by reason of insanity—on the same day. He was recommitted to Central State Hospital for the Criminally Insane. The trial of the man who had committed the must gruesome set of crimes in Wisconsin history had reached its predetermined end.

Before Gein was returned to the mental institution, the press was given a brief opportunity to meet with him. The ten-minute interview was conducted in a book-lined conference room in the courthouse. Eddie sat at a small table, answering questions in a voice so quiet that the reporters in the back of the room had trouble hearing him.

He was dressed in the same blue suit he had worn throughout the proceedings. It was the only one he owned, and by now it looked as baggy and wrinkled as his work clothes once had. Like the other spectators at the trial, it was hard for the newsmen to envision the shy little figure who sat before them as a monster. He seemed, as one of them later wrote, like "a plaintive, almost pathetic looking old man."

Asked how he felt about the verdict, Eddie replied that he was mostly relieved that the trial was over. He hadn't counted on being set free and was, in fact, looking forward to getting back to the hospital. "They treat you pretty good there."

As he had in the past, he blamed his troubles on external circumstances. "Locality has an awful lot to do with a person's life," he mused. "I believe if we'd have stayed in La Crosse, this thing would never have happened. I believe it was just my bad luck to go to a locality where the people were just not as friendly as they should have been."

One of the reporters asked what he would have done if he had been released. "I can't say," Eddie answered. One thing was certain, though—he wouldn't have returned to Plainfield. "There's nothing there anymore, nothing of interest."

He concluded by stating that he held no grudge against society and, in general, did not feel bitter at all about the way things had turned out. During his stay at the hospital, he said, he had seen lots of "others worse off than me."

"At least I have my health," he declared.

A few moments later, the press conference was over, and Eddie was led to the patrol car that would drive him to the mental hospital. He was on his way back home.

# 44

*"A man that doeth violence to the blood of any person shall flee to the
pit; let no man stay him."*

*Proverbs* 28:17

Judge Gollmar's order recommitting Gein to Central State did
not entirely preclude the possibility of Eddie's eventual release,
since it provided that Gein should only remain institutionalized
until hospital officials deemed he was sane and that his discharge
would not be a danger to society. Still, though Dr. Schubert
wouldn't rule out the remote possibility that a miracle cure for
schizophrenia might be discovered in Eddie's lifetime, the chances
that Gein (who was by that time sixty-two years old) would ever
recover his sanity seemed slim, to say the least.

It came as a shock to most people, then, when in February 1974,
Eddie Gein filed a petition with the Waushara County clerk of
courts, claiming that he had "now fully recovered his mental health
and is fully competent and there is no reason why he should remain
in any hospital."

In discussions with newsmen, Dr. Schubert continued to portray
Gein as well adjusted to life in Central State. During the past few
years, Eddie had been working as a carpenter's helper, mason, and
hospital attendant, earning a dollar fifty a week. He had opened a
savings account and accumulated nearly three hundred dollars.
During his spare time, he watched TV (he was especially fond of ball
games), listened to his shortwave radio, read books and magazines.
He was free to roam the building and the grounds. Though he
continued to be a loner and had little to do with other patients (who

regarded him as "strange"), he had never caused a moment's trouble.

Nevertheless, after spending seventeen years locked up in the mental hospital, Eddie had begun to feel trapped. "I doubt that anybody would be happy there," he would later say to newsmen who asked if he was content at Central State. "If you want to go someplace, you can't go. It is human nature to want to go someplace." Eddie wasn't exactly sure where he would go if he gained his release. But one thing was certain—he wanted out.

Eddie's petition was reviewed by Judge Gollmar, who ordered several psychiatrists to reexamine Eddie and scheduled a hearing for June 27. On the day of the hearing, a hot, sunny Thursday, Eddie showed up at the Waushara County Courthouse in his blue suit, striped tie, and white shirt, looking considerably older than he had six years earlier. Before the hearing began, he met with the press, smiling for the television cameras, joking with a TV artist who dashed off a quick sketch ("You could have made it a little more handsome," Eddie said with a grin), and quietly answering questions.

What, asked one reporter, did Eddie regard as an important issue in the world today?

"Work," said Eddie. "In some places more fellows want to work than there is work, and other places it's the other way around."

Where would he go if he were released?

Eddie said he would probably move to a big city, where there were better job opportunities. "I know several trades. I can do most anything."

When one newsman asked if he would consider moving back to Waushara County, Eddie shook his head. There was no reason to go back there, he said, though he believed that if he did, he "wouldn't have trouble from the people."

What about his relationships with women? one reporter wanted to know. What were they like these days?

Eddie smiled shyly. The only women he had contact with were the nurses at the hospital, he explained, and his relationships with them were completely normal. After all, he said with a wink, "they are all married."

As far as the reporters could tell, the most remarkable thing about the white-haired little man was how ordinary he seemed. He was amiable, polite, soft-spoken—a little nervous, perhaps, but perfectly lucid. He certainly didn't look or sound like a madman. Maybe (unlikely as it seemed) he had recovered his sanity after all.

Then the doctors' testimony began.

The first psychiatrist to testify was Dr. Thomas Malueg. Earlier in the year, after completing his examination of Eddie, Malueg had forwarded a report to Judge Gollmar in which he confirmed that "to any casual observer" Gein "would present no obvious evidence of serious mental disorder." He was "friendly" and "willing to talk openly" (at least "when discussing relatively non-threatening material"). His "thought processes were generally intact and reasonably well organized."

Nevertheless, Malueg reported, there were unmistakable indications that Gein's psychosis was simmering just below the surface, ready to be reactivated under the right conditions. Whenever Malueg had asked Eddie direct questions about his crimes, for example, Gein would become highly agitated. "I don't want to rake up the past," he would say angrily. "If you stir up the past you might get burned up in your own fire. Psychiatrists are probably responsible for a lot of trouble in the world because of making people dig up the past. I think a lot of the prisoners from here might go out and kill 'em, rob 'em, club 'em because of digging up the past."

Eddie's interpretations of common proverbs were also, in Dr. Malueg's words, "very personalized." Malueg had presented Eddie with a few well-known sayings and asked what he thought they meant.

Malueg began with "People who live in glass houses shouldn't throw stones." Gein answered without hesitation: "Everybody has something he wants covered up."

"Don't cry over spilt milk," said Malueg.

"Don't dig up the past—what's done is done," Eddie replied.

"Still waters run deep," said Malueg.

Eddie thought for a moment, then answered, "Some people are calm on the surface and hotheads underneath."

Malueg had one more: "A bird in the hand is worth two in the bush."

For some reason, Eddie seemed amused by this proverb. He laughed, Malueg wrote in his report, "somewhat inappropriately" before giving his interpretation. "If you have a bird in your hand," said Eddie, "you might squeeze him too much and kill him."

Clearly, Gein was still a sick man, a conceivable threat to himself and others. Nevertheless, it was Malueg's belief that—though Gein should certainly not be released or even transferred to a halfway house—he might do well in a different hospital and suggested that he be moved to the Winnebago Mental Health Institute, a "less restricted facility" than Central State.

The remaining three witnesses, however, didn't share Dr. Malueg's belief. Dr. Leigh M. Roberts, head of the department of psychiatry at the University of Wisconsin Medical School, testified that Gein's condition—specifically his "tolerance of stress"—had actually deteriorated in recent years and advised against a transfer to Winnebago because of the "accessibility of women" there. Dr. Schubert and Dr. George Arndt (who, years earlier, had researched and written about the phenomenon of "Gein humor") agreed that Central State was still the best place for Gein. Sending him out into the world—or even into a less closely supervised institution— would be a mistake. "I don't think he has the strength to cope with society now," Schubert said, "and I don't think he ever had the strength to cope with society." Gein, he asserted, was absolutely alone in the world. In all the years of his confinement, he had never had a single visitor. Left to his own devices, he "would be a pathetic, confused, out of place person," a social outcast and potential victim of exploitation.

In the end, after a long day of testimony in the small, over-crowded, sweltering courtroom, Judge Gollmar had no choice but to reject Gein's petition. Noting that, had Eddie been sentenced to life imprisonment for the murder of Mrs. Worden, he would already have been eligible for parole, Gollmar said he wished he knew of a way to give Gein a little freedom. But it was not in his power to transfer Eddie to Winnebago.

As for "plucking" him from Central State and "putting him back on the street," Gollmar agreed with the experts. "I don't know whether it would be dangerous to Mr. Gein to release him. I do know that it would be horribly frustrating to him. This is a Rip Van Winkle situation. The simple day-by-day concerns would be impos-sible for him to handle. Simply crossing the street or getting food and a place to sleep would be very difficult for Mr. Gein after his many years in an institution.

"People might not treat him very well. Some people might even try to exhibit him."

After announcing his decision to return Gein to Central State, Gollmar adjourned court. Eddie, who accepted the ruling with his usual equanimity, got up and shuffled toward the exit. As he passed the spectators in the front row of benches, he noticed a little girl sitting beside her mother and smiled broadly. "It sure is awful warm," he remarked softly.

The next morning, Eddie was driven back to Central State Hospital, where he quietly returned to the pursuits that made up his life—putting his handyman skills to work around the hospital, listening to the news on his shortwave radio, and dreaming of the round-the-world trip he planned to take someday, once he had saved enough money.

Eventually, Eddie did make it out of Central State—but only by being transferred to another institution. In 1978, when Central State was converted into a "correctional facility," Gein, along with nine other patients, was moved to the Mendota Mental Health Institute in Madison. According to a spokesman for the State Health and Social Services Department, Gein had been deemed eligible for the transfer "by virtue of a stable condition and a low security status." By then, he was seventy-two years old, frail, in declining health, and beginning to show the first signs of senility.

He immediately became the hospital's resident celebrity. New employees—nurses, orderlies, administrative staffers—could hardly wait to get their first glimpse of the notorious Edward Gein. And they could hardly believe, when he was pointed out to them, that the gentle little man, shuffling slowly down the hallways or around the sprawling grounds of the institution, was the monster who had haunted their childhood dreams.

He still had ways of making news. A year after Eddie's transfer to Mendota, a particularly gruesome murder took place in Milwaukee. An eighty-six-year-old woman named Helen Lows was found bludgeoned to death in her bedroom. Her eyes had been gouged out, and slits had been cut into her face, apparently in an attempt to peel the skin off her skull.

The suspect arrested for the crime turned out to be a former mental patient named Pervis Smith, who, in 1974, had been committed to the Central State Hospital. There, he told police, he'd learned all kinds of interesting things about murder, mutilation, and the manufacture of human face masks from his best friend at the hospital, "Little Eddie" Gein.

Gein was seventy-eight years old, senile, and suffering from cancer when he died of respiratory failure in the geriatric ward at Mendota on July 26, 1984. Newspapers around the world printed the obituary of the man whose crimes had been the basis of Alfred Hitchcock's *Psycho*, by then long recognized as a classic of the American cinema.

The following night, sometime between three and six A.M., Gein was buried in an unmarked plot in the Plainfield Cemetery. Only a few employees of the Gasperic Funeral Home were present to witness the interment.

A woman who lived nearby, however, noticed some lights coming from the cemetery at that ungodly hour and, the next morning, notified her friend, a news correspondent named Linda Akin, who drove out to the graveyard to investigate. It took her a while, but Akin finally located the spot. "They had it look like there was no new grave," she later explained. "After the next time it rains, nobody will know there is a grave there." But there was a fresh grave, and it had been dug in the only appropriate spot.

Eddie had been laid to rest directly beside his mother.

Among the mysteries left unresolved at the time of Gein's death was the exact number and identity of his victims. From the time of his arrest to the present day, many people have believed that Gein committed far more murders than the pair he confessed to. They seem especially convinced that he was responsible for the disappearances of the two young girls, Georgia Weckler and Evelyn Hartley.

Others, however, feel that Gein was, as he claimed, innocent of these crimes. Clearly, he was capable of the most deranged and horrifying acts—grave robbing, necrophilia, sexual mutilation, and more. But child snatching, according to many people who knew him, simply wasn't his style. Eddie, they argue, wasn't interested in children. As the cases of both Mary Hogan and Bernice Worden show, his particular dementia involved the abduction and slaughter of mothers.

Besides the unsolved questions, Eddie left behind something else—a legacy of horror. By now, he is only a bad memory to the older citizens of Plainfield. But he's a memory that won't go away. Even today, most of the townspeople would prefer not to talk about him or even hear his name mentioned. Indeed, their most ardent hope is that one day, his name will be entirely forgotten and their community will no longer be instantly identified in the public's mind as the hometown of Wisconsin's most notorious and perverted killer.

Increasingly, however, that hope seems unrealistic. Indeed, in the thirty years since his crimes first became known to an appalled and disbelieving public, Gein's notoriety has actually increased, thanks largely to his impact on American popular culture. In 1975, a young Austin filmmaker named Tobe Hooper—who, as a child, had heard tales of the Wisconsin ghoul from visiting relatives—transformed his childhood recollections of the Gein horrors into one of the most harrowing movies ever made, *The Texas Chain Saw Massacre*. A triumph of drive-in Grand Guignol, Hooper's film let loose a flood of teenage slice-'em-ups known collectively as "splatter" movies— movies with titles like *Driller Killer*, *The Tool Box Murders*, and *Motel Hell*. Besides Hooper's exploitation classic, two more of these films were based directly on the Gein legend: a low-budget shocker called *Deranged* and an even lower-budget gore fest with the improbably perky title *Three on a Meathook*.

Indeed, it can be argued that insofar as Hitchcock's *Psycho* was the prototype for every "slasher" film that followed, the figure of Eddie Gein stands behind all the knife- and ax- and chainsaw-wielding psychos who have stalked the screen during the past decade, preying on oversexed adolescents in films like *Halloween*, *Friday the 13th*, *A Nightmare on Elm Street*, and all their imitators and sequels. If there can be such a thing as a seminal psychotic, that dubious honor must surely belong to Eddie Gein—the patron saint of splatter, the grandfather of gore.

Even today, public fascination with his case continues. As recently as November 1987, the *Madison Capital Times* ran an article about one of the psychiatrists who had interviewed Gein at the time of his arrest. Headlined "INFAMOUS KILLER ED GEIN WAS 'SENSITIVE,' PSYCHIATRIST SAYS," the article quoted Dr. Leonard Ganser, a retired psychiatrist for the State Department of Health and Social Services, who described Eddie as "always considerate and courteous," a "sensitive man" who "did not want to give offense."

In October 1987, Judge Robert Gollmar died at age eighty-four after a long and illustrious career, during which he had presided over scores of sensational murder trials. But, as his obituaries made clear, it was for his role as judge in "the 'Psycho' trial" (as the *New York Times* called it) that he would forever be remembered.

During the past few years, Eddie has been the subject of a play, a documentary, even a comic book. In the early 1980s, a Minnesota filmmaker announced his plans to make a movie called "A Nice Quiet Man," based on the story of Gein. It would not, the producer insisted, be a "guts and gore film" but rather a "message movie" (the message being "that it is society's responsibility to detect bizarre behavior and help those who need it"). The producer did not expect to land a big-name star for the role of Eddie Gein. For the part of Bernice Worden, he hoped to secure the services of Joanne Woodward.

Perhaps the most succinct and eloquent proof of Gein's ongoing fascination, however—of his status as a contemporary cult figure and pop immortal—was a classified advertisement that appeared not long ago in an issue of a publication called *Fangoria*, a monthly newsstand magazine devoted exclusively to "horror in entertainment." The ad (from a company called Bates Enterprises) was for a silk-screened T-shirt created in tribute to "the guy who got it all started."

The message on the T-shirt, printed in letters of blood, bones, and body parts, reads "Ed Gein Lives."

# ACKNOWLEDGMENTS

Thanks to the support and encouragement of many people, the writing of this book proved to be a much pleasanter experience than it might have been, given the grimness of the subject matter.

My researcher, Catharine Ostlind, provided invaluable assistance at every stage of the project. Her professionalism, energy, and generosity were enormously sustaining. Without the enthusiasm of Stacy Prince and Elizabeth Beier, this book would never have been more than an interesting idea, and I am grateful to them both, as I am to my agent, Jonathan Dolger, who offered the kind of advice, aid, and comfort I've come to depend on.

During the time I spent in Wisconsin, I was treated with unfailing kindness by everyone I met. Among the people whose thoughtfulness I will always be grateful for are Michael Bemis of the Wisconsin Department of Justice Law Library; Joan and Fred Reid of Plainfield, who opened their home to me; Irene Hill Bailey, who, in spite of the evident pain they are still capable of causing, spent an afternoon recalling the memories of three decades ago; the late Judge Robert Gollmar, a thoroughly gracious gentleman, and his equally gracious wife, Mildred. I would also like to thank Roger Johnson, Floyd and Lyle Reid, Dr. George Arndt, and the Honorable Jon P. Wilcox.

Many other people offered me various kinds of assistance during the researching and writing of this book, among them Nancy Alquist, Howard Bjorklund, Robert Bloch, Mindy Clay, Debra Cohen, Jim Donna, Daniel Dowd, Dominic Frinzi, Jim Hansen, Georgina Harring, Sid Harring, Dawn Hass, Mark Hasskarl, Rick Hayman, Jack Holzheuter, Andrea Kirchmeier, Peggy Klimke, Ann Lund, Dennis McCormick, Linda Merrill, Sally Munger, Roberta

Otis, Eugene Perry, John Reid, Jo Reitman, David Schreiner, Darold Strege, Robert E. Sutton, and Myrna Williamson. I owe a debt of gratitude to them all.

As always, Jonna Semeiks provided the most constant and crucial support. Without her, this book simply couldn't and wouldn't have been written.